Internation

BOTTLED NOTES FROM UNDERGROUND
Contemporary Plays by Jewish Writers

Edited by Sonja Linden and Marion Baraitser
Introduction by Tony Hammond

CAROLE BRAVERMAN
MARION BARAITSER
SONJA LINDEN
DAVID SCHNEIDER
JOSHUA SOBEL

LOKI BOOKS

LB LOKI BOOKS

Loki Books is financially assisted by the Arts Council of England, UNESCO Publishing, the Institute for the Translation of Hebrew Literature, the Jewish Book Council, the Israeli Embassy, the British Council and the European Jewish Publication Society.
First published in Great Britain in 1998 as a paperback original by **LOKI BOOKS** LTD, 38 Chalcot Crescent, London NW1 8YD.

Printed and bound by Antony Rowe Ltd, Bumper's Farm, Chippenham, Wiltshire SN14 6QA, England.

ISBN LOKI 0 9529426 2 3

Cover drawing by Alexandra Baraitser

CONTENTS

Foreword

Bottled Notes From Underground is the first international anthology of plays by contemporary Jewish writers to be published in Britain. It is an expression of a new confidence in Jewish identity in playwrights in Britain today, whether they choose to see themselves as playwrights who happen to be Jewish, like Arthur Miller, or Jewish playwrights, like David Schneider (the grandson of a Yiddish playwright), who stayed on at Oxford to research a PhD in Yiddish drama and who made his debut as an actor in Joshua Sobol's *Ghetto* at the National Theatre. His first play, *The Eleventh Commandment*, published in this anthology, about the triumph of a mixed marriage, shows all the confidence, Jewish wit and fantasy of a stand-up comic.

Why has this anthology been so long in the making? Perhaps Shylock cast a long shadow of self-consciousness and confusion over Jewish playwrights, discouraging them from seeing the Jewish experience as a valid one to stage, or from daring to create a flawed Jewish character.. An unspoken taboo was handed down, rooted in the fear that such material would provide fuel for anti-semitism (a fear underscored by the Holocaust), and apprehension about the response from a mixed audience. Consider how it would be if Arthur Miller had made the Loman family Jewish, or if Mamet had made the professor in *Oleanna* Jewish, or Pinter had declared the dysfunctional family in *The Homecoming* not to be just from the East End, but also Jewish.

Bottled Notes From Underground breaks further ground in that women and men are published alongside one another for the first time in a British publication of a collection of dramas by Jewish playwrights. Carole Braverman's play, brimming with characteristic American Jewish humour, shows us the lives of three feisty Brooklyn sisters. Marion Baraitser's play about the life of the communist philosopher Louis Althusser sympathetically treats the viewpoint of his Polish Jewish wife in their complex and shifting mixed marriage relationship. Sonja Linden dares to represent on stage the magnificent and flawed character of the musician Victor Ullman and his relationship with two women in the Terezin concentration camp.

Why publish plays? It seems right to encourage the idea that plays are not only worth the enjoyment of performance, but are also worth reading for pleasure and for study, because new writing is an important and integral part of the performed play. More contemporary plays are being published and read in Britain today. A collection of plays by Jewish writers is evidence of a new energy in British theatre in general. This collection is aimed at giving lively, thoughtful plays of excellence a longer life, promotion, and a greater availability to the general public, to students and theatre practitioners, as well as allowing access to the texts by those who cannot always reach them.

Marion Baraitser
Sonja Linden

January, 1998

Introduction

It is a simpler matter to talk of plays by Jewish writers than it is to talk of Jewish plays. Unlike *Yiddish, Jewish* does not denote a language, which otherwise would provide a neat category, but it does, perhaps, raise among other expectations, anticipations about a *style* or use of language. In this regard, paradoxically, Sobol's play, published here from the Hebrew, stands apart

Simpler, too, if there were a way of designating Jewish plays as we might designate French, Spanish or North American plays, by reference to language or country of origin. But that is not the case and therein lies just the interest and specificity of such plays as the five collected here. It may be possible, but not easily justifiable, to wrench out of these five present works, a kind of collective identity or common thematic ground, such as may be proper in the case of a collection of works by a single playwright. But they have roots in no single dramatic tradition: thematically they draw on no single national history: there is no unifying Jewish identity such as Zionism or orthodoxy.

And yet... because each of these plays can be shown to be weighted by a collective historical experience, which is that of modern Jewish history, their field of cultural reference extends across certain borders, and what is perhaps foreign to the language of its expression, is none the less integral, both to the characters and perspectives of the plays and, of course, to their playwrights. It is in that extent of blend and engagement that we are invited to become aware of the presence of a common though varied background culture, elusive though definition continues to be.

It is in this awareness that a preoccupation with designation comes about. While it is surely true that each of the playwrights represented here has no intention of writing for a single 'national' audience - the breadth of reference of the plays explicitly runs counter to such narrowness - it is also the case that there is everywhere a connectedness to a history and culture which may, at any one time, prove to be either informing or a dead hand. As a dynamic engagement between tradition and the existential present, Judaism, in its broadest sense, offers perhaps the longest surviving, most fully recorded example. And that longevity has incurred many a brush with extinction, not least in the 20th century in Europe and the Middle East. Jacob and the Angel wrestle and Israel is created - in every generation.

Joshua Sobol's *The Palestinian Girl (Shooting Magda)* is a Jewish-language play. It, unlike the others, belongs to a Jewish nation-state culture. Its very subject matter draws on, or reflects into, the politics and prejudices of contemporary nationalisms. Indeed, in the struggle to 'portray' the eponymous Palestinian girl, Samira, as Magda in the film-within-the-play, identities - Jewish, Muslim, English Christian - all prove both inadequate and, worse, oppressive:

> Magda is something that nothing sticks to. No label. Magda is the kind of stuff that can't be frozen in any form. Magda is just the opposite. Magda isn't the result. She isn't the continuation. Magda is what happens one minute to the next... Magda is something that doesn't belong, something that'll never belong to anyone.

Against the pejoratively intended 'assimilation', from which the Palestinian Samira is warned off, we are invited by Samira herself to understand and embrace something like the 'existential present'. For, in one sense of the term, assimilation might after all equally as well involve in her case, converting to Judaism or 'learning the duties of a Muslim wife'.

Samira's potential embodiment of a quite contemporary Israel, is but one of the several radical perceptions of the dynamic struggle between tradition and the 'existential angel' these plays offer.

Sonja Linden's *The Strange Passenger* takes place in Terezin. Here the dead hand of history promises not only physical extinction, but its spiritual reductiveness, internalised by its victims, threatens to turn all struggle into the most self-destructive of all struggles, that for the barest means of survival. It is against this, rather than the external 'national' threat, that her protagonist composer Victor Ullman, ultimately finds himself engaged. With him, and through him, the play refuses to be assimilated into the European. Instead, the conflict of duties and responsibilities which the artist Ullmann had been largely unsuccessful in resolving, both with respect to his family and to his creativity, before their incarceration, is brought more urgently and vividly to light in the camp. The play embodies a fierce affirmation of life and creativity, by asserting the necessity of giving meaning to, and of engaging with, the existential present up to the very brink of extinction.

Jewish Brooklyn and its distinctive inflection of the language of Carole Braverman's *The Yiddish Trojan Women* are in large part responsible for the seamless connection between the Yiddish-speaking Europe of a grandmother, and American present of her granddaughter and nieces. But while this traditional continuity is the medium, it does not constitute the whole message. The classical parallel drawn by the title of the play, and other structural references, as well as the granddaughter's study of anthropology, invite us to perceive how this Yiddish-American culture provides not simply a thoroughly contemporary perspective on the wider world, but is uniquely equipped in some regards to engage with it. The integration of past and present through the tricks age plays on memory is remarkably carried over in Braverman's play to inform, for example, not only contemporary suffering in Guatemala through past Jewish suffering in Europe, but the lawless urgency of sexual desire. The action is none the less essentially all present. No weight of tradition or history can contain, or in the end outweigh, the possibilities of the present, but without them, as the unrooted, under-educated Luke testifies to, we are dangerously adrift and unable to engage with it.

In quite different ways, Marion Baraitser's *Louis/Lui* engages with memory and selfhood. Drawing on Louis Althusser's autobiography, the play enacts a pattern of alternative readings of past actions and shifting identities. Althusser seems to embody something of the political and historical derangement of the century through most of which he lived. The figure of his Polish-Jewish wife, on whom he felt he depended but whom he strangled, provides a chilling parallel action to the history of a century on which Althusser reflected, and his ambivalent embrace of the Jewish woman haunts the play.

An ingredient of *The Yiddish Trojan Women* which balances and provides a counterpoint to the tragic subtext of the play is the comic routines of Brenda Brodsky, who plays the nightclubs and during course of the play manages to achieve her goal of material success. She deserves it. Her routines are good, but they also depend on a working-over of the stereotypes. Such stereotypical material is well-known and well-used as a shorthand for Jewish identity, both by Jew and by Gentile, (accompanied by the full range of amusement, affection, ambivalence and distaste on both sides!). It is the very material and substance, however, of one of the deadest hands that Judasism can lay on itself. In the *Eleventh Commandment* David Schneider plunges into a theatre of stereotypes with such verve and inventiveness that we might think Dario Fo had had a hand in things. Danny is being investigated by the authorities for remaining single. He is sexually subverted by his mother's 'presence'. His room piles up with food in Tupperware pressed on him by his mother. He plans to 'marry out'. And without so much as a missed beat, or saying 'no, but seriously - though the play engages with the anxiety that underlines much of our jokiness - the anxiety that Judaism is disappearing:

> ANGEL. Look. I understand that your concern but I'm afraid there's nothing we can do about it. It's the inevitable result of free will, the enlightenment and the great taste of crispy bacon.
> ABRAHAM. But what about my people?
> ANGEL. Who understands God's plans? Listen, your people re not the same as they were two, three thousand years ago. They're always changing... Maybe its time for one of those changes.

Schneider manages to arouse a remarkable empathy and attention for his vision of the Israel that may be ready to emerge, because his comic stereotypes are understood to be the defensive carapace from within which the jokey Jacob must emerge to meet his angel.

In their diversity, energy, wit, seriousness and range, these plays point out a number of important directions, not just for Jewish playwrights, but for Jewish theatre.

Tony Hammond
January,1998.

THE YIDDISH TROJAN WOMEN

by

Carole Braverman

I began writing this play while on sabbatical almost ten years ago. The core thematic urgency was expressed inTess' line: 'The world is filled with decent people and heinous crimes', with all its harrowing and mysterious implications. But there are other threads: the first time I saw the film version of Euripides' *The Trojan Women*; the lingering memory of my grandmother Regina, singing an old Yiddish 'torch song' into a reel-to-reel tape recorder; the haunting (and totally imagined) image of Rivka looking out of the window, begging Devorah to teach her the simple human trick of 'looking away'; fragments from a love story; a newspaper article; the repressed desire to be a stand-up comic.

The Yiddish Trojan Women was originally produced under the title *The Brooklyn Trojan Women* by The Women's Project (Julia Miles, Artistic Director) in New York City, in Ist June, 1993.

CAST

TESS BRODSKY	Ariane Brodsky
TBRENDA BRODSKY	Lucille Rivin
ABIGAIL BRODSKY	Stephanie Clavman
DEVORAH BRODSKY	Joanna Medin
LUKE HARRIS	Adam Barnet

The play was produced in the American Jewish Theatre (Stanley Brechner, Artistic Director) in January 1996, and by the Soho Theatre Company (Abigail Morris, Artistic Director) in London, January 1996.

CHARACTERS

Tess Brodsky
Brenda Brodsky
Abigail Brodsky
Devorah Brodsky
Luke Harris

Setting: Brooklyn, NY early 1980s, Most of the action takes place in the apartments of Devorah or Tess. There are brief interludes in various nightclubs, a union hall, and a college lecture hall. The set should be minimal and suggestive, rather than realistically detailed.

ACT ONE

Scene 1

Devorah's Apartment in Brooklyn, 1982. As the lights rise, we hear a Yiddish torch song of the 1930s. The singer is Devorah Brodsky, who is recording the song into a tape recorder. Tess Brodsky, Devorah's granddaughter, a woman in her early thirties, is dressed for her grandmother's wedding, about to take place that afternoon. She is reading. Brenda Brodsky, her cousin, also in her thirties, enters.*

BRENDA. You should see her in there. The mike in one hand, the schnaps in the other. What the hell is she straining her tonsils for? Doesn't she know she lost her voice years ago?
TESS. She's recording the music for her wedding.
BRENDA. She's going to walk down the aisle to that crap?
TESS. It's Morris' favorite. Very sexy stuff. A few bars of it and he gets hard.
BRENDA. That old fart?
TESS. Well, hard enough.

BRENDA. She'll kill him you know. This one's frail. He won't even last as long as the third. Someone ought to warn him.

TESS. People don't like warnings.

BRENDA. Why is it so hot in here? The super shoots that steam up the radiator like he was heating Hell. Which in a way he is. *(Trying to pry open the window, wiping off the dust)* Look at that. She still keeps this place a pigsty. I was embarrassed to bring friends up here, you know that?

TESS. It wasn't that bad.

BRENDA. Sure, for you. You didn't have to live with Grandma.

TESS. What's with you? Why are you so on edge?

BRENDA. What? You mean besides having to sit through another one of her weddings? I don't know. You should see the joint I'm playing this week.

TESS. I was there, remember?

BRENDA. So what do you want, a medal?

TESS. Why do you work places like that?

BRENDA. Oh I don't know. I guess I got tired of Caesar's Palace. You got to pay your dues in this business, toots. Besides, it beats the Catskills.

TESS. You've been paying dues for fifteen years.

BRENDA. Don't give me that. I don't need that 'when are you going to make it?' crap from you.

TESS. Okay, I'm sorry.

BRENDA. At least I don't play it safe, Miss Tenure-Puss. At least I don't waste my time teaching. And that's why I'll have it all and you won't. Because I got nothing to fall back on, because for me it's either having it all or cutting window shades in Woolworth's.

TESS. I said okay, didn't I?

BRENDA. I'm sorry. His apartment makes me nervous. You know I love you, Splendid Cousin. Come to my show again tonight, and we can hang out a little afterwards.

TESS. Not tonight.

BRENDA. Please?

TESS. I can't tonight.

BRENDA. Just one show. You can leave before the strippers.

TESS. It's not the strippers. I promised Abby I'd go somewhere with her after the wedding. There's this guy from Kentucky she wants me to meet.

BRENDA. Kentucky? If you need a date that bad why don't you ask me?
TESS. It's not a date. He's been helping her with some union stuff down there.
BRENDA. I'm always offering to fix you up aren't I? And I'm not talking red neck here, I'm talking quality men.
TESS. Don't use that expression I hate it. It reminds me of fabric.
BRENDA. Look you can't go this long without a man. It's not healthy. Your skin will dry up.
TESS. Look, just leave me alone, okay?
BRENDA. One hellish marriage, six or seven disastrous affairs, of course you can begin to think they're all *shmucks.*
TESS. I never said they were all *schmucks.*
BRENDA. That's because you're an idiot. Of course they're *shmucks.* What do you think, it was just a run of bad luck? You have this unconscious desire to choose the wrong man? They're *shmucks*. All of them. But that doesn't mean you give up sex for two years. Jesus, even saying it aloud gives me the chills. Don't you get lonely?
TESS. I have you, don't I?
BRENDA. Yeah? Well, if I mean that much to you, come to the club tonight.
TESS. Come on, Brenda, I haven't seen Abby for months. She just got back a few hours ago. Maybe afterwards, maybe the two of us could go.
BRENDA. Right. Like she would really come to one of my shows.
TESS. I'll ask her.
BRENDA. I don't want her there. (*Abby Brodsky enters. She has been inside in the living room with Devorah. She is in her middle thirties, a little older than her sister Brenda, but not by much.*)
ABBY. Grandma's ready to leave.
TESS. Isn't Morris coming here?
ABBY. No. He's meeting us at the Synagogue. I told my friend Joe Miller we'd meet him after the wedding, about seven, is that okay?
TESS. Sure.
ABBY. We're working on an Op Ed piece for the New York Times an I thought you could help us edit it.
BRENDA. Sounds like a hot date.
TESS. What's the article about?
ABBY. We were in Kentucky for months organizing a textile factory.

The workers finally vote to join the union - and we just found out, hours before we left yesterday, that the company is moving the whole operation to Guatemala. Nearly 400 people will be out of work.

BRENDA. See. Next time mind your own business.

ABBY. We can't fight these battles just locally any more. If we keep closing our eyes to working conditions in other countries there won't be one functioning union left here.

BRENDA. Just what I was in the mood for. A harangue from the Red Virgin.

ABBY. It's not just coincidence that Reagan and Company are supporting the thugs in Central America while they break the unions here. You saw what he did to the Air Controllers? God, the bastards in this Administration - the bastards. Even the way they talk... That sickening combination of sanctimony and meanness... The one in the State Department? With the eyebrows out to here? God, every time he opens his mouth it's a deliberate test of my endurance.

BRENDA. You're nuts, you know that?

TESS. She has a big heart, that's all. I wish mine were half as good.

ABBY. Your heart is fine.

TESS. No. I'm selfish, Abby, and envious. I want the world too much.

ABBY. So. It's natural to want the world for awhile.

TESS. Is it?

ABBY. Sure. Even God had to want the world before he made it.

TESS. *(Laughs.)* That's true. *(Beat.)* Why do you have such faith in me?

ABBY. Because you have an immortal soul.

TESS. Really?

BRENDA. Is it? Really? What is she, the Pope?

ABBY. Yes, but it means you have to take it seriously. You have to be worthy of it.

TESS. Doesn't Brenda have one too?

ABBY. No one who paints her toe nails can have an immortal soul.

TESS. Really? They disqualify people for that?

ABBY. And she's too serious about getting a tan.

BRENDA. Oh yeah, what do you mean - Tess gets tans.

ABBY. But she's not serious about it.

TESS. That's right.

BRENDA. Not serious? She used to spend more time on that roof than the chimneys.

TESS. That's a lie.

BRENDA. You know the trouble with you, don't you? You don't know how to enjoy anything.

ABBY. She didn't lie there with her lips parted in a small ecstatic 'O'....

BRENDA. One of your genes is missing or something...

ABBY. A small ecstatic 'O' of such total self-absorption, I have often considered your lips a partial explanation of the problem of Evil in the world.

TESS. Wow. Just from her lips?

BRENDA. Shut up! You were the most methodical tanner in the building. The Sun couldn't make a two degree move without you adjusting the angle of your lounge chair.

TESS. That's a lie.

BRENDA. It was so fine-tuned the neighbors used you as a Sundial.

ABBY. You don't have a soul, accept it.

BRENDA. Who needs it? At least I don't put out cigarettes in the palm of my hands.

TESS. Come on, Brenda.

BRENDA. It's true, isn't it?

TESS. She was thirteen years old.

BRENDA. She's crazy.

ABBY. I'm crazy? We open factories where workers are kept in line with death squads and I'm crazy?

BRENDA. Yes. Yes.

ABBY. In the year 1982, in the richest country in the history of the world, an old man is living in a cardboard box right across from Grandma's building, and I'm crazy?

TESS. *(Looking for him through the window*) Jesus. Where?

BRENDA. The whole neighborhood knows you're crazy.

ABBY. Half frozen, wearing a coat even I wouldn't put on, picking through garbage for his dinner.

BRENDA. They would talk behind my back. There she goes. The *meshugana's* sister.

TESS. Where?

BRENDA. What are you looking for? What? Don't you know she's crazy?

ABBY. Unfortunately, not everyone has your high threshold for other people's pain.

BRENDA. Everything is your business. Everything! *(Devorah enters.*

She is eighty, still a vigorous and handsome woman.)

DEVORAH. Oy shut up already, shut up! What's going on!?

BRENDA. The concert's over?

DEVORAH. Always fighting, always fighting. I didn't have enough from you when you were children?

DEVORAH. *(Turning her attention to Abby.)* Why aren't you dressed?

ABBY. I am dressed.

DEVORAH. This is dressed by you? Put on some shoes, you're not going in sneakers this time.

ABBY. I'm wearing sneakers. I don't have to destroy my feet every time you get married.

DEVORAH. Saul's family, may he rest in peace, they couldn't get over it. To a wedding she comes in sneekers. People said to me I don't even want to say. 'Sha I said... Sha..she broke her foot.'

ABBY. Will you stop treating me like a child, I'm 35 years old.

DEVORAH. And you still make trouble for me. The caterer found out she was coming, he almost refused the affair. You listening? I had to *shtup* him extra. He remembered from when she made trouble with the waiters trying to organize them.

BRENDA. She's nuts.

DEVORAH. Sha. Don't talk about your sister that way. *(To Abby.)* And comb your hair a little. Put on a little lipstick. Make yourself representable. Such an educated girl you always look like a *schnorrer*.

ABBY. *(Spotting the old man out the window.)* There he is again.

TESS. Who?

ABBY. The old man.

DEVORAH. Who does she take after that's what I'd like to know. Not me.

BRENDA. Why don't you just admit that she's adopted.

DEVORAH. Oy shut up already. You're no prize yourself.

TESS. (*At window with Abby.*) I don't see him.

ABBY. Not there. There.

TESS. Where?

ABBY. Crossing Bay Parkway.

DEVORAH. (*The image of them both at the window triggers an old memory.)* What are you doing?

ABBY. *(Turning Tess' head in the right direction.)* There.

DEVORAH. What are you doing?

TESS. Hm?

DEVORAH. What are you looking at? Get away from there.
ABBY. What?
DEVORAH. (*Pulling them away.*) Get away from there I said!
TESS. What's the matter, Grandma?
DEVORAH. (*She's not sure herself.)* Nothing. (*Pause*) All day long she would stand there.
ABBY. Who?
DEVORAH. (*Beat.*) Rifka.
TESS. Who is Rifka?
DEVORAH. No one. Nothing. (*But the image persists.)* She was your Grandpa's sister.
TESS. Grandpa had a sister?
DEVORAH. She could see things through the window.
BRENDA. So could we if you'd wash them once in awhile.
DEVORAH. Things no one else could see. Things that hadn't happened yet.
TESS. No kidding?
DEVORAH. But no one ever listened to her. People saw her coming, they would walk the other way.
TESS. Why didn't you ever tell us about her?
DEVORAH. She would shout all day sometimes, wild with grief. They were going to take her away.
TESS. What happened to her?
DEVORAH. I don't know. (*For a fleeting moment, she is a little puzzled herself by this reply.)* Why doesn't she know?)
TESS. Grandma...?
DEVORAH. Her mother, Malka, was a real witch. That I remember. Such a mother-in-law I wouldn't wish on my worst enemy... Always cleaning, always cleaning. Every night she would come into Grandpa's butcher shop to wash up the blood. He would yell at her, 'What are you doing? I'm a butcher, not a florist, there has to be some blood.' But you couldn't reason with her. Every night she'd be there with her pail scrubbing... two, three hours. She wouldn't rest till she got the blood off everything. And in the morning when the meat came in, it would start all over.
TESS. What happened to Rifka? Did she come to America with you and Grandpa?
BRENDA. Will you stop encouraging her? I want to get out of here.

DEVORAH. When Grandpa fell in love with me, his mother wanted I should cut my hair off. But I refused. She was always jealous of me, always. Hair I had, redder than fire. And a voice on me. I was the star of the whole village. In the Purim plays, I was always Esther the Queen, always, because of my voice, and because I was so beautiful. *(She begins to hum one of the old Purim songs.)* Even when we came to this country I was a star.

TESS. Tell us about the Yiddish Carmen.

BRENDA. Jesus. I want to get out of here.

DEVORAH. On second Avenue I was playing 'The Yiddish Carmen'...

BRENDA. Yiddish Carmen - what did you do, work in a blintz factory?

DEVORAH. I was a beautiful young Gypsy fortune teller. It was my most tragic role. *(She sings a little of the opening song.)*

BRENDA. I'm going to get the car. (*She exits.*)

DEVORAH. There is a scene where I am predicting my own future from the cards... (*She sings with intense feeling, miming the cards, a few bars of the song.)*

Queen. (*She sings another few bars)* King... I see there will be a man... that there will be a fire in my soul for a man... *(Staring at the imagined card.*) They all thought he was dead.

TESS. Who, Grandma?

DEVORAH. It was Purim - I remember because I still had on my costume. She was looking out the window, like she always did. And then she saw him. We both did. Walking toward the house dressed like a Russian peasant - big boots, a white shirt, no beard...

TESS. Who was it?

DEVORAH. Daniil back from the dead.

TESS. From the dead?

ABBY. Who was he?

DEVORAH. A troublemaker. Just like you. Always minding everybody's business. They threw him out from the town before I even met your Grandpa. They hadn't heard from him in years. They thought he had died in a Siberian prison.

ABBY. Was he a Bolshevik?

DEVORAH. He was the handsomest man I ever saw. The sun's face didn't glow like his.

TESS. Wow.

DEVORAH. His hair was black as burnt *kugel*. His cheeks were like the apples of *Simchus Torah*. His eyes like the sky in summer. Women couldn't resist him. He had a mark on his forehead. A love mark. Once you saw it, they had to tie you up.

TESS. What happened to him?

DEVORAH. When he came into a room it was like a storm, like the force from magnets....

TESS. Grandma?

DEVORAH. *(Long pause.)* What?

TESS. What happened to him?

ABBY. And to Rifka?

DEVORAH. What happened? *(Another long pause as if struggling to remember - then pushing it down.)* Nothing happened.

TESS. Why didn't you ever tell us this story?

DEVORAH. Nothing happened I said! What do you want from me? Who remembers these things. It was a long time ago. Hurry up already. Morris will be waiting. Get going. Look what time it s already. *(They exit.)*

Scene 2.

A nightclub in Hoboken. Brenda walks on with a mike, accompanied by stripper music.

BRENDA.. Thank you. Thank you very much. I'm Brandy Brod and I'm thrilled to be playing here again at *The Hot Box.* What a classy place. But let's get one thing straight, okay? I am not the stripper? Not to be fooled by this gorgeous bod, not the stripper, okay? She's still backstage waiting for the elastic marks from her underwear to fade, okay? Men like looks, am I right? You, what do you look for in a women? Blindness I bet, huh? Ever see that commercial on television - the one for the cereal? The bitch in the white bathing suit with a body that makes you want to flush yourself down the nearest toilet? And she's taking this slow jaunt over to her pool like she has all year to get there, but you never see her face, right - she's so good they show her in parts, right, like its a mini series and we got all week. Neck... shoulders... cleavage... tasteful crotch shot... And just before she takes the big plunge she shapes her legs into this perky little 'Special K' - I mean thank God they didn't call that crap 'Special V' right? *(To another heckler.)* I'm not taking it off okay. Can't you tell a classy broad when you see one? I am so classy, my gynecologist wears white gloves. Oh please. I sit in those stirrups side saddle. I take my pap tests in French. Will you shut up? What's the matter with him he can't wait a few minutes to see a pair of tits?

Stripper music drowns her out. Blackout.

Scene 3

Tess's Apartment. About nine months later. Luke and Tess enter. It is raining outside, and their jackets are wet. They have just met. He is in his late twenties, good-looking, feeling awkward, nervous, wanting to appear more relaxed than he is. A fantasy seems about to be played out for him if he can play his cards right. Luke has never spoken to someone even remotely like Tess, and he already thinks her a little weird. She has invited him here on an uncharacteristic impulse, and is also a little nervous.

LUKE. This is your place?
TESS. What?
LUKE. Your place? You live here?
TESS. Oh... yeah. Yeah, I do. You're wet.
LUKE. Nah... nah.. I'm fine. Just a little damp. Really started coming down heavy, huh? Cats and dogs, huh? Thanks for stopping.
TESS. You know why I did?
LUKE. I think I got some idea.
TESS. You don't. It's too magical and amazing.
LUKE. Yeah?
TESS. Want to at least take your jacket off?
LUKE. Sure. (*He doesn't feel as easy about it as he affects.*) I wouldn't smell it if I were you, though.
TESS. Okay. But it's usually the first thing I do with a guest's jacket.
LUKE. Really?
TESS. I'm kidding. Did I look like I was going to smell it?
LUKE. No, just warning you. It stinks from my dog. So, this is where you live, huh?

TESS. Yeah.

LUKE. Nice place. You certainly got a lot of books.

TESS. What?

LUKE. It looks like a library.

TESS. Oh yeah. I love to read - ever since I was a kid I've forgiven my brain almost everything for providing me that... pleasure.

LUKE. It must save you a lot on paint, huh? I mean the way they cover the whole wall like that.

TESS. Yeah. That's true too.

LUKE. I like to go to the library sometimes.

TESS. Yeah?

LUKE. I like their books about eatin'.

TESS. About who?

LUKE. Eatin'. Cookbooks.

TESS. Oh. You like to cook?

LUKE. Yeah.

TESS. What else you like to do?

LUKE. Me? I don't know, the usual - watching the games on TV, poker with the guys, lifting weights, the dog races when I can afford it. Sometimes I like to hunt squirrels. Not shoot them or anything, just shake them out of the trees.

TESS. Really? Is that a sport?

LUKE. I don't know. One of my stepfathers taught me how. You got to wait for just the right moment cause the best part is the look on their faces. God do they looked surprised, like 'hey what's happening, you know.' Sometimes the nuts just shoot right out of their mouths like bullets.

TESS. Doesn't it hurt them?

LUKE. Nah... mostly they survive it. They're graceful. Like cats. What time is it?

TESS. Four ten. Want to call home or something?

LUKE. What do you mean?

TESS. Home. Where you live. Your wife.

LUKE. Nah. I'm not married.

TESS. You live alone?

LUKE. Yeah. I was just thinking maybe I should call my boss about the truck. God he pisses me off. For weeks, I've been telling him the drive train is shot, you think he gives a shit? He's always fucking me over, excuse my English.

TESS. Its hard to find another job, huh?

LUKE. Are you kidding, with my background? I'm not even supposed to be driving the damn thing, I don't have the right license. I'm supposed to be baking the bread not delivering it. I'm just helping him out for a few weeks because his regular driver quit sudden - the jerk can't keep any help because he doesn't know how to treat people. Also I can use the extra money, not that it comes to much. But I need the bread. Get it. I knead the bread? That's the only reason I put up with the asshole.

TESS. It's a very honorable living, I think, baking bread.

LUKE. Oh yeah, honorable. What I really wanted to do was 'Mixology.'

TESS. No kidding.

LUKE. Yeah. I actually went back to school to take a course in it a few years back -

TESS. Really, I teach it.

LUKE. No kidding. You're a bartender?

TESS. What?

LUKE. A bartender.

TESS. What does teaching mythology have to do with being a bartender?

LUKE. Jesus, you got to know how to mix the drinks, don't you. You can't get your license without it.

TESS. Oh MIXology?

LUKE. Yeah, how to mix the drinks.

TESS. I'm sorry, I thought you said mythology.

LUKE. I thought you lisped. What's mythology?

TESS. Just stories, stories that all people make up to explain the mystery of things. Why we're here, what we're like why I picked up a total stranger hitching a ride on the BQE.

LUKE. Like I said, I think I know why.

TESS. There you were, standing on the shoulder of the road, your jacket torn, looking miserable and wet, like an exhausted Greek god down on his luck, come down to earth to test the hospitality of mortals. You're not Greek are you?

LUKE. I don't know. I never asked.

TESS. What do you mean? Are you adopted?

LUKE. You mean when your mother gives you up?

TESS. Yeah.

LUKE. Nah... I had my own mother.

TESS. And you never found out your nationality?

LUKE. What's the big deal, I never asked.

TESS. Asked? Who asks? Usually they work it in while you're struggling through the birth canal. Where would the world be without xenophobia?

LUKE. Without what?

TESS. You know, 'we and them', 'us and they' - tribes, nations. What's your last name?

LUKE. Harris.

TESS. Uh, uh. Too nondescript - could be anything - even Jewish.

LUKE. Yeah, right, Me. My uncle would have knocked the shit out of me. Do I look that weird to you?

TESS. Hey, what do I have here, a genuine anti-Semite?

LUKE. A what?

TESS. Jesus, you're ignorant. A Jew-hater.

LUKE. Who me? I don't hate no one. Now my uncle, yeah - he hates a lot of people - niggers, spicks, faggots, commies, but Jews is the worst to him. He's always saying how they got what they deserved. Something really bad happened to them in World War II, didn't it? A lot of them got murdered, right?

TESS. You have got to be the most ignorant person I have ever personally met.

LUKE. Hey, lady, stop calling me that. Maybe if you talked English once in a while -

TESS. I'll talk whatever I want. I don't tell you how to talk, do I?

LUKE. Hey, look, why did you ask me up here? I just came up here to get laid if you want to know the truth.

TESS. Not a chance.

LUKE. You don't want it, that's fine. You're not that irresistible yourself, if you want to know the truth. - You were just there, you know what I mean, looking like you wanted it... And I happen to be horny.

TESS. You happen to be a jerk. Will you just get out of here?

LUKE. *(He begins to exit, but by the time he reaches the door, his instinctive good nature regrets having said something that hurt her.)* Look, I'm sorry. I didn't mean to hurt you. I just got the wrong idea is all. Okay?

TESS. *(Who knows a real apology when she hears one)* Okay.

LUKE. Thanks for the lift. It was nice of you. I was out of line to say those things. You know, about getting laid.

TESS. Nah, You were right.

LUKE. Yeah?

TESS. But it was a mistake.

LUKE. Yeah. *(Re-entering the room.)* And I'm sorry for... you know... about your not being irresistible.

TESS. Thanks. I'm sorry too... about your being ignorant.

LUKE. It's okay. So good-bye, huh?

TESS. Yeah, and good luck with the 'mixology', and everything, okay?

LUKE. You too. *(He leans over to give her a perfunctory kiss on the lips. He kisses her again, a little longer this time. She backs off. He reseats himself.)* Maybe I should just stay to hear the end of the story... About how come you gave me that lift.

TESS. It's too amazing, you won't believe it.

LUKE. Try me.

TESS. Okay, there you were, on the Brooklyn-Queens Expressway - a god down on his luck..

LUKE. I'm going to get a new jacket.

TESS. Every impulse in my nature whispered I should stop.

LUKE. Well good for me you did, or I'd still be out there.

TESS. I didn't -

LUKE. You didn't what?

TESS. Stop. Every impulse whispered 'stop', but every cautionary tale I'd ever heard about hitchhikers shouted it down. I passed you.

LUKE. You passed me...

TESS. This is a strange story.

LUKE. I get it... Then you turned around?

TESS. On the freeway? No, no. Once I had chosen, there was no turning back. It was an offering from heaven and I had refused it, like a coward -

LUKE. You were right to be scared -

TESS. No, no, there are those moments when you hear a voice and you know it comes from your truest self and you have to risk all and act. For about twenty minutes I debated with myself and felt ashamed, and then, in the wonderful safety of your being twenty miles behind me, I decided to pick you up - well, decided that I would if I had it to do over. I would be braver if I had a second chance. No sooner had I said it... Then what do I see looming in the distance? YOU.

LUKE. Me?

TESS. You, standing exactly the way I had last seen you, even to the angle of the thumb, even to the way you feet were grounded in the shoulder of the road. 'I've been dreaming' I said, 'dreaming,' but I looked at my watch and no, twenty minutes had gone by. It was like an episode in the Twilight Zone.

LUKE. I saw that episode. She keeps passing the same hitchhiker. I saw it. God you must have been scared, huh?

TESS. Terrified, mainly because I realized I wasn't going to stop now either, that I do all my changing in my head. You got closer and closer, you were exactly as I had seen you twenty miles before. Surely, this was an act of grace, a second offering from a merciful Heaven, and miserable coward, I wasn't going to stop. But finally, it was too magical. All my terror was swallowed in the magic of it.

LUKE. I got it. I got it. I know what happened.

TESS. Don't tell me.

LUKE. No listen, this is great. Are you a slow driver?

TESS. Yes.

LUKE. This is great. Listen, this guy picks me up, see? He just shoots across three lanes of traffic like a bat out of hell and picks me up. A big guy maybe 300 pounds, you know, who turns out to be a strongman in the circus at Madison Square Garden.

TESS. No kidding?

LUKE. Can you believe it? I mean weights is a hobby of mine. I go to all the weight exhibitions. So we get to talking about this and that, you know, and we get into this argument about who's the strongest man in the world. He claims it's this guy who held the tail of a Cessna and kept it from going off.

TESS. You're kidding. You mean an airplane?

LUKE. You never heard of that? Okay, it was a very impressive thing, I admit it, but it was nothing to what I saw this other guy do two years ago, this guy that climbed up a pole with a 700 pound horse on his back. Do you know how hard that is? I'm serious.

TESS. Really?

LUKE. What am I kidding here? It was the most beautiful thing I ever saw.

TESS. Come on.

LUKE. So help me God.

TESS. But how did the horse hold on to him? What did he do? Put his front legs round the guys neck?

LUKE. I know, I know, it looked funny. Cut it out, I'm serious.

TESS. Well I think you won then. That's harder than holding back a Cessna.

LUKE. Damn straight. But he couldn't accept it. He got so mad he just stopped the car and threw me out.

TESS. And left you there for me to find again.

LUKE. I guess so.

TESS. God the choices that we make. The way the smallest of them alters our direction. And to get a second shot at one like this. What happens to all our lost alternatives, do you think? Are they played out in some parallel universe? What would have happened to Oedipus if he hadn't solved the riddle of his own identity? What would have happened to Andromache if Troy hadn't been destroyed? So much in life depends on where you stop the story, doesn't it? I used to do that a lot when I was a kid. - I would stop reading 'Romeo and Juliet' right before he takes the poison. I'd stop Othello when he was still happy with Desdemona in Cyprus. But stopping in stories can be dangerous. Once, because I didn't have the stomach for the crucifixion, I stopped the New Testament at Good Friday and destroyed Christianity. The Jew who unkilled Christ.

LUKE. Lady, you are lucky I got guts, because you are scary.

TESS. I was sort of going on a bit, huh?

LUKE. You are weird. You are the weirdest person I ever met.

TESS. Look, maybe you should just leave.

LUKE. I didn't say I wanted to leave.

TESS. You didn't have to. Mind-reading runs in my family. We've been weird for generations.

LUKE. Yeah? So what else is on my mind?

TESS. Not much else.

LUKE. One thing, though. One thing is on my mind. *(He moves closer.)* Come on lady, your heart is beating so loud your neighbors are going to start pounding on the ceiling in a minute. And then your books might come crashing down.

TESS. Stop calling me lady.

LUKE. So what's your name?

TESS. Tess.

LUKE. Tess... *(Kisses her.)* Tess... *(She kisses him back. They exit.)*

Scene 4

Abby is addressing the national meeting of delegates from her union - the Confederation of American Textile Workers.

ABBY. Members of Local 109. My name is Abigail Brodsky. I was honored to introduce to you earlier this evening our guest speaker, Mr Jaime Ortega, from San Pedro, Guatamala, who reported to us on trade union activities in his country. The history of the labor movement in our own country has been one of struggle against enormous power - from the days when striking miners were mowed down in the streets - to the relentless Cold War assaults on organized labor - to today, the worst era of union busting since Taft-Hartley. Factories are closing here by the hundreds and relocating in places where workers are paid pittance wages and kept in line by horrible repression. The struggle for a humane society where ordinary people can live decent lives continues everywhere. We can't detach our struggle from people even worse off than ourselves. Mr Ortega has described the appalling conditions in one textile factory in his village in Guatemala. He has requested that we send American observers there - to give practical support to the strikers, and to also provide by our presence some protection to the organizers. I urge you to pass this resolution. (*She exits.*)

Scene 5

Tess' apartment, one hour later. Enter Tess and Luke. He is buttoning his shirt, looking nervous, awkward, trying to be casual, but feeling guilty, worried.

TESS. You okay? What's wrong?

LUKE. What? Nothing? What do you mean? It was great. Thanks.

TESS. Thanks?

LUKE. I mean I enjoyed it a lot.

TESS. What's bothering you? (*He can't bring himself to tell her*) What?

You have a disease?

LUKE. Hell no.

TESS. What? A girlfriend? You're feeling guilty about a - (*She guesses)* Oh shit.

LUKE. I'm sorry.

TESS. You're married? Shit. I asked you, didn't I?

LUKE. I know, I lied.

TESS. You said you lived alone.

LUKE. I lied.

TESS. Shit. And kids too?

LUKE. Three. And one on the way.

TESS. That's great.

LUKE. You're upset?

TESS. What do you think?

LUKE. I'm sorry.

TESS. I asked you.

LUKE. Would you have done it if you knew.?

TESS. No.

LUKE. That's what I figured.

TESS. So you lied. Jesus, I hate being lied to. I hate it.

LUKE. It was wrong. I said it was wrong. Look I'll make it up to you.

TESS. How can you make it up to me?

LUKE. I don't know. You like flowers?

TESS. Flowers?

LUKE. Okay, let me think. I'll think of something.

TESS. I don't want anything. Just go.

LUKE. Can I come back?

TESS. No.

LUKE. I don't mean for that. Not if you don't want it. Look, I like you, you're weird, but I like you. Look I've never done this before.

TESS. Oh yeah, and I'm a Rabbi.

LUKE. It's true. I never cheated on my wife. I mean I've wanted to, I've thought about it a lot. We were married when I was nineteen. That's a long time with one woman even if she is gorgeous. But I don't know, with the kids and work and things. Then all of a sudden I'm caught in this fantasy here, except its really happening.

TESS. A fantasy? Me?

LUKE. Yeah. I still can't believe it, it's like a dream.

TESS. What about your wife? Wouldn't you feel guilty?

LUKE. About her? Nah? It's you I'd feel bad about. She doesn't want me that way much. She's always telling me I need another woman.

TESS. She doesn't mean it. Believe me, she would be so hurt if she ever found out. I don't want to cause someone that kind of pain .

LUKE. How would she find out? We won't tell her.

TESS. No, no, I couldn't lie to another person like that. I hate lying.

LUKE. You wouldn't be lying. I'd be lying. You'd have nothing to do with it.

TESS. You're not good at it. You'd make a mistake. Then she'd know and her world would cave in.

LUKE. She won't know. She doesn't notice things as much as you do, believe me. It'll be fine. I won't make a mistake. Jesus, Tess, all I want is a little fun. A person only got one life.

TESS. You really never cheated on your wife before?

LUKE. No.

TESS. Look me in the eye. A person only gets one lie with me and you've had it.

LUKE. Really... I've never even gone to prostitutes. (*Tess takes his palm, as if to read it.*) You read palms too?

TESS. Fortune-telling runs in my family.

LUKE. I once had a blowjob. Once, that's all.

TESS. You don't count that as being unfaithful?

LUKE. She came up to me in the street, I didn't even know she was a pro. She was young, you know, and very pretty, had these gorgeous white teeth. I noticed that right away. It surprised me you know when she asked, so I said 'How much for a blowjob?' And she said - 'Twenty', and ... we... uh... she took me up to her apartment. It was a nice place. She kept it clean, introduced me to her neighbors and everything, like I was a date. Asked me if I wanted coffee. We talked for awhile. It was weird. Then she took her clothes off and did it.

TESS. And that was it? You just left... you didn't -

LUKE. I was tempted, she was really pretty, especially her teeth. God,I still remember them. But, I don't know - they don't really want you, you know what I mean? When it comes to that, I want a woman who wants it, like you.

TESS. Your wife doesn't -

LUKE. She's okay. She's had some bad luck with men, you knew. Her father was a real creep, then she was raped by three drunks in a bar when she was fifteen -

TESS. Jesus.

LUKE. I mean she shouldn't have been there - in a way she was asking for it - but it was a raw deal. She got pregnant... Her father threw her out.

TESS. She had the baby?.

LUKE. Yeah. The kid was a year old when we got married. Still doesn't know I'm not her father. We'll probably never tell her. Hell, she feels like my own. We've known each other all our lives, Holly and me, grew up in the same neighborhood, dropped out of the same high school. - Jesus we had nothing when we got married. I don't know, one night... she was seventeen... I was nineteen... we both got drunk and she was crying in my arms you know... She felt good to hold and she's so pretty and I said, 'Hell, I'll marry you myself.'

TESS. This is too much. How can I do this to a woman who's been through this kind of shit? Why did you tell me?

LUKE. What do you mean? You told me I only get one lie...

TESS. I know, I know. I don't know what I'm saying. Look, look. - just give me some time, okay... Call me in a few weeks.

LUKE. A few weeks?

TESS. I need some time to think.

LUKE. Come on, Tess. Look, she's not that innocent herself. She can be pretty nasty. (*She takes his palm.*) Okay, she's not that bad - average, I would say, average, but Jesus, she's not that delicate She can take care of herself. Besides, she's not going to find out. (*The phone rings.*)

TESS. That's probably her now.

LUKE. What do you mean? Even I don't have the number.

TESS. Hello. Grandma. What's the matter? Slow down, I can't... Oh Jesus. Is he conscious? Where are you? What? They have to... It's to monitor his heartbeat. Where are you? Why didn't they take him to Coney Island Hospital, it's closer... Nevermind, I'll be right there.

LUKE. Bad news?

TESS. Yeah.

LUKE. I'm sorry. You need a lift somewhere?

TESS. How are you going to give me a lift? Your truck is in the middle of the expressway.

LUKE. Oh yeah. You want me to come with you?

TESS. No.

LUKE. Can I see you again?

TESS. No.

LUKE. Come on, Tess. *(They exit.)*

Scene 6

Devorah's Apartment in Brooklyn, two weeks later. Morris has died, and Devorah is sitting 'shivah' for him. She is presently off-stage, resting. Tess, who has come to visit, is also offstage. Brenda enters, calling off some parting words to a neighbor who has stopped her in the hallway of the building.

BRENDA. Right. Right, I'll tell her... I'm sure she'll be very touched. *(Entering the room)* Jesus. I can't stand it with these women. Tess? Grandma? Hello?

TESS. *(Entering, writing some notes.*) Hi.

BRENDA. Where is she?

TESS. Resting.

BRENDA *(Looking out the window.)* Look at them sitting down there.

TESS. Who?

BRENDA. Who.These stupid women.They make me sick.You have to pass fucking inspection just to get into this building.

TESS. Where should they sit? Scarsdale? It's their neighborhood.

BRENDA. Oh please, they've been down there on that sidewalk since the Diaspora. That's why no trees grow in this fucking borough you know, because they take up the whole street.

TESS. 'So Brenda, you came to sit *shivah* with your Grandma? Such a pity, such a fine man, Morris, and so sudden, so young to go, a man only 200 years old. *Nu*, that's the way it is, one minute so alive - eating, blinking, sitting, snoring, choking on his phlegm, the next pussssht.'

BRENDA. What, you're a stand-up comic now?

TESS. Afraid of the competition?

BRENDA. Why don't you write me up some of this stuff?

TESS. Come on.

BRENDA. I mean it. I always need new material.

TESS. Come on, I was fooling around. I got my own work.

BRENDA. Work? You call this work? (*Reading the front page of the manuscript.) By the Breath of God Made Wild: Desire and Corruption in the Myth of the Trojan War.* Oh give me a break.

TESS. It's there, Brenda. In all the old myths - the secret of our nature.

BRENDA. Oh, who cares? I'm talking big bucks here, Tess, I'm talking the - *The Tonight Show.*

TESS. You got a spot on *The Tonight Show?*

BRENDA. No... no yet... but I had an audition.

TESS. No kidding.

BRENDA. And I was great. It's finally going to happen, I can feel it. And no thanks to my agent, believe me. I've been cultivating their casting director for a year - hiring limos, bribing the waiters for the right table, being seen talking to the right people. Oh don't look at me like that, Miss Prim, that's how you get points with people who count. You think just because you got talent, everyone comes running. Unless you're hot, no one gives a shit how good you are. You have to force it on them.

TESS. I hope you get it. I really do.

BRENDA. So help me with my act.

TESS. Will you leave me alone?

BRENDA. Right. God forbid you should write something people could actually enjoy. You're becoming as grim as my sister.

TESS. Have you heard from her Brenda?

BRENDA. Me? I don't even hear from her when she's in New York.

TESS. I don't know how to get in touch with her.

BRENDA. She's always disappearing you know that.

TESS. Yeah, but she's not in Kentucky now, she's in Guatemala.

BRENDA. What the fuck is she doing in Guatemala? No, don't tell me.

TESS. Even her union doesn't know where she is exactly.

BRENDA. Oh please, sweet one, Splendid Creature... just one routine.

TESS. You'd ruin it.

BRENDA. I'll work on the accent.

TESS. It's not the accent.

BRENDA. What then?

TESS. You just make *shtick* out of it. You don't really like them.

BRENDA. I will. I'll like them, I'll love them .- Please, I've had such a depressing week and all I want is to make you stinking rich.

TESS. Could I have a grand house in the country with a swimming pool, and three bathrooms?

BRENDA. Yes.

TESS. And a Jacuzzi?

BRENDA. Yes.

TESS. And one of those circular driveways?

BRENDA. Yes, yes, yes.

TESS. God how I envy the rich those driveways. You can live your entire life without ever once having to put your car in reverse.

BRENDA. We could have it, Splendid Cousin, we could have it all.

TESS. God, Brenda, it's weird how many different selves can fit into so small a space. *(Pointing to her head.)* It's like Hong Kong in there.

BRENDA. I'm shitting a brick over this audition, I really am.

TESS. What would you give to get a break like that?

BRENDA. Anything. Absolutely anything, short of my life, and eyesight. I don't know. Maybe short of your life.

TESS. (*Genuinely touched.*) Really?

BRENDA. I said maybe, didn't I?

TESS. Would you do something wrong? Would you do something really wrong?

BRENDA. No, I draw the line at anything wrong. You're such a jerk.

TESS. Oh Brenda...

BRENDA. What?

TESS. I have just begun this sordid, meaningless affair.

BRENDA. Really? That's great. Why didn't you tell me? Who?

TESS. Just a guy. Don't tell Abby.

BRENDA. I'm running to tell Abby. What, he's Republican?

TESS. No. Well, maybe, I don't know, I don't think he votes.

BRENDA. One of your anarchist College Professor assholes?

TESS. Not exactly, he makes bread.

BRENDA. Good, you're getting smart.

TESS. I don't mean... that kind of bread.

BRENDA. Then what?

TESS. Bread. Real bread.

BRENDA. What, you mean that you eat?

TESS. Yes, that you eat, Jesus. And he has a wife.

BRENDA. Yeah?

TESS. And almost four kids...

BRENDA. Yeah?

TESS. And no capacity at all for abstract thought.

BRENDA. So what's the problem?

TESS. It's just... Jesus, he's so dumb. I spent the first hour we met with my sex instinct desperately trying to dodge my brain.

BRENDA. Is he good?

TESS. And that's another thing. He's a really decent guy. And his wife... she's been through a lot, you know.

BRENDA. Who hasn't?

TESS. But really a lot. Luke's the first decent thing that's ever happened to her.

BRENDA. So. You're taking him away from her?

TESS. Are you kidding? We couldn't even spend a whole weekend together.

BRENDA. So.

TESS. It's just, well, you know, he's lying to her.

BRENDA. No. He doesn't go home and tell her that he's screwing you?

TESS. I would hate that most if I were her. It's a sin to keep someone so much in the dark about her own life.

BRENDA. It's true. I think you should give him up.

TESS. Yeah?

BRENDA. Sure. She'd do it for you.

TESS. On the other hand, she's twenty-six and gorgeous. And... and I was really lonely, you know?

BRENDA. Oh for Christsake, you're such a jerk, just enjoy it. Is he good?

TESS. I don't know. It's hard to tell when you're that hungry for each other. All he has to do is look at me. *(Devorah Enters. Brenda kisses her.)*

BRENDA. How you doing, Grandma?

DEVORAH. I still can't believe it. To see what happens to a person. I was talking with him just last week.

BRENDA. So what's the miracle? He was alive last week.

DEVORAH. How fast it all goes by. It seems like only yesterday I married him... It seems like only yesterday I married Grandpa. And the years go by and your children grow up and you drop dead and that's it, you say good-bye and new people come.

BRENDA. You drop dead and then you say good-bye. - That's a new one.
DEVORAH. We were arguing over which show to watch on the television. One minute he's yelling, the next minute he's on the floor. He started turning blue, he couldn't catch his breath, I got so scared. But I got down right away on my hands and knees and tried to survive him. Didn't know how but I tried. It was no good, he looked at me, and then I saw his soul leave his body.
TESS. You actually saw it leave?
DEVORAH. The light went out in his eyes, he opened his mouth and it went. When the soul goes out of you, you're finished, no matter who you are, a king, a doctor, that's it.
BRENDA. He was alive for a week after the stroke, Grandma.
DEVORAH. Machines. Nowadays they have these machines that keep you alive for years - without a heart, without a brain even you're okay. But the soul leaves, that's it, you can say good-bye. I saw it once before. When the light goes from the eyes like that. It seems like only yesterday...
BRENDA. She always gets so depressing when she's between husbands. Look, you want me to fix you up with someone?
DEVORAH. I need you to fix me?
BRENDA. Come on, there are no men in this building. They've all been shipped down to relatives in Miami until you get married again.
DEVORAH. Fix yourself up better. I'm an old woman. You should have children before it's too late. And that other one who didn't even come to the funeral? Forget it, from her I'll never see a child.
TESS. We couldn't get in touch with her, Grandma. She doesn't know.
DEVORAH. She doesn't know?
TESS. She's far away.
DEVORAH. Far away. Poor girl. She always was so different.
BRENDA. She's nuts.
DEVORAH. She wanted so much to be normal. She would cry in my arms sometimes. 'Help me Devorah,' she would say, 'teach me how to look away.' (*Walking toward the window)* She would look out that window for hours. Hours. She would see things that weren't there. (*Lost in an old scene.*) 'Shut up. Shut up. No one wants to hear you. Why did you let her out. I told you not to let her out.' 'She was lonely, Mama, she wants to be with people.'
BRENDA. What is she talking about?

DEVORAH. She saw him through the window. Saw him walking toward the house. I did too. It was Purim. I remember because I still had on my costume. His eyes were like the sky. His face... his face... I could stare at him for hours. I could die just from watching him read. 'When you run,' he said to me, 'your hair is like fire in the wind.' My body ached to touch him. When he was in the room it was like a storm in my soul. Can you understand? It was like the force from magnets.

TESS. Who was he?

DEVORAH. Daniil. Grandpa's brother...

BRENDA. Her own brother-in-law?

DEVORAH. We thought he had died in Siberia.

BRENDA. She's really something.

TESS. What happened to him, Grandma?

DEVORAH. One morning she was wild with grief - shouting, banging on people's doors. 'Listen to me, please listen.' People complained. They were going to take her away.

TESS. What happened ?

DEVORAH. She had seen something terrible. Terrible. It broke her heart.

TESS. What?

DEVORAH. I was picking strawberries in the field. I remember... They were so big and luscious I ate them from the ground. I didn't even wait to wash the dirt off. She was running toward me... I think she was running... We saw her... We both did...But his hand, his hand was on my mouth... *(A long pause, and then she returns, disoriented, to the present.)* They left already?

TESS. Who?

DEVORAH. Who? Who else? The Fishbeins.

TESS. The Fishbeins?

DEVORAH. Fishbein. Fishbein. From upstairs. Who were paying condolence. What's the matter with you lately?

TESS. They left hours ago.

DEVORAH. They left? Look at that, they didn't even say good-bye.

BRENDA. She knows you got your eye on him.

DEVORAH. You saw the way she held on to him? Like I would want an *elter cocker* like him.

BRENDA. Come on, come on, you got Fishbein marked.

DEVORAH. Oy, leave me alone already, mark for yourself better.

(They exit. Tess is silent for a beat, looking after them. Then she turns,

collects her thoughts, and begins a lecture to her class.)

Scene 7

Lecture hall. Tess addresses her students.

TESS. Force. Naked brutal force. Everything has been crushed before that reality. Picture it. The men have all been killed. The women are huddled among the ruins waiting to be carried off into slavery. All around them are the dying flames and the rising smoke of a city that is no more. Troy is no more. On the ground, banging her head against a rock is Hecuba, Troy's Queen. Just a few hours before she was an Empress. Dukes and ambassadors tiptoed when she took a nap, her daughters and sons were alive and safe, her grandchildren were jumping in her bed, her husband was with his young mistress in another part of the palace, things weren't a hundred percent, but hey, it was a good life. At one side of her, rocking back and forth upon the ground, is her daughter Cassandra. Wild-eyed Cassandra, to whom the gods gave the gift of prophecy. Some gift. It drove her crazy because no one ever believed her. To the left of Hecuba is her daughter-in-law Andromache. Jill? No, I'm not talking politically here, she just happened to be on that side. Actually, she was the most conservative of all the women. Virtuous, gentle, obedient, the kind of woman who follows the world's hard rules as proudly as if it were a third grade teacher coming down the aisle with gold stars to paste in her book. But at this moment, what is the world to Andromache but hate and madness and red death? A beloved husband slain, her country destroyed, her child ripped from her arms and thrown off the walls of the city, its broken body brought back for her and Hecuba to bury. She has lost everything. The last we see of her she is in chains, driven like a beast is driven onto the Greek ships. Euripides ends his story here. But what happened to Andromache after this? And to Hecuba? And the others? What happens when every taste is gone but the taste of ashes in your mouth?

ACT TWO

Scene 1

Tess' apartment. The phone rings.

TESS. (*Tess rushes in to answer it.*) Hello. Yes. Yes, I'll accept. Abby? I said I'll accept. Abby? Where are you? I know but... What? Jesus I can hardly hear you. That's great. When? Okay, let me get a pen. (*She searches frantically for a pen. Finds one.)* Okay. Flight 34... (*It's out of ink.*) Shit. Wait... wait a minute... (*She finds a pencil*) Okay. Flight 34... Tomorrow... 6:13pm... What? Right now?... Okay... You go... I know, I love you too... Abby, wait a minute... Abby?

LUKE. (*Entering, buttoning his shirt*) What's the matter?

TESS. Nothing. One minute this thing is connecting you with someone and the next it's just a piece of plastic in your hands.

LUKE. Who was it?

TESS. My cousin.

LUKE. The one we went to see at that club?

TESS. Not that cousin.

LUKE. She's really something.

TESS. You were pretty dazzled by her, huh?

LUKE. She's okay.

TESS. She thinks you're gorgeous.

LUKE. Cut it out. Come here, I got some stuff for you.

TESS. Stuff? What kind of stuff?

LUKE. Just some things I bought for you.

TESS. Presents? You mean presents?

LUKE. Wait a minute, will you?

TESS. I love presents.

LUKE. They're not presents, I wish I had the money for presents.

TESS. What is it?

LUKE. Will you wait a minute, you're worse than my kids. *(As she grabs the bag away.)* Hey.

TESS. (*Pulling out the first present.*) A... small towel. Oh, thank you.

LUKE. It's a washcloth. Jesus.

TESS. It's wonderful.

LUKE. I noticed you didn't have one when we were, you know, in the shower.

TESS. That's what you noticed, when we were you know in the shower?

LUKE. I can notice more than one thing, can't I?

TESS. That's what you noticed in a moment so joyful that nothing else that ever happens to me in this life, no matter how horrible, can ever make me wish I wasn't born. - That I needed a washcloth?

LUKE. What do you mean?

TESS. I love it. Thank you.

LUKE. You ever did it like that before? I mean in a shower?

TESS. Sure. Haven't you?

LUKE. Sure. (*She grabs his palm to check for truthfulness.*) Okay, okay, I didn't... But you got to admit it sounds like a pretty stupid idea. I mean standing up like that... Everything so slippery we can barely get a hold of each other... Water pouring down all over us. This is turning me on.

TESS. Hey, I got presents here. (*Unwrapping another which at first she doesn't quite place.*) A... a...

LUKE. Knife sharpener.

TESS. God I needed one.

LUKE. Tell me about it. I don't know how you cut anything with those things you got in there. They're like blocks of wood.

TESS. Thank you.

LUKE. There's more.

TESS. More? Oh Luke, you have to stop this, this is too much... A bottle opener. A bottle opener. I needed one. You notice everything I need.

LUKE. It's got all the gadgets on it, like the one I got at home.

TESS. Luke, you really are a generous man.

LUKE. Cut it out. It's nothing. I wish I could get you a real present.

TESS. Yeah? What would you get?

LUKE. I don't know. A diamond necklace maybe.

TESS. Yeah?

LUKE. Yeah. And you'd pick up your hair and I'd stand behind you and clasp it and I'd say - 'Hey there's lots more where that came from, Baby.'

TESS. I don't want a necklace.

LUKE. You want a washcloth?

TESS. Yeah.

LUKE. That's because you're weird. (*Starts to kiss her.*)

TESS. Wait a minute. Tell me about your day.

LUKE. What do you mean my day?

TESS. What you did?

LUKE. The same like I always do. What's there to tell? I got up, I took a shower, I got dressed, I ate.

TESS. What did you eat?

LUKE. Who cares?

TESS. Me.

LUKE. Cornflakes, I ate cornflakes okay, and the kids were throwing it all over the place, and the baby was squalling, and my shirt wasn't ironed yet, and the landlord didn't fix the radiator yet, and she was bitching at me to fix this, fix that, meanwhile I got to get the truck ready and drive it through the snow for eight hours,so we have this big fight, and now we're not talkin. That's my day.

TESS. If you could listen to what she's saying, she would probably listen to you.

LUKE. She doesn't hear anything I say, I told you.

TESS. Maybe she doesn't feel that you hear her.

LUKE. No matter what I say all she ever says is 'yeah, yeah, yeah.' - Her and my boss - 'yeah, yeah, yeah, yeah.' - Its their favorite sentence.

TESS. Maybe if you were more specific about what you want from her.

LUKE. What I want from her? What I want from her is that she be more like you. Is that what I should tell her?

TESS. Oh God. I'm doing something really wrong here. You've got to stop coming here.

LUKE. You want me to stop coming here?

TESS. No. No, it was easier to say it than hear it. Just stop liking me so much.

LUKE. Really?

TESS. No. Just don't tell me that you like me.

LUKE. Yeah?

TESS. No... just... I don't know... remind me of something I'm forgetting, something that makes this all right.

LUKE. What, you mean like I'm a better husband?

TESS. Yes. Good, that's good.

LUKE. That she's gorgeous.

TESS. That's it. Good.

LUKE. Men turn around to look at her in the street. It drives me wild, I nearly belted someone last week.

TESS. (*Without much conviction.*) Great.

LUKE. And anyway, I'd never leave her.

TESS. Okay, I think I have a handle on it now.

LUKE. Our fights don't last long. Even if we go to bed mad, you know how it is with married people... This touches this, that touches that...

TESS. I said okay, didn't I?

LUKE. What's the matter now?

TESS. Nothing. What else did you do this weekend?

LUKE. This weekend... Lets see... Friday night we took the kids to McDonalds - that's a fast food place, you get hamburgers and fries and stuff.

TESS. I know what McDonalds is. - What am I, from Mars?

LUKE. What's the matter?

TESS. Nothing. Then what?

LUKE. Then on Sunday, I took my son to see my grandmother in Baltimore.

TESS. You drove down to Baltimore?

LUKE. Well I haven't seen her for while.

TESS. Yeah? How long?

LUKE. About twenty years I guess. Didn't even know where she was. A cousin found out for me. Oh, by the way, I'm half Italian and half Scottish.

TESS. You found out your nationality?

LUKE. Big deal. I was there already, wasn't I? So I asked her.

TESS. Oh Luke.

LUKE. What?

TESS. My life is strewn with your gifts.

LUKE. Cut it out. (*She kisses him.*) I got to go.

TESS. Yeah. I know. (*They hold each other. They exit.*)

Scene 2.

Devorah's apartment, a few weeks later. Brenda enters and makes a call.

BRENDA. Brandy Brod. What do you mean call back? I've been calling back for three weeks. You told me to call back at two, it's two. When? Then give her this number. Then give it to her again. Thanks. 212 375 7766. Thanks. *(Hangs up.)* It better be ten minutes. I'll smear your fat ass all over the sidewalk if you keep me waiting one more day. (*Tess enters.*) How is she?

TESS. Restless.

BRENDA. I wonder how much more of that sedative we can give her without actually killing her.

TESS. Why such sentimental restraint?

BRENDA. Oh please, that's no hothouse flower in there, toots.- We're talking about a woman with the hots for her own brother-in-law.

TESS. Will you shut up about that already?

BRENDA. You didn't tell Abby?

TESS. No.

BRENDA. Or about your own little lovenest?

TESS. That was the first thing I had on my mind to tell her.

BRENDA. Oh what are you so uptight about? (*Seeing there is something)* What?

TESS. I have to give him up, Brenda.

BRENDA. Yeah? Well how about to me? The guy would cream up a corpse, even if he can't put three words together in a sentence. He's not actually retarded, is he? *(Pause*) What? She found out?

TESS. No. No, it's not that.

BRENDA. So? *(Abby enters.*)

ABBY. She thought I was Rifka. She started shaking me and screaming at me to stop looking. 'Stop Rifka, stop, there's nothing there, stop looking.' Then she suddenly recognized me. (*To Brenda.*) Have you taken her to see a specialist?

BRENDA. Have I taken her? I? What about you?

ABBY. I should call Goldfarb from Guatemala for a doctor's appointment? I didn't even know that she was sick.

BRENDA. (*Imitating the Spanish accent*) Guatemala. Cuba. Nicaragua. Listen, whatever else you can say about the left-wing Yids, they got the Spanish cities down.

ABBY. What did I say? I asked her if she took her to a doctor?

TESS. (*Hugging her*) It's so good to have you back home, Abby.

ABBY. I hadn't meant to stay that long.

BRENDA. (*To telephone.*) Call, you fuckhead.

ABBY. People are just disappearing there, Tess - health workers, union leaders, teachers, priests, anyone who speaks out. (*She picks up the telephone and begins to dial.*)

BRENDA.. Hey, I'm expecting a very important call.

ABBY. *(Telephone.*) Jim Arnold, please. (*To Tess.*) And we're supporting the bastards. I want you to take a look at some material I brought back.

Hello Jim? Abigail Brodsky.

BRENDA. You better make this quick.

ABBY. Did you get the packet I sent you? What do you mean? Who did you speak to? You believe that shit? Oh come on, you expected them not to deny it?

BRENDA. Will you get off the fucking phone? Jesus. I am expecting an important call.

ABBY. I know you've been there too, but unfortunately, not everything worth reporting in that country happens in the Hilton Bar. People are being mowed down in the streets for godsake, for the heinous crime of wanting to feed their children. (*He hangs up on her.*) That's a free press for you.

BRENDA. Did he hang up on you, you old diplomat you?

ABBY. He's terrified that if he actually wrote something that suggested we murder people to protect profits, he won't become Washington Bureau Chief.

BRENDA. The guy wants to have a few drinks in the Hilton, it kills her. They should come and arrest him for the crime of knowing how to enjoy himself.

The phone rings

BRENDA. Jesus, do you see what you almost made me miss? *(Answers phone)* Hello. Speaking. Right. *(As she's put on hold.*) Why should I mind holding you slob? I got all day.

ABBY. (*To Tess, taking some documents from her bag.*) Tess, I want to show you something.

BRENDA. Hello Angela? Hey, it's good to finally hear from you. I was in Atlantic city for a few weeks at a gig and my grandmother's fifteenth husband *plotzed* and she's not doing so great so I'm back for a few.... What? Yeah... uh... what's the story? We expected to hear... Really? Uh huh.... So what was wrong? I mean it felt good. Uh huh... Well, I could tone it down, that's no... Look we've known each other for a year, if you just give me this shot, just a shot, I'll owe you forever I swear it... Uh huh. Can I call you when... Uh huh... Well keep me in mind. Thanks. (*Hangs up.*) Shit. I have been crawling on my belly for over a year, I've gone without food to send the bitch flowers, a year, a year of sucking up and kissing ass down the toilet. Damn. Damn. Too dirty my ass. It's the most original act in the business. I've got to get something on her. And I know how, don't worry. I know how. They won't wear me down... Never. I'll wear them down first. Don't worry, this is just added motivation for me, just added motivation. Oh the pleasure of one day ramming it down her throat.

ABBY. Will you shut her up? She is plunging the whole world into darkness.

TESS. Don't exaggerate, it gets a little hard to read that's all.

BRENDA. Very funny. My life is falling apart and this is what I need right now - sarcasm.

ABBY. You're getting meaner, Brenda, meaner every day.

BRENDA. My hopes are in shambles, I'm getting screwed over by everyone, and I happen to feel like shit, but hey, it's great to have a family.

ABBY. Mean, grubby, self-serving, self-important, depressing -

TESS. She's not depressing.

BRENDA. It certainly took you long enough.

TESS. She's too funny to be depressing.

ABBY. She's funny? That's it? That excuses the fact that behind that face lurks a bottomless chasm of self-interest?

BRENDA. Oh what do you know about being funny? You never laughed once in your life.

TESS. That's not true. She has a great sense of humor.

BRENDA. Please. If there was a hymen in those lips it would be just as intact as the other one.

ABBY. Even her humor is mean-spirited.

BRENDA. And how would you know that, huh? How would you know, have you ever been to one of my performances? Have you ever encouraged me in anything?

ABBY. What am I supposed to cheer you on for? A mansion in Beverly Hills, a fleet of cars, the adoration of millions, and the chance to ram it down the throat of everyone who didn't believe in you enough?

BRENDA. That will do for starters. My values don't suit you well big deal, big fucking deal. (*Gathering her stuff to leave.*)

TESS. Brenda...

BRENDA. The world agrees with me, you fucking loser, not you... And you want to know why? You want to know why? Because no one in his right mind wants to live in a roach-infested apartment over a car wash in a neighborhood of junkies.

ABBY. They're not junkies, they're working people.

BRENDA. You're a victim groupie. You always were. Anyone but your own family.

TESS. Brenda

BRENDA. You leave me alone, too... Get your hands off me... (She exits.)

TESS. Brenda.

ABBY. Let her go.

TESS. Don't you care about her at all?

ABBY. No. I don't know. She makes me so angry.

TESS. She's more honest than I am.

ABBY. Oh don't give me this 'she's selfish but she's honest' crap. I hate people who are honest about their selfishness. It's not enough they go around screwing everyone in their way, they have to make a virtue out of it. Like having a conscience is an affectation.

TESS. Conscience. A lot of good that does most of us.

ABBY. Yours isn't so bad.

TESS. (*Smiles.*) Really? There's another explanation for why it doesn't work?

ABBY. Tess, I want to show you something.

Abby wants to show Tess some material from Guatemala, to ask her help with something. She walks over to the pile of stuff she left by the telephone, begins looking through it. Tess, half self-mocking, half serious, is still absorbed in speculation on the limits of human conscience.

TESS. Maybe they're all just badly designed. The human conscience—put together on the cheap. Like one of those fake security cameras you see hanging in stores that can't afford the real thing. Glaring down on you, flashing a red light but not really attached to anything that works.

ABBY. (*Looking at some of the photographs in the pile.*) It's so strange.

TESS. It is. (*Realizing Abby is talking about something else.*) What's strange?

ABBY. How one minute you're living something, and the next it's just an image on a piece of cardboard. *(Tess goes over to look at the photographs with her.)*

TESS. Is this where you were living when you were in Guatemala?

ABBY. Yeah. In that cottage. It's the home of a woman who works in the textile factory there. Two rooms - dirt floor, no telephone, no toilet, no running water. There's a river at the end of the road where I bathe in the mornings. The water is so clean. I haven't seen water that clear since I was a kid. Do you remember that river in the Catskills where we had a bungalow, before my parents died? You'd come up there sometimes...

TESS. Yeah. The Neversink.

ABBY. There was a rock right in the middle where Brenda and I could rest when we swam the width. There's one just like it in this river. The woman's kids sometimes come there with me. The oldest is about eight and takes care of all the younger ones. They all have diseases - parasites, diarrhea... The three year old has patches of hair missing from her head. She looks like a doll that some kid got mad at, but it's a skin disease that comes from malnutrition. Tess, I need your help with something.

TESS. What?

ABBY. The workers in the factory there have organized a union, but their leaders are being arrested, their meetings broken up by thugs, their houses bombed, people kidnapped off the streets. - And we're supporting the bastards. Tess, I have to go back.

TESS. You're going back?

ABBY. That's why I need your help here. I need to document our involvement. I have material, but I need hard proof.- There are things that need to be checked out here, people in Washington I need to talk to. But I don't have time. If you could -

TESS. Abby, are you crazy? You can't go back there.

ABBY. It won't be for long.

TESS. It's too dangerous.

ABBY. I can help them.

TESS. No.

ABBY. Tess, if you could just help me with some of the research, the publicity... A few weeks.

TESS. No. You can't go back there.

ABBY. I can't just see it and then go home. It's not a movie. People have to know the truth about what's happening there.

TESS. Why? What do people do with the truth when they get it? Nothing.

ABBY. I can't believe I'm hearing this from you. How can we change anything if we don't know what's going on?

TESS. The world is filled with decent people and heinous crimes and it's not just because we don't know what's going on. Is it?

ABBY. Look, I haven't got time for this.

TESS. I'm just trying to understand.

ABBY. Understand what? The complexities of your own personal psyche? The mythic dimensions of good and evil. I haven't got time. *(Devorah enters, dazed and frightened.)* What is it, Grandma?

DEVORAH. *(She stares at Abby, then takes her hand.)* Come, come inside, there's fire... There's fire everywhere, come inside with me.

ABBY. It's okay, Grandma, it's okay, it's just a dream.

DEVORAH. What happened that morning?

ABBY. What morning?

DEVORAH. The way you looked at me. Did you see something, Rifka? Something I forgot?

ABBY. It's me, Grandma. Abby.

DEVORAH. Abby?

ABBY. Don't you recognize me?

DEVORAH. Abby?

ABBY. Yes.

DEVORAH. Zayner. Look. Look how I forget things.

ABBY. You want me to come lie down with you a little?

DEVORAH. Yes. Come lie down with me. *(Devorah exits. Abby begins to follow, but Tess calls her back with a sudden cry of fear.)*

TESS. Abby. Don't go back. *(Abby turns again to follow her grandmother into the bedroom.)* Please. I'm scared.

ABBY. I'm scared too. What do you think? You know things - but it's different when you see it. It's different. I was invited one day to go home with a friend for dinner. He was telling me about his family as we walked - his new baby, how good a cook his wife was, how he'd met her. He called to her as we opened the door to come and meet me. When she didn't answer, we walked into the kitchen. They were all there, his whole family. His wife, his three children, his sister, his mother, the new baby. They were all seated around the table as if about to eat. But they had all been murdered. The heads had been cut off and set before the bodies like dishes. All of them. Even the baby.

TESS. Oh God.

ABBY. I don't understand either, okay. I was in despair for days. What is it we're up against here? What? What am I doing trying to document a force like that? Trying to drag it politely before subcommittees. What am I doing?

TESS. Forgive me.

ABBY. What if it is stronger? What if it is really stronger than anything that resists it?

TESS. No....

ABBY. The only thing is - what are we if we consent to live blindly in a world in which that happens?

TESS. I know. We can't.

ABBY. What are we if our only response is despair?

TESS. Forgive me.

ABBY. I didn't mean to blame you. I don't understand either.

TESS. You do. It's you who has it right. (*Hugging her.*) Oh Abby, of course I'll help you. Of course, I will.

ABBY. You will?

TESS. Every time I'm with you I want to live a larger life. I'd do anything for you. I love you.

ABBY. I love you too.

They hold each other. Finally Abby releases her and begins to exit to Devorah's bedroom. Abby turns and pauses at the door for a moment, as if about to say something, but doesn't, and exits. After a beat, Tess begins to gather up, with some urgency, the political documents that Abby has left behind. Luke enters.

Scene 3

Tess's apartment. Tess is reading through Abby's documents, deciding which ones she needs to take with her. Luke is nervous. He wants to tell her something, but can't find the words.

LUKE. Tess?

TESS. Um?

LUKE. I need to tell you something.

TESS. What?

LUKE. (*Beat. It's not what he has to tell her.*) When's your train?

TESS. A few hours.

LUKE. You have to go?

TESS. There's stuff I have to do for Abby. I promised her, I told you.

LUKE. But why do you have to go for so long? Why can't you do it here?

TESS. Because there's some research that can only be done in Washington, and... Is this what you had to tell me?

LUKE. No.

TESS. What then? Luke you're scaring me. Oh my God, she found out.

LUKE. My wife? Nah.Though I sometimes think she must have rocks in her head not to.

TESS. Why? You never spend the night here. I never call. I've given up wearing lipstick. We're so careful, sometimes even I don't know you're having an affair.

LUKE. What do you mean you don't know?

TESS. Nothing. I'm just saying there's no reason for her to suspect.

LUKE. What do you mean no reason? I'm different, aren't I? Everything is different.

TESS. What would you do if she found out?

LUKE. I don't know. I'd have to stop seeing you, I guess. Isn't that what you want?

TESS. Yes.

LUKE. It's what you're always telling me.

TESS. I said yes, didn't I?

LUKE. You think we'd have a shot at it?

TESS. No. Why, do you?

LUKE. No.

TESS. Good. How come?

LUKE. She's my wife. I live there. My kids live there.

TESS. *(Reminding herself as well.)* Your kids, that's right, your kids.

LUKE. And she loves me.

TESS. She tells you that?

LUKE. Yeah, sometimes she tells me that. She can be sweet sometimes. We've been though a lot together, you know. She's stood by me in hard times. Sometimes I don't even know why I'm cheating on her like this.

TESS. So don't. Don't come here anymore.

LUKE. Come on, don't be mad.

TESS. No, really, I'm going away for awhile anyway, this is a good time to break it off.

LUKE. Don't say that.

TESS. No, really, let's just end it -

LUKE. Tess...

TESS. Stop it.

LUKE. Tess, look at me. What I needed to tell you is this. - You see, you were nothing to me. I was just having fun. You think you know what you want from a woman You make it clear, she makes it clear - it's so simple, and then you wind up thinking about her all the time, day, night. So I'm thinking how can I have all these feelings for a woman who's nothing to me? And then I figured it out. It suddenly came to me. You're not nothing to me. I love you.

TESS. Don't say that.

LUKE. You think I don't mean it?

TESS. It's not real.

LUKE. It's real. You want to know why?

TESS. No.

LUKE. Well I sure do. I wish to hell I could figure it out. You're not even pretty.

TESS. Thanks.

LUKE. Half the time I don't even know what you're talking about.

TESS. This is the lousiest declaration of love I've ever heard.

LUKE. I'm coming to the good part. (*But not quite yet, his mind is still on the other track.*) You give lousy head.

TESS. That's the good part?

LUKE. I'm just making the point that it isn't only sex.

TESS. What's the good part!?

LUKE. You're different.

TESS. That's it? I'm different?

LUKE. When I'm with you my life seems less... I don't mean less, I mean, I don't know the word I'm looking for... You're just better than anyone I know. I'll never meet anyone like you again no matter how hard I look. When you're gone, that's it. It's forever. It scares the shit out of me. (*From Tess a low, dull moan.*) I can't leave her. I really can't.

TESS. I don't want you to.

LUKE. What do they call it again when you got mixed feelings about something?

TESS. Ambivalence.

LUKE. Yeah. And what is it when the mixture is eating your guts out?

TESS. Conflict.

LUKE. More.

TESS. Torment.

LUKE. That's it. Tess, sometimes I think I'm going crazy.

TESS. Forgive me.

LUKE. It's not your fault.

TESS. It is. I have deliberately pretended to be looking out for her and all the time I was making her look small in your eyes, teaching you to value everything I have and she doesn't.- I loved your preferring me, I loved it. I have put my own vanity over everything.

LUKE. (*A realization.*) You love me too, don't you?

TESS. No.

LUKE. Yeah, you do.

TESS. We've never even spent a whole night together...

LUKE. Don't go.

TESS. I have to. (*A long beat in which Luke struggles with the dilemma to which there seems no answer. He makes a tentative, confused decision to try to break it off.*)

LUKE. Tess, I don't know where I am anymore... The thought of leaving her kills me... The thought of losing you kills me... and now you're going away... I don't know...Maybe what you said before... I don't know... (*He puts his jacket on and begins to exit. She tries to stay calm in the face of what she knows is the right decision, but panic at losing him wells up in her too forcefully.)*

TESS. (*Calling him back.*) Luke? *(Beat.*) Are you happy with her?

Luke I told you how it is.

TESS. I can't do without you. Stay here with me.

LUKE. What? You mean now?

TESS. I mean for good.

LUKE. You mean leave her? *(A beat Then Tess nods assent.)* But... you're going away.

TESS. I won't... (*She goes to him.*) I won't. (*They cling to each other, a tender and troubled embrace.)*

Scene 4

A Club in Atlantic City. Several months later.

BRENDA. Thank you. Thank you. It's a pleasure to be here in Atlantic City. Umm. A lot of gorgeous guys here tonight. You, you're very cute. Is he yours? YES. So defensive. YES. You married? GET MARRIED. Oh yes. Don't fall for this woman's lib crap, get married young. I don't care who the *schmuck*, get married. Because the same *shmuck* you wouldn't even dance with in high school, you're thirty-five, he's a catch. Oh yes, yes. Because men get established and women go on sale. Am I right? The most fabulous DESIGNER women, thirty-five - CLEARANCE...You... Can you take it? BARGAIN BASEMENT. Oh she's insulted. Oh sure blame me, it's my fault. I invented biological clocks. Is God cute? 'And now, on the occasion of your thirty-fifth birthday - a biological clock.' 'For me? Oh gee, thanks, just what I needed.' I'm telling you, women have it rough. Is God cute? How many of you are like me and read the Bible every night? In the Bible women had it rough. First of all, the least thing you did wrong, you got stoned. And in those days it wasn't hard to mess up because the only thing you had to do to get pregnant was to 'know a man'. That's it. Oh sure, in those days If you just said 'NO', you were a tramp. 'I hardly knew him.' - You heard that a lot. It meant, 'Boy, was he quick.' 'I thought I knew her.' - A wet dream. And it was so dark in those tents, no one ever knew anyone well. You could get up in the morning and find out that the woman you thought you knew, you didn't know. You really knew her sister. This happened a lot, because getting stoned a lot affects your night vision. True. I mean this is the only way to explain some of the guys I've been waking up with in the morning. Just kidding. Actually it's my grandmother who's the wild one in our family. She's had four husbands. And that's not counting her own. (*Blackout.*)

Scene 5

Tess' apartment, several months later. Tess is sleeping fitfully, a pile of papers having fallen from her grasp. She awakens from the nightmare with a start of terror, then half orients herself to the waking world. The phone rings, triggering a flash from the dream. She rushes for it, thinking it might be Abby.

TESS. Abby? (*It's Luke's wife.*) Oh... hello Holly. How are you? No, of course, I under - I know, I know that... I'm not trying... If there's anything... I know, I know how it must feel... Yes... Yes, he is here... Just a second. (*Calling inside.*) Luke. (*He doesn't answer.*) Luke? (*Wondering where they are. Shouting.*) Brenda? (*Realizing they aren't there.*) I'm sorry, Holly, I think he must have gone down. What? No, no, of course not It's because he was here when I fell... What? I know... I know how it must... I'll have him call as soon... (*Holly hangs up. So does Tess.*) Shit.

(*These calls upset her. And she's still a little woozy from the nightmare. She tries to get her bearings. Wonders where Luke and Brenda are. Calls once more inside to bedroom.*) Luke? (*To Kitchen.*) Brenda? (*She picks up some material she was working on, but finds it hard to concentrate. She hears them come in. Luke enters, followed by Brenda. He looks uncomfortable.*) Where were you?

BRENDA. We went down for cigarettes.

TESS. Holly just called.

BRENDA. So, what else is new?

TESS. She said it's important. (*Luke goes to the phone and dials.*)

BRENDA. You were out like a rock. You feel rested?

TESS. No... I... I had a nightmare.

LUKE. (*On telephone.*) Hi Holly, how are...? What? I can't understand a word you're... What? Oh come on, Holly, they're my kids too. Your mother said it would be okay... I just took them to MacDonald's... Slow down will you, I - (*Holly hangs up the phone.*) She's pissed because I went to see the kids at her mother's house.

BRENDA. Oh for Christsake. You tell her you'll stop the checks. Didn't I tell you what to say if she keeps pulling that?

TESS. We have to give her time.

BRENDA. Time, *schmime*. You want to see them or not?

LUKE. Sure. I miss them.

BRENDA. God, you let her walk all over you. Both of you. You should threaten her with a custody fight - That would keep her in line.

TESS. That's all she needs is to be dragged into court now.

BRENDA. They're his kids too.

LUKE. I can wait.

BRENDA. After what she pulled in this living room, you could probably have her declared an unfit mother.

LUKE. Will you butt out. I said I could wait.

BRENDA. Fine, be a *schmuck*. (*Looking through some of the papers on the floor.*) Is this the extra material for the routine?

TESS. No. That's stuff for Abby.

BRENDA. Look, I got a show tomorrow night, and we're still five minutes short. Did you come up with anything?

TESS. Yeah. I think so. I was working on it.

BRENDA. Well is it possible to take a look at it before the actual show?

TESS. It's inside. (*To Luke, who's pacing.*) Are you okay?

LUKE. Sure, what do you mean?

TESS. I don't know. You seem nervous.
LUKE. I'm fine.
TESS. You're not sorry, are you?
LUKE. What do you mean? About what?
TESS. I don't know. Everything.
LUKE. No. Why, are you?
TESS. No. What then? Your kids?
LUKE. They'll be okay.
TESS. You still love me?
LUKE. Sure. (*As she playfully takes his palm.*) What are you doing?
TESS. Just checking .
LUKE. Cut it out.
BRENDA. He loves you, he loves you Can you get the new material? (*Tess exits. To Luke.*) She's can't read palms you idiot.
LUKE. I know that.
BRENDA. So what are you afraid of?
LUKE. Who's afraid? It's stupid, that's all.
BRENDA. Will you calm down?
LUKE. I'm fine.
BRENDA. If you can't hold it together, take a walk or something.
LUKE. I said I'm fine.
BRENDA. (*Beat.*) It was nothing, okay?
LUKE. Jesus. In the car like that. - With her right upstairs.
BRENDA. It was nothing. We just got carried away. If you ever open your mouth -
LUKE. Right. I'm dying for her to know.
BRENDA. Then she won't.
LUKE. She's pretty smart.
BRENDA. Oh please. I could count her smarts on the fingers of one hand - and still have enough left over to get you very hot.
LUKE. You're really something you know that?
BRENDA. So are you. (*Tess re-enters. Brenda takes the material and hugs her.*) I'm sorry I snapped at you.
TESS. It's okay.
BRENDA. Wait till you see the house I rented for us in Vegas.
TESS. I can't go with you to Vegas.
BRENDA. What do you mean, you can't go? You're my partner. You

have to see how new material works with an audience. I mean didn't I tell you they wouldn't get the Faust joke in Vegas? (*To Luke.*) Do you know who Faust was? (*To Tess.*) I rest my case.

TESS. So drop it. I hate what you do with some of that material anyway.

BRENDA. What do you mean? I have to fit it into my own rhythms, don't I?

TESS. I can't go to Vegas. I have to go down to Washington. I have stuff I have to do for Abby. I told you. I should have done it months ago.

BRENDA. Look, who's paying you, me or Abby?

TESS. I haven't heard from her for weeks, Brenda.

BRENDA. I mean you don't expect me to support his wife and kids, do you?

LUKE. I said I'd make it up to you.

BRENDA. You? On $250 a week?

TESS. Do we have to talk about this now?

BRENDA. You know what we promised her.

TESS. I know.

BRENDA. It was the only thing that calmed her down.

TESS. I know.

BRENDA. *Gelt*, baby, it does it every time.

TESS. Look, what do you want?

BRENDA. I'm sorry. I'm just nervous. I'm sorry, okay? I'd do anything for you, sweet one, you know that. But you can't just leave me in the middle like this. Do you know how big an opportunity this is? I need you there... Just for a few days?

TESS. All right.

BRENDA. You know how much is riding on this.

TESS. I said okay.

BRENDA. Thank you, thank you, Splendid Creature... I just don't know why I always have to fight with you to make you a rich woman.

LUKE. They really paying you twenty grand a week?

BRENDA. Show biz, baby.

LUKE. Jesus. I'll never see that much money in my life.

BRENDA. It's hard to believe it's finally happening. I knew once I got that spot on the Carson show, the offers would come pouring in.

TESS. What did you finally get on her, anyway? The casting director?

BRENDA. What do you mean? Talent and persistence, baby, talent and persistence. Okay, maybe I had a few angles.

LUKE. Bet you're excited about seeing Vegas. It's probably even better than Atlantic City, huh?

BRENDA. Atlantic City's a pisspot compared to Vegas. Want to see it?

LUKE. Are you kidding? When would I ever get a chance?

BRENDA. Now. My treat. Come with us.

LUKE. I got to work.

BRENDA. Come for the weekend.

LUKE. All the way to Vegas just for the weekend?

BRENDA. Sure. Why not? It'll be a blast.

LUKE. Nah, I don't want to go.

TESS. Why not?

LUKE. It's just not a good idea, that's all.

TESS. Why?

LUKE. It's just not. (*The temptation is too much.*) I don't know. What do you think?

TESS. I think it would be fine. (*He hesitates.*) What?

LUKE. Nothing.

BRENDA. Look, if you're coming, go pack a few things. We're leaving in half an hour.

LUKE. Yeah. Okay. (*Luke exits to bedroom.*)

BRENDA. Jesus, if this lasts six months, what do you do with him when you're not in bed?

TESS. Don't talk about him that way.

BRENDA. Oh please...You've been in a cold sweat since the day he moved in -

TESS. That's not true.

BRENDA. A cold sweat baby, because now that he was yours forever, you might have to spend the whole weekend with him.

TESS. Shut up. You don't understand him.

BRENDA. Don't I?

TESS. There are depths to his nature.

BRENDA. It was a match made in heaven, okay. Just pack your stuff and let's get out of here. (*Pause. She sees Tess is upset.*) I'm sorry. I know I'm being a bitch. I'm just nervous, Sweet One. No one matters to me as much as you do. I'm really grateful that you're coming. What is it?

TESS. I'm worried sick about Abby.

BRENDA. You're being stupid, she's disappeared before for weeks.

TESS. Not like this.

BRENDA. Exactly like this.

TESS. Something's wrong... I feel it... I have dreams.

BRENDA. Wonderful, another clairvoyant in the family. Hello, Aunt Rifka.

TESS. She's in a room with nothing in it but a pay phone, and she's trying to call me, and the operator keeps telling her I won't accept the charges... 'I accept,' I keep telling her, but they don't hear me... And then I hear... this horrible banging on her door...

BRENDA. All right, okay, when I get back from Vegas, I'll check out who I can speak to over there. I'll find out something.

TESS. They won't talk to me.

BRENDA. That's because you're a nobody. To me they talk.

TESS. So what are you waiting for? Let's go now.

BRENDA. Are you crazy? I got a show in Vegas tomorrow night.

TESS. Vegas? You got a show in Vegas? We're talking about Abby.

BRENDA. So what else is new? We're been talking about her all our fucking lives.

TESS. You don't give a shit whether she's alive or dead? She's your sister.

BRENDA. Don't give me that 'I don't give a shit' crap. It's she that doesn't give a shit. Where was Abby when Luke's wife was flipping out all over your living room, huh? You called Abby? You called me. Where is Abby anytime you ever needed her? Down in some hellhole getting herself killed.

TESS. What are you saying?

BRENDA. I'm saying she's a nut.

TESS. Has something happened to her? Have they been in touch with you? (*Luke re-enters.*)

BRENDA. No.

TESS. Do you know something you're not telling me?

BRENDA. No. I didn't mean it the way it sounded.

TESS. Something happened.

BRENDA. Nothing happened.

TESS. Brenda, please just tell me.

BRENDA. There's nothing to tell.

TESS. You wouldn't try to keep it from me... Not about something like this?

BRENDA. Look, don't get paranoiac on me, okay? Nothing happened.

LUKE. Just tell her the truth for Christsake.

BRENDA. Shut up, Luke.
TESS. Oh God I felt it.
BRENDA. Nothing happened.
TESS. You're lying. Tell me, Luke.
LUKE. Jesus, Tess, I'm so sorry. We just got carried away, you know...
BRENDA. Will you shut up? She's asking about Abby.
LUKE. Abby? I don't know nothing about Abby, Tess.
TESS. What's he saying?
BRENDA. Do I know?
TESS. You slept with him?
BRENDA. Are you crazy? No.
TESS. Luke? (*He doesn't answer.*)
BRENDA. He's lying. (*To Luke.*) I don't know why the fuck you're doing this. (*To Tess.*) He's lying.
TESS. Luke? Luke is a lover of truth.
BRENDA. Luke is a lover of anyone who can put the request into simple sentences.
LUKE. Hey, wait a minute. You threw yourself at me. I mean it was my fault too. I'm not trying to excuse myself here.
BRENDA. Your taking him seriously was a joke...
LUKE. Hey, I'm this close to smashing your face in, you know that?
BRENDA. She would feel a lot better if you'd get out of here, okay?
LUKE. A lot you care about what she feels.
BRENDA. You shut up. I'd do anything for her. Anything. What do you know about it?
LUKE. Tess, are you okay?
BRENDA. Will you get out of here, you're just making it worse.
LUKE. Shut up Brenda. Tess? (*Wanting to touch her, give comfort.*) Tess? (*Beat*) Is there anything I can do? (*Long beat. He recognizes, sadly, that he can't, that the hurt has gone too deep. Lights dim as Brenda tries to repair the damage with apology.*)
BRENDA. I'm so sorry... It was wrong, I know it was wrong. I'll make it up to you, I swear. Please... I love you... you know that... I wasn't thinking... I didn't know it would hurt this much. (*Blackout.*)

Scene 6

Devorah's apartment. Devorah enters carrying a Yarhzeit candle, singing to herself a hymn of mourning. She lights the candle, then exits. Tess and Brenda enter, taking off their coats. They have just returned from burying Abby, whose body they have brought back from Guatemala. Tess takes off her coat .

BRENDA. You okay?

TESS. Yeah.

BRENDA. You sure you want to stay here?

TESS. Yeah.

BRENDA. You could spend the night at my place.

TESS. I'm okay.

BRENDA. You could say two words to me. She was my sister. (*Calling inside.*) Grandma? (*To Tess.*) Is the woman still here?

TESS. She leaves in the evening. (*Picking up the 'yarhzeit' candle.*) What's this? You told her?

BRENDA. About Abby? No. She doesn't remember anything anyway. I have to make a call, okay?

TESS. Sure.

BRENDA. (*On phone.*) Harry? My grandmother's. Because I just walked in the door this minute what do you want from me? What do you think? It was a nightmare. I couldn't even recognize her. I wouldn't wish on my worst enemy what I just went through. She drowned herself. It was horrible - I don't even want to talk about it You're telling me? She was in way over her head down there. They think she may have been involved in drugs. (*Devorah re-enters.*)

BRENDA. Hi, Grandma. No, not tomorrow, I'm exhausted. I've just got back from burying my sister for Christsake. No kidding? It came through, that's great. So, so, you did one thing right. Okay, just a second (*She fishes out a pen to take a message. Devorah gazes at the candle.*)

DEVORAH. Poor Rifka. She came to me last night. Their world is so dark. I lit a candle for her.

TESS. Dark as their world is, it's they should light candles for us.

DEVORAH. At night, there are yellow stains on all the mirrors. That's not good. It means there are demons in the house. Well, *zei gesunt*, I have to go home now.

TESS. This is your home.

DEVORAH. What are you talking, are you crazy? I come here to visit a little you shouldn't be alone, but Grandpa's waiting for supper. Where is my purse? What did you do with my purse?

TESS. Grandpa is dead. He's been dead twenty-five years. This is your home.

DEVORAH. Did you ever? Get out of my way. My husband is hungry.

BRENDA. Could you keep her quiet, I'm on the phone?

TESS. He's working late, remember he told you he'd be very late, so you should stay with me.

DEVORAH. Here I'm supposed to wait for him? See how I forgot? What's happening to me?

TESS. It's okay. Come, sit down.

DEVORAH. Whose apartment is this? I have to pay you something to stay here?

TESS. No, nothing. This is your home.

DEVORAH. I'm not a stranger here?

TESS. No. You live here.

DEVORAH. You live with me? I know you?

TESS. I'm Tess.

DEVORAH. My mama's name.

TESS. I was named after her.

DEVORAH. My Mama is also dead?

TESS. Yes.

DEVORAH. Look how people are dropping like flies. It's like a pogrom in here. Like Europe in the old days. And my in-laws? Malka and Chaim? Also dead?

TESS. Long ago.

DEVORAH. See? See how I caught you? Everyone is dead by you. I just saw them this morning. They looked fine. How do you like that?

BRENDA. (*Finishing the call.*) Isn't there a sedative we could give her or something?

DEVORAH. Leave it to you, the world would be a graveyard There'd be nobody left. See how I caught you? Wait, wait. I'll go and bring them in. See for yourself my mother-in-law still has that big mouth on her. Wait you'll see. (*She exits.*)

BRENDA. She's losing her mind.

TESS. Amazing how much you can lose and still continue to exist, isn't it?
BRENDA. It's just a matter of time before this woman quits too. We have to put her in a home, that's it. No one's going to put up with her no matter what I pay them.
TESS. Okay.
BRENDA. Yeah? Okay, so I'll have my secretary start working on it. (*Taking out an empty pack of cigarettes.*) Jesus. They just disappear on me. *(About the yarhzeit.)* How long do they burn?
TESS. They burn till they're finished.
BRENDA. It's so grim right in the middle of the room like that.
TESS. I'll take it inside.
BRENDA. I didn't say you have to take it inside.
TESS. It's okay.
BRENDA. It's okay, it's okay. Everything is okay by you.
TESS. Look, what do you want?
BRENDA. I want you to forgive me.
TESS. I do.
BRENDA. You were sick of him anyway. I did you a fucking favor. Okay, I was wrong. I know I was wrong. I wanted him. But I didn't know it would hurt that much. I didn't know. I took him like I'd take an orange. Forgive me!
TESS. I do. I do. How many times do I have to tell you? What am I? The Morality Mavin? You wanted him. I wanted him. We reduce everything to our own needs. We can't help it. It's the way we're made. We poison the earth with our selfishness. Abby was a stranger to this world. It was you who had it right.
BRENDA. Look, I just found out about a movie deal. I'm going to Greece in a few days.
TESS. That's great.
BRENDA. Come with me. The script needs a consultant. I mean I don't think there's myths in it, but it's Greece, right. You know a lot of stuff that's bound to come up -
TESS. I can't.
BRENDA. Okay, just come for a holiday, just get away from here. Greece, for Christsake. Come on, Splendid Creature, come with me.
TESS. I can't.
BRENDA. Why?
TESS. I'm busy.

BRENDA. Doing what?

TESS. Leave me alone.

BRENDA. You don't have to work, just be with me. I'm alive, me, not her. Jesus, Tess, you want to lose me too?

TESS. I left her to die.

BRENDA. It's she who should feel guilty, not us. After what she put us through. I still get nightmares.

TESS. You too?

BRENDA. What do you think? She was my sister. Seeing her like that.

TESS. Why do you tell everyone she killed herself?

BRENDA. What everyone?

TESS. Before we were even out of the airport terminal.

BRENDA. It's my fault they were there? They're animals. They'd stick that fucking mike in your face in the middle of a funeral.

TESS. But why do you tell them that it was suicide?

BRENDA. Why do I tell? Because it's the truth.

TESS. They murdered her, Brenda..

BRENDA. You saw the letter. And the witnesses? And the drugs for depression all over the apartment.

TESS. They murdered her. You know it as well as I do. Whatever line you take in public, you know it as well as I do.

BRENDA. You still can't face the truth about her, can you? She was a depressive all her life. A grim, joyless, self-punishing depressive.

TESS. That's a lie.

BRENDA. You could hear it in her voice that she was cracking up.

TESS. She would never have killed herself, never.

BRENDA. You're getting crazy, you know that? This whole ordeal is making you crazy.

TESS. It doesn't matter.

BRENDA. Let me help you for Christsake. Come to Greece with me.

TESS. I said it doesn't matter.

DEVORAH. (*Re-entering.*) Help me... Help me... Tess.

BRENDA. I'll make it up to you, I swear it.

TESS. Leave me alone.

DEVORAH. She blames me.

BRENDA. Grandma, please go inside, I have enough problems here.

DEVORAH. She just stands there... And him too... All of them... All around my bed, like *Dybbucks*. All of them... Waiting.

BRENDA. I've made mistakes, I know it. Big ones. But how many times can I say I'm sorry? You have to forgive me.

DEVORAH. 'Tell them' she says to me, 'tell them what happened.' What does she want from me?

BRENDA. Grandma, please go lie down.

DEVORAH. Help me.

TESS. How?

DEVORAH. Tell me what happened.

TESS. I can't.

BRENDA. (*Trying to lead her back to the bedroom.*) Go back inside.

DEVORAH. (*To Tess.*) Tell me.

BRENDA. I will... I'll tell you, first let's take some medicine.

DEVORAH. No medicine, get out of my way.

BRENDA. You have to go inside.

TESS. Leave her alone.

BRENDA. You butt out.

DEVORAH. Get out of my way. (*In a last surge of strength, she knocks Brenda to the floor. The three of them are stunned by the force of the blow.*)

BRENDA. You stupid, crazy old woman. Get inside.

TESS. Leave her alone.

BRENDA. Will you butt out?

TESS. Leave her alone I said.

BRENDA. Okay, okay, she's all yours. I wash my hands of it. You hear me? I wash my hands of both of you. I am so sick of this shit. (*She takes her coat to exit.*) You know your problem? You're a fucking loser. Jesus, Tess, a fucking loser, just like Abby. (*She exits.*)

DEVORAH. Please... tell me ....

TESS. I can't tell you. I said I don't know.

DEVORAH. All right. Who needs you, I'll do it myself. You'll see. I'll... I'll ... (*A wail of helplessness.*) I can't remember.

TESS. It's not your fault. (*Beginning the story.*) You were born in a *shtetl* in Poland. Remember? And your family was very poor.

DEVORAH. It's true. Sometimes my mother would boil water so people passing wouldn't know there was nothing to eat in the house.

TESS. But it didn't matter to Grandpa. He fell madly in love with you, and swore that if you didn't have him he'd drown himself in the river.

DEVORAH. That's true too. Once he saw me he had to have me... He was lovesick.

TESS. His mother Malka was against the marriage.
DEVORAH. My family couldn't even afford a dowry for me. In those days, that was a terrible thing for a bride.
TESS. That's right. And she always brought it up to you... How poor you were.
DEVORAH. She was a witch that one... (*Devorah becomes lost in an old scene between her mother-in-law and her younger self.*)
'Stop singing already. Do something. Make yourself useful. Who were you before you married our Heshel? A nobody. A nothing.' 'I didn't tell you three times, Mama, I have a rehearsal for the *Purim Spiel*?' 'Ah, the rehearsal, excuse me. - An excuse for parading around showing yourself to men.' Then I enter, Esther the Queen. The King, Ahasahasahasaha - I can never pronounce his name, takes one look on me and that's it, he's finished. He grants me anything. My heart's desire... My heart's desire... (*Struggling to remember something.*) What else?... Tell me... there was something else...
TESS. Your husband had a sister Rifka, and a brother Daniil who everyone thought was dead.
DEVORAH. Yes, that's right. What happened to her?
TESS. I don't know.
DEVORAH. Tell me.
TESS. I don't know.
DEVORAH. Tell me.

We hear Rifka offstage before she enters. She appears either behind a scrim, or a back area of the stage, lit as if in fire. Beginning in Yiddish, which blends into English, ,she is frantic with fear and grief. The character is played by the same actor as plays Abby.

RIFKA. *Di Shtetl brent*
Mamehs farbrechn di hent un veynen
Di erd vaykt mit blut.
The village is burning - mothers wring their hands and weep. Children screaming for their parents, old people lined up and shot, girls raped and torn apart, the ground is soaked with blood -
DEVORAH. Rifka?
RIFKA. Listen to me. Listen. What has happened is happening and will happen again.
DEVORAH. Rifkeleh, be a little quiet, you're depressing people.
RIFKA. Devorah, you promised.

DEVORAH. Promised what?

RIFKA. To help me. To tell them what I saw. They'll listen to you.

DEVORAH. Rifkeleh - Nobody's going to listen, because you're crazy, and you upset people.

RIFKA. I only tell what I see.

DEVORAH. What difference would it make to you if you saw something nice once in awhile? Who would it hurt? You have to learn to look away a little.

RIKFA. Can you learn to do that?

DEVORAH. Why not?

RIKFA. Then teach me. Teach me how to look away.

DEVORAH. Teach you? How can I teach you? It's like talking, walking, you just put one foot in front of another and you do it.

RIFKA. Please, Devorah.

DEVORAH. You'll listen to what I tell you?

RIFKA. Yes.

DEVORAH. Okay, now look out the window like a normal person. What do you see?

RIFKA. I see the village of Kuzmeen in flames.

DEVORAH. Okay, shake your head, quick. Good, Now look away a little. Good. What do you see now?

RIFKA. You don't want to know.

DEVORAH. Because you're not looking away enough.

RIFKA. Show me. Show me how to do it.

DEVORAH. Get up. Okay, watch me closely how I do it. (*Devorah arranges herself by the window, trying to analyze the way she does it.*) I'm not sure how I do it. I just look. Like this.

RIFKA. What do you see?

DEVORAH. What I see? I see the Rebbitzen in her new black dress walking like she owns the street.

RIFKA. And what else?

DEVORAH. I see Chava staring into the eyes of her betrothed, that *schlmiel* Velvel, like he was Moses about to lead her out of Egypt. I see that big mouthed Yenta, Mrs.Glotzer walking with her *cholent* pot....

RIFKA. Yes, but what else? Don't you see something else? Don't you see it?

DEVORAH. What? Whatever is there, I see.

RIFKA. It's no use... I'll never get the hang of it.

DEVORAH. Don't' give up. Try again. (*Rifka tries again.*) What do you see?

RIFKA. Chava, arm in arm, with Velvel?

DEVORAH. Good, good, now quick look at something else.

RIKFA. *(Feeling a little encouraged.)* Miriam, the goosedealer, is trying to get away from the Rebbetizen and her advice?

DEVORAH. (Very excited, very encouraged.) Yes... Yes... Very good.

RIFKA. (*RIKFA too is excited until she looks again.*) I see... Uhoh... I see my brother Daniil, who died in Siberia, walking down the street dressed like a Gentile.

DEVORAH. Rub your eyes quick.

RIFKA. (*It doesn't help.*) He's still there walking toward our house.

DEVORAH. You're tired, Rifka, we'll try again tomorr... (*She sees him too, the handsomest man she ever saw.)* My god.

RIFKA. He has no beard and big black boots, and a white shirt like a Russian peasant. And the jacket... The jacket I made for him so long ago.

DEVORAH. Hair black like burnt *kugel.*

RIFKA. Yes.

DEVORAH. Cheeks like the apples of *Simchus Torah.....*

RIFKA. Yes.

DEVORAH. A body like the young David when he went dancing through the streets of Jerusalem.

RIKFA. Yes... Yes - (*There is a knock at the door.*) What should we do?

DEVORAH. Answer it. (*To Tess.) Azoi ist gevane.* It was like he'd come back from the dead. (*Rifka looks at her, sad and intent. To Rifka.*) What is it, Rifka? (*To Tess.*) Why did she look at me like that?

TESS. I don't know. (*Rifka turns and looks out the window with a growing sense of horror.*)

DEVORAH. What happened? What did she see?

TESS. I don't know.

DEVORAH. Tell me, Rifka, tell me. (*With a cry of horror and despair at what she sees, Rifka runs out.*) I remember now. I remember. (*The old memory floods back.*) I was picking strawberries in the field. They were so big and luscious I ate them from the ground. I didn't even wait to wash the dirt off. Then I heard the horses and the screaming. When I ran back to the village there was fire everywhere. I didn't know what I was doing. I ran into the house. There was no one there. But out the window I could see, I could see it now... They were killing people in the streets. I could hear the screams... I could see them chasing Rifka in the street, two of them on horses, the others running after her. I started to cry out, when all of a sudden there was a hand on my mouth... His hand. I could feel it was Daniil's hand. When I was quiet, he picked me up and carried me to the cellar, and we hid there, we hid in a corner underneath a blanket and wept and clung to each other. We heard them chase her into the house... There was screaming everywhere, poor Rifka, her cries were right on top of us. But my heart was beating fast because he was so close to me. Because his mouth was on my mouth. And then... Then we couldn't hear them anymore We were in each other's arms and we couldn't hear them anymore.

TESS. While they were killing her?

DEVORAH. They could have killed the whole village at that moment, I didn't care - Rifka, my husband, the whole world, I didn't care. In the morning, when it was quiet, we went upstairs. She was lying there in her blood. It was the saddest sight... I couldn't look. He took her in his arms and wept and wept. We couldn't pull him off her body. Then suddenly he got up and walked out the door. There was no light in his eyes. We never saw him again... Never, never... And I never said anything. Not a word. Not to your Grandpa, not to anyone. I never told anyone.

TESS. What could you tell them? That while they were murdering her, all you could think about was him?

DEVORAH. She had seen it all. She wasn't crazy...

TESS. Don't think about it.

DEVORAH. (*A realization.*) She wasn't crazy.

TESS. Where are you going?

DEVORAH. To my village in Poland.

TESS. Grandma, It doesn't exist anymore. It's vanished.

DEVORAH. I have to go back. They have to know. I have to tell them what happened.

TESS. They're dead. They're all dead.

DEVORAH. Dead? (*Looking at the Yarhzeit candle.*) Oh Rifka...

TESS. It's for Abby.

DEVORAH. Abby?

TESS. Yes.

DEVORAH. My Abby is also dead?

Devorah almost loses her balance, has to hold on to something, then nearly crumbles to the floor. Tess comes to help her, but the sight of her Grandmother rocking on the floor undoes her, and she just sinks down with her and begins to weep, though trying not to. Devorah tries to comfort her.

DEVORAH. Sha... don't cry.

TESS I'm not. It's better to be dead.

DEVORAH. No.

TESS. They feel no pain.

DEVORAH. Death cannot be what life is. Death is empty. Only life has hope.

TESS. Hope? All we ever do is betray each other. All we ever lose is everything. Our hearts are so small, so small, and even that gets broken. Even that gets broken.

DEVORAH. Who are we? - The world isn't good enough? We live here.

TESS. Help me.

DEVORAH. Yes, I will.

TESS. Help me, Grandma.

DEVORAH. I will. I'll think of something....

TESS. It's too late.

DEVORAH. I promised her. I have to try. You heard I promised her.

TESS. That's true.

DEVORAH. Come darling, get up. *(Tess rises from the ground)* You'll do it? You'll come with me?

TESS. Yes.

DEVORAH. We'll tell them what happened?

TESS. We'll tell them.

DEVORAH. *(Beat.)* You think maybe, we're there already, we could look for him?

TESS. Yes

DEVORAH. He's probably an *elter cocker* by now, huh?

TESS. Look you're no prize yourself.

DEVORAH. Thats too true. *(They laugh. They hold each other.)*

THE END

The author recommends '*Ikh Hob Dikh Tsu Fil Lieb*' by Alexander Olshanetsky and Chaim Towber. Copyright permission is required.Director may also use any Yiddish song in the public domain.This sequence may be performed on or off stage.

LOUIS/*lui*

A tragicomedy
based on Louis Althusser's 'The Future Lasts A Long Time'

by

Marion Baraitser

The philosopher Louis Althusser's autobiography *The Future Lasts a Long Time* is a tissue of shifting possible interpretations of a life that spanned two world wars, the 1968 Paris riots, the collapse of Communism, and his own 'madness' which culminated in the strangulation of his Polish Jewish wife. It is a life that speaks for our century.
The book's obsessive exploration of the nature of identity and of selfhood, or the lack of it, led to the play's themes, which ask what it means to be a stranger to oneself - to be 'lost in translation'. These questions concern me as a woman living in the late twentieth century, as a Jew and as my mother's child. I wanted to explore the identity not only of Althusser, but of his Jewish wife.
The play's formalism reflects the uncertainty of meaning and of memory. It combines a musical structure of repetitions and variations, with a score for sound and lighting.

LOUIS/lui was written with the help of an Arts Council Options and Award Scheme for Shaker Theatre Company.

A reading of extracts of the play takes place at the New End Theatre, Hampstead, in March 1998, with The Lime Tree Productions.

PREFACE:

'Hallucinations are also facts'
(Louis Althusser in *The Future Lasts a Long Time*)

'Nothing begins - simply a drifting or a disorientation from which one never moves away.' (Jacques Derrida)

'Life is always someone's death.'
(Antonin Artaud)

'Imposters can be an action for the good.'
(Machiavelli, as quoted by Louis Althusser)

CHARACTERS

LOUIS, a French boy
LOUIS, as a young man, played by the same actor
LOUIS, as an old man
HELLY, a young Polish Jew
HELLY, as an old woman
HELLY, LOUIS' wife as an old woman
LUCY, LOUIS' mother as a young woman
LUCY, LOUIS' mother as an older woman, also as HELLY
CHARLEY, LOUIS' father as a young man
CHARLEY, LOUIS' father as an older man as LOUIS
STUDENT, a young woman
NURSE
THE HANGING FIGURES OF LUCY/MARX/CHRIST
COLLEGE MASTER
ANALYST
YOUNG AIRMAN LOUIS

NOTE:
The character of Louis/lui is presented by the actor as a 'double' personality - he is both himself and outside himself. In the playing of the events, we witness the gap between these two positions through which Louis/Lui escapes us and the play. As the piece will be performed for both English and French audiences, the director may play with each culture's sense of the ridiculous in the 'other'. The HANGING FIGURES may be represented on film, or video, or as giant hanging puppet figures.

SET

The set is divided into three areas that represent three places in Louis' mind, simultaneously imaginary and real:

THE RED R(W)OMB: a dark red vast interior that also suggests a puppet theatre, with a free-standing door in its frame (but no wall), which opens on to a space with a huge bed with red covers, floor to ceiling windows opening to the darkened back, framed in old, tattered red velvet curtains. This room contains piles of precariously balanced books and yellowing papers, old plates of food, a wooden figure of Christ on the cross, a giant furled Communist flag, a War 1 rifle, a full-length mirror.
THE WHITE R(W)OMB: a small area, empty except for a small battered iron bed neatly made with white sheets and covers, reminiscent of an army, hospital or child's bed.
THE YELLOW OUTDOORS: an area suggestive of a sandy beach or a cornfield.

TIME

There are four time periods: 1920s, 1940s, late 1960s and 1980. Each period in time is clear from the clothing worn and the subliminal music score. We move freely in and out of these time periods as we move between the three levels of reality, memory and fantasy.The play ends in the 'future' i.e.the 1990s.

LIGHTING

To help the audience, any action happening in the present is lit in red; any event occurring in remembered time is lit in blue; fantasy actions are lit in white.

FILM SEQUENCES

Recurring through the piece are two black and white two-minute film sequences. One shows a vast white worm emerging from the top of a cupboard. A second film sequence shows a large, fat and naked woman taking a young clothed boy onto her lap and counting his boy parts. The director may include short pieces of archival film thrown up against the walls, or onto a gauze backdrop, behind which the action can be seen.

FRENCH/ENGLISH LANGUAGE TAPES

Short sequences of language tapes preface some scenes. They are invented to introduce and distance the action of each scene, but sound like a beginner's audio language course. Each sentence is given first in English, then in French, in LOUIS' and HELLY's voices, or if the director wishes, the actors can say these words on stage.

MUSIC/SOUND SCORE

Taped music scores and sound scores accompany some scenes as an ironic counterpoint to the action.

SCENIC FORM
The play is built round three main sequences:
THE RED R(W)OMB Sequence
THE WHITE R(W)OMB Sequence
THE YELLOW OUTDOORS Sequence.

The formal structure is based on:
REPETITION
REPETITION WITH VARIATION
SUBSTITUTION
BLACKOUT - 'gaps' or disappearances

THE RED R(W)0MB SEQUENCE
VARIATION 1

SET/TIME

1980: Winter morning light kept out by drawn tattered red curtains. Piles of books and yellowing papers teeter in one corner. A huge Red flag stands rolled in another. Water-jug, medicine bottles and a telephone stand on a large untidy desk. A Crucifixion hangs above the bed.

ACTION 1

LOUIS (Old man), wearing a dressing-gown and with his back to the audience, bends over HELLY (Old woman) who lies fully-dressed, face upwards on the bed. LOUIS is massaging her shoulders, at first with great gentleness and love. Soon, we cannot tell if he is caressing or attacking her. She is silent and still, while he grunts, hisses with the effort. This process takes at least three minutes.

LIGHTING: Red.

SOUND-TRACK: Subliminal sound of continuous pealing church-bells.

FRENCH/ENGLISH TAPES:
This is him - Louis.
This is her - Helly.
Louis and Helly are preparing for bed.
Louis has brushed his teeth.
Helly has also brushed her teeth.
Helly has washed her face.
Louis has not yet washed his face.
But Louis has washed his hands.
It is good to wash before you go to bed, isn't it?
Louis is in his dressing-gown.
Helly is not in her pyjamas.
Have they said their prayers?
Helly is resting.
Is Helly sleeping?
I think Helly is sleeping.
Does Louis think Helly is sleeping?
Louis kisses Helly goodnight.'

ACTION 2

LOUIS (Old man) falls silent and uses his thumbs to massage the neck of HELLY (Old woman) in long, slow forward movements. After a while, he stops. He tips backwards, knocking down a pile of books. He freezes, staring at HELLY. He steps forward. He stares for long moment. He begins to tremble. Still fixated by HELLY, he becomes agitated. He runs to the door, scattering books and papers. The flag falls, the rifle drops. He wrenches open the door and runs out.

LOUIS. *(Shouting.)* Help! Come quickly. I think she's dead.

LOUIS (Old man) re-enters the room. He stares at HELLY, still lying face-up on the bed. He reaches across to the red tattered curtains and tears off a strip which he folds into the shape of a rose. He lays it on HELLY's breast. He steps back and stares at her. He crosses himself. Off-stage, we hear the sound of the approaching voices of the COLLEGE MASTER and the DOCTOR.

RED R(W)OMB SEQUENCE
VARIATION 2

REPETITION: Repeat RED R(W)OMB SEQUENCE until 'LOUIS (Shouting)'

ADDITION

LOUIS (Old man, *beside himself.)* Help. Come quickly. My wife is dead. She is dead! *(Rushes off-stage, right. Rushes back in again.)* I have strangled her. I have strangled my wife! *(Rushes off-stage.)*
COLLEGE MASTER. *(Off.)* Has it come to this?
DOCTOR. *(Off.)* I shall examine him at once.
COLLEGE MASTER. *(Entering stage, left.)* It's her...That woman! Drive anyone insane. Not one of us - you take my meaning. *(Quickly crosses himself.)* And he a man of such stature, such intelligence... One of the best we have. Oh, this is awful, awful.
DOCTOR. But is he in his right mind? I must go to him at once. What about the police?
COLLEGE MASTER. Examine him first, I think.
DOCTOR. Yes. He's had a bad bout recently...

RED R(W)OMB SEQUENCE
VARIATION 3

REPETITION: THE RED R(W)OMB SEQUENCE:

VARIATION 1. Repeat sequence until 'LOUIS (Shouting)'

SOUND-TRACK: Subliminal 1980s French light, popular love songs.

SUBSTITUTION: Light on HANGING FIGURE OF LUCY (Young woman). The front of her dress is bloodied.

ACTION

LOUIS. Poor old girl. Do I frighten you? *(Taking her hands in his.)* Poor hands. Poor worker's hands. *(Kissing them.)* Poor wounded hands. I worship these hands.

HELLY. They're ugly. Old woman's hands. What do you know about peasants' hands? - Comrade! *(Touching his head.)* It's all up here with you. Worker's hands... And you? Where have you got us after all these years? - All your talk...

LOUIS. Marry me. Marry me now! *(HELLY snatches her hands away.)*

HELLY. *(Laughs.)* What! Marry the Jew at last will you? What's your hurry, after all these years? Now that your father's dead and gone you'll marry me, will you? Now that he can't witness the shame of it. His precious Catholic boy will marry the little Jew from Poland. That gutter-snipe, that Paris tart, that dirty little Communist.

LOUIS. All right, so he was a lousy banker from Lyon. Is that my fault? He was a banker but he didn't give in to Petain. What're you bringing him up for? I've spent my whole life trying to get away from him. Leave me alone!

HELLY. *(Getting off the bed, reaching for her clothes.)* I've had enough of you. I'm leaving. I can't stand you a moment longer. *(There is a grim comic struggle as HELLY tries to get to the door. LOUIS suddenly lets go of her and they fall, breathless. They lie still.)*

HELLY. Monster!

LOUIS. When it's all collapsing, that's when you'll walk out on me... Yes, yes... When there's finally nothing... An... absence... Quite numb... Oh, if you knew... I'm so frightened, Helly...

HELLY. I've got to get out of here. Once and for all. I've got to make a life. Be myself.

LOUIS. You know I can't survive without you. You are everything I have, Helen.

HELLY. Who is he then - this great big Louis! Haven't you had enough of him? - Well I have! I'm sick of him sucking blood from my breasts. - I'm sick of counting for nothing. I'm sick of being the nasty little dog at his feet. Do you think that telephone ever rings for me? Do you think any of your friends would care if I died today? Look after yourself, Louis!

LOUIS. I'll die without you.

HELLY. Too bad.

LOUIS. Monster!

HELLY. Bastard!

LOUIS. Harridan!

HELLY. Coward!... Mummy's boy!

LOUIS. That's your idea, not mine. You put that into my head.

Silence. HELLY gets up as if to go to the door again. LOUIS throws her back on to the bed

LOUIS. No! *(Pause.)*
HELLY. Let me out... This bloody womb. I won't stand it a moment longer! *(Pause.)* I want a flat of my own. *(Pause.)* Do you hear me? I want to move out of this hole!
LOUIS. Don't abandon me Helly.
HELLY. You telling me that? Where do you think I've been half my life? Up and down on that bloody Métro to hell and gone, freezing to death, worrying myself sick over you, holding your hand in asylums. Where did it got me? Look at me! Look at what's left! And you're famous! Everyone loves you!
LOUIS. Oh my saint. My little saint. I adore you.
HELLY. All my life, worked like a dog for you. And for what? So God's gift to the world is in working order? I want a bit of peace and quiet. Before it's too late.
LOUIS. I had a dream... Such a terrible dream last night... I dreamt I had to kill my sister - but she had to agree to it.
HELLY. Your sister...

Silence. HELLY stares at him. LOUIS pushes her back on to the bed.

LOUIS. Relax. I'll massage your shoulders. Just as you like it... There... You see. I'll look after you... You're mine now. Little mother... Poor little mother... You're mine now... And I love you... Look how I love you! It makes you happy. I know it makes you happy and I want you to be happy...
HELLY. You're kind... Good to me... Just like...

LIGHTING: White lights on THE HANGING FIGURE OF LUCY.

MUSIC SCORE: 1920s popular songs.

LOUIS. Yes, I'll protect you mother... Now you just lie down, put your feet up. You'll be wanting something to read. I'll do the dishes... Spotless, no germs... 'Everything has its place, everything in its place'...

LIGHTING: White light on CHARLEY (Older man)
CHARLEY enters and watches LOUIS (Older man). CHARLEY (Older man) is dressed as a banker and smokes a large black cigar and gives the

impression of sinister strength and power.

LOUIS. I'll study... I'll read till my eyes drop out... just like Uncle Louis did... Just like you and Uncle Louis did... I'll be clever. And good like Uncle Louis... And - say my prayers.

REPETITION: Repeat RED R(W)OMB SEQUENCE to end.

BLACKOUT

RED R(W)ROOM SEQUENCE
VARIATION 4

REPETITION: RED R(W)OMB SEQUENCE, VARIATION 1, To 'LOUIS (0ld Man) massages HELLY (Old woman).

TIME: 1918.

LIGHTING: Blue.

SUBSTITUTION 1

CHARLEY (Young man) massages LUCY (Young woman) who lies face up on the bed, in a summer dress of the period.. He is bare to the waist. Next to him lies a rifleman's uniform of the 1914—1918 War, and the rifle.

SUBSTITUTION 2

Enter LOUIS (Boy) who watches.

SUBSTITUTION 3: HANGING FIGURE OF CHRIST, White lighting.

MUSIC SCORE: French and English War songs of the period, sound of rifles cracking, marching - louder, suddenly stops.

FRENCH/ENGLISH TAPES :
Louis' father, Charley, is going to bed.
Louis' mother, Lucy, is going to bed.
They are both going to bed.
Louis' father wants to be a banker.

Louis' mother wants to be a teacher.
What do you want to be?
Write it down.
Louis wants to study at the École normale supérieure.
They make a happy family.

VARIATION, ACTION

CHARLEY's action becomes more sexual. CHARLEY force himself on LUCY, who resists, bewildered and hurt by the force of his desire/rape. When he is satisfied, CHARLES lies next to her and smokes a large black cigar. LUCY pulls down her dress. It is stained with blood.

CHARLEY. You're mine now. *(LUCY begins to whimper and cry.)* My brother is gone. Louis is gone. You'll just have to accept this. What happened to Louis over Verdun - happened. That's war for you. There is no justice. He's gone and I'm here. You must accept it. It is what happened. My brother's not coming back. It's finished and done with. It's no use crying any more. So finish your crying and be done. I know you want him - Louis - I know you think I'm not good enough. But it's me you've got now. Louis didn't come back from the skies of Verdun, and I did. I came home. On my two feet. I walked home. I am not clever like Louis. I am not an airman. I am only a rifleman but I'm strong ... My body is strong. I came back and he didn't It was my duty to marry you... I know I'm only a banker's clerk and he was going to the university. Always had his head in a book.. But then Louis didn't come home. You must be satisfied... Stop crying, do you hear me!

LUCY stops crying. CHARLES starts to dress in his uniform He takes a large slab of meat wrapped in brown paper from his rucksack, and a bottle of wine.

CHARLEY. Here, I'm starving. Got it on the black market. A celebration. Be quick about it. It's a long way back.

LUCY gets up and fastidiously and reluctantly starts to clean and prepare the grotesque and giant slab of meat.

CHARLEY. By the way, you won't be going back to teach at the school any more. When I come home, you'll stay home and look after me... And our family. You're mine now.

LUCY serves the meat to CHARLEY, who eats and drinks hugely and greedily. He wipes his mouth, picks up his rifle.

CHARLEY. I'll be back... As soon as this damn war's over.

He kisses her. Exit CHARLEY with his rifle and kit. LUCY stands paralysed under the

BLACKOUT

SUBSTITUTION: MUSIC SCORE: 1940s French songs.

SUBSTITUTION: THE FIGURE HANGING from the wall is LOUIS (Airman)

VARIATION: ACTION

Lights up on LOUIS (BOY). He is sitting on a kitchen chair watching LUCY (Young woman) wash sheets. She has stopped for a moment, and is dreaming, gazing at LOUIS (Boy) but looking right through him to THE HANGING FIGURE OF LOUIS (Airman).

LOUIS (Boy). Mother? Mother! *(Looking behind him.)* Who are you looking at, Mother? Mother... It's me... Louis... Look at me, Mother... Do you know who I am? I wish I were just called plain Jacques, or Pierre, like grandad. Can I be called Pierre? Why did you have to call me Louis? Lui! I don't want to be Uncle Louis. I want to be Pierre Berger. Or Pierre Fermier! Like grandad. That's what they call me when I go to stay with grandad on the farm. The workers call me Pierre. Then I can be me for a change. Mother? Mother! Look at me. I don't want to be ... him... Louis. *(Looking over his shoulder.)* He's someone else... Mother... Look at me! Let me be Pierre for a change

LUCY. *(Still looking behind LOUIS boy.)* Never leave me, Louis, not for an instant! *(Suddenly looking directly at LOUIS boy.)* Where would I be without you! *(Embracing LOUIS boy.)* Oh my dear boy. My dear, dear Louis.

FILM SEQUENCE 1: Huge white worm comes out of top of the cupboard.

ADDITION

CHARLEY (Older man) enters and watches. He carries a rifle and smokes a large black cigar. He is dressed as a banker.

LOUIS. Mother, is Uncle Louis still alive? Why have I never seen him - except in the photo?

CHARLEY laughs. LUCY gazes at LOUIS (boy) who studies. She continues to wash the sheets.

LUCY. *(Her speech is non-stop and like a fast-forward tape, crescendo.)* Louis... Louis darling. Read - Study. Then one day, you'll study at the finest university. *(Pushing books at him.)* Study. You must study. Your Uncle Louis, he did so well in his examinations. He was going to be famous. Yes, everyone would have known about him one day... You know why? Because he always had his head in a book.

CHARLEY. (To LUCY.) Vautre! Wallow!

LUCY. (Ignoring him and hurrying on.) Money! He had no head for money!... He understood... spiritual things... Yes, things of the spirit. Do you know what that is? He had a clean spirit. A pure spirit. And gentle... His touch... It was the gentlest touch in the world. That is how you must be - good and clean and pure.

CHARLEY starts to walk backwards towards the bed.

CHARLEY. Vautre... Vautre... Vautre... Wallow... Wallow... Wallow...

LUCY. Body and mind. Have you washed your hands? You can't be too careful. There are germs everywhere. In the air. They wait to invade your body. Through the wounds. So we don't want any sores on your body where germs can penetrate. No football, do you hear? No fooling around with the boys in the playground. Keep yourself to yourself. You could graze a knee, or an elbow. Ah! - It doesn't bear thinking about. We have to watch out all the time. Germs are just waiting to invade your body. Through the holes - just think of your nose, your mouth, your ears. - Gaping holes! There's no letting up. Now say your prayers.

CHARLEY gets on to all fours and slowly starts to crawl under the bed.

CHARLEY. Wallow... Wallow... Wallow...

LUCY. There are the beans to string, the tomatoes to skin, the peppers to slice, the radishes to scrub, the cabbage to stuff and tie, the stock to skim, the leaks to soak, the carrots to scrub, never mind the peas to shell, the potatoes to dice, the mushrooms to wipe. Your father can have his gammon. - Yes, your father will have his red meat! That's what pleases him. Red meat. He is made that way. There is nothing to be done. Tell your father there's meat for his dinner.

LOUIS. *(Yells)* Pa! Ma says there's meat for your dinner.

CHARLEY. *(Emerging from under the bed.)* Louis, tell your mother, 'Good, I'm starved.'

LOUIS. Ma, Pa says he's starved.

LUCY. Tell him he's got ten minutes not a minute less.

LOUIS. Pa, Ma says you got ten minutes.

CHARLEY. Tell her I'll come when I'm ready.

LOUIS. Ma, Pa says he'll come when he's ready.

LUCY. Tell your father I'm not a waitress.

LOUIS. Pa, Ma says she's not a waitress.

CHARLEY. Tell her then I'm not a banker.

LOUIS. Ma, Dad says he's not a banker.

LUCY. *(To the audience)* See what I'm up against?

CHARLEY starts to howl like a dog from under the bed. LOUIS puts his hands over his ears.

LUCY. *(Like a fast-forward tape.)* I have put out the money for tomorrow's *pain chocolat*. It is exact of course. Imagine if you were attacked on the way to school. Imagine if someone wanted to get at you for the money. There is not a penny more than you need. Just keep an eye out in front and behind. Imagine the harm such a person could do to your body! It doesn't bear thinking about.

LUCY lifts a dirty sheet to the light. She stares at it for a long moment. She points at a stain.

LUCY. (Like a slowed down tape.) And what have we here? What does this mean my boy? - This... mark here ... This brown stain?

LOUIS slowly gets up and stands, motionless, hands to his sides.

LUCY. You know what this means my son? This means you can be happy, my boy. This means - you are a man... Yes - a man - a Louis. At last my son is a ... *(Holding the sheet close to her.)* Louis. *(Calling to CHARLEY.)* Charles! Charles! Come here at once. I have something to show you.

CHARLEY's howling is silenced. He comes out from under the bed. He lights a large black cigar. He saunters over to LUCY, who shows him the stain on the sheet.

LUCY. Just take a look at that! Isn't that a sight and a half! Look at that!

Smoking his cigar, CHARLEY examines the sheet. Slowly, he grins.

CHARLEY. Make 'em happy, son. Make 'em happy!

LUCY whispers something into CHARLEY's ear.

LUCY. Go to your father, son. Go on. Go on. He just wants to check everything is as it should be.

CHARLEY grabs LOUIS by his pants and attempts to stick his head down LOUIS' trousers. LOUIS resists.

VARIATION: LIGHTING: White lighting makes LOUIS' face disappear.

A comic, violent pantomime ensues in which CHARLEY gets his head down , and his hand up, LOUIS' trousers.

CHARLEY. *(Laughing.)* He'll make 'em happy. He'll make 'em happy!
LUCY. That settles that then!

LUCY washes the sheet. Exit CHARLEY.

SOUND-TRACK: Long sound of lips making a deflating balloon sound.

LIGHTING: White lighting makes LOUIS' body disappear.

FILM SEQUENCE 2: A large fleshy naked woman takes LOUIS (Boy) on to her lap and counts the invisible parts of his body.

LIGHTING: The lighting remains white.

YELLOW SPACE
SEQUENCE 1

Enter GIRL in bathing costume on bicycle. She and LOUIS (Older) sit down on the ground together. LOUIS picks up a handful of sea-sand and trickles it down the girl's cleavage... The girl giggles. She slowly lifts the leg of her bathing costume, and her leg, so that LOUIS can see her crotch as the sand trickles down her leg.

GIRL. Pierre... Pierre... Pierre...
LUCY. *(Calling, off-stage.)* Louis... Louis... Louis.
GIRL. Jacques... Jacques... Jacques...
LUCY. Louis... Louis... Louis...
GIRL. Pierre Berger.
LUCY. You're to leave that girl alone, Louis - she's far too old for you! Do you hear me? I won't have you getting involved with an older woman! It's not nice!

Exit girl on bicycle, in fright. Enter CHARLEY with rifle.

CHARLEY. What do you want for your birthday, son?
LOUIS. A rifle like yours, papa.

CHARLEY hands LOUIS his rifle.

CHARLEY. *(Laughs, using the gun as his sex.)* You'll make 'em happy. Make 'em happy. Make 'em happy, boy!

CHARLEY shows LOUIS (Boy) how to work the gun. CHARLEY pulls LOUIS to the ground and shows him how to position the gun to shoot. LOUIS fires the gun.

CHARLEY. Missed!

LOUIS fires the gun again.

CHARLEY. *(Laughing.)* Missed. - Big-head!

CHARLEY takes the rifle and fires three shots. LOUIS is terrified.

CHARLEY laughs.

CHARLEY. One cartridge left. You know what to do with it.

Exit CHARLEY. LOUIS examines the rifle awkwardly. He aims it in several directions. He aims it at himself and fumbles for the trigger. Long moment. He lowers rifle, opens cartridge container, shakes out a single bullet. He throws down the rifle. He exits, running.

BLACKOUT

RED R(W)OMB SEQUENCE
VARIATION 5

TIME: 1980.

REPETITION: LOUIS (Old man) massaging HELLY (Old woman), ACTION 1.

VARIATION 1: HELLY lies on the bed face downwards.

SUBSTITUTION: HANGING FIGURE IS LUCY.

SOUND TRACK: Subliminal church-bells.

FRENCH/ENGLISH TAPES:
Louis is not well.
Louis is going to visit the doctor. ('Visit' - to pay a visit)
Helly does not have to pay a visit.
The doctor has given Louis medicine.
Louis does not like taking his medicine.
Do you like taking your medicine?
I do not like taking my medicine.

HELLY. *(Muffled, dreamily.)* Ah! Lovely! Marvellous. I'm in heaven. Thank you. Thank you...

LOUIS continues to massage her shoulders.

HELLY. That new student rang... The one with the angelic profile... Just your type... I encouraged her... You might like to take her to bed... She's a beauty. Classic... Oh - a little more to the left... Yes, that's it, just there. Lovely... Marvellous. I'm in heaven. She wants to talk to you about translating your pamphlet. Into Spanish. Just think of the millions who could read it then! Half the world!... We could spread Mao right across South America! *(Pause.)* Louis... Louis! Are you with me?

HELLY sits up, pushes LOUIS away from her, stares at him. She gets up, alarmed.

HELLY. Oh my God!

HELLY goes to table and checks the bottle of pills. She throws them down.

HELLY. Where are the new ones? You haven't taken the new ones... What's the matter with you? What the hell do you think you're doing? Louis! I can see from your eyes... Why are you doing this to me?

LOUIS sweeps the pills off the desk. HELLY tries to stop him. He throws handfuls of pills out of the window. They circle each other like boxers, taking occasional slaps at each other.

HELLY. *(Stands, gasping.)* OK. So you want to get it over with. Well why not? Go ahead. What do I care? Look at you... Like an old whale out of water... A mammoth stuck in the ice-age. *(Approaching him.)* Oh my poor one... My poor little one. *(Taking him in her arms.)* What are we going to do with you now? How will we manage? My only love...

LOUIS. It's finished.

HELLY. No... You'll last forever. *(Pause.)* And there's that nice young student to look forward to...

LOUIS. I'll never get out of here... Has anyone offered me a place?... Has anyone invited me...? And the new ones, driving their darts... Oh quick-silver fish .with their mouths full of such beautiful pearly little teeth! Leaving politics out of philosophy! Where is there for me to go now? A Machiavelli - alive to see my work fail!

HELLY. Don't say that! So, you learned Stalin was wrong...

LOUIS. And socialism.- River of mushy shit, socialism.

HELLY. But your wonderful, fantastic... imaginary new Marxism - you invented that!- You changed things. Put your wonderful mind to it - Freeing us up, praised be Marx, from some out-dated frozen old story with a hero and a plot and a fixed ending told by a lot of old farts!

ADDITION: SOUND-TRACK: Subliminal Beethoven's Ninth Symphony.

LOUIS. *(Laughing.)* Gentle breezes... Free fruit and flowers for everyone to pick in the promised land of no market forces, eh? *(Laughter getting more hysterical.)*
HELLY. *(Laughing, too, now.)* That's what you wrote!
LOUIS. (*Hysterical.)* Was I manic or depressed?
HELLY. *(Wiping her eyes.)* My poor dear man.
LOUIS. *(Suddenly quiet.)* What do you know? Just an old women too far gone. Don't speak for the Party. The Party doesn't want you!
HELLY. *(Quiet.)* Please Louis.
LOUIS. Please Louis... Please Louis what! Who has to beg for you? Plead for you? Louis... Lui. He has to tell the Party committee you weren't a double agent - not a Nazi spy... *Lui* has to say you did not side with pro-Russian Germans as a Communist in the Resistance... That's what *lui* has to say to the Party, isn't it? But we all know you are a Pole, a Polish Jew - and they were Russian.
HELLY. (*Quietly.)* You know I betrayed nobody.
LOUIS. Know? What do I know? And who puts me in such a position with the Party? - Intolerable! Humiliating! I picked you up out of the gutter!
HELLY. So who thinks of voting against me? - Who actually considers casting his own vote against me so I can't get back into the Party? Who, Louis - my own dear old man. - Don't give me that 'holier-than-thou' bit. You know the Party is my lifeline. Fraud!
LOUIS. The Party insists that I throw you out of here... That you're a bad influence on me - What do you want me to say? Huh, huh? What do you want me to do? Leave the Party? Throw myself into the wilderness? Because of you?
HELLY. Yes. *(Begins to cry.)* Where is my child? My child.

Silence.

LOUIS. Well I did, didn't I.
HELLY. *(Sitting on the bed.)* I don't know what you did, do I? You'll never be sure I'm innocent, will you? Will you actually do it, Louis? - Testify against me. - Agree with them - take sides against me. - What am I to you, then? Nothing! Have you even married me? *(Silence.)* You'll never change. You're numb inside. Not one of us. It's like talking to a wall.

LOUIS. *(Sitting next to her.)* Quiet!
HELLY. You enjoy it, don't you? You enjoy hurting me. How have I stuck it so long?
LOUIS. When I think what I've done for you! Given you a position, a life... Dried up old cuttlefish!
HELLY. Go on. Wallow in your pain! Stuck in here... You're right. Who would have you now? Louis. Where would you be without me! *(Pause.)* But this is what you want. You like it here. It's your amniotic fluid. Look how you float in it! Think how long it has held you up... This womb, the university room. Never cut the umbilical cord. You're safe, safe here. You don't have to go anywhere... Well, I'm going to get out!

Silence.

LOUIS. You won't leave me?
HELLY. *(Moving to telephone.)* Behave yourself, then. Calm down. Take your pills.
LOUIS. *(Batting the telephone out of her hands.)* I feel good. I feel wonderful. I'm walking on the moon... I'll visit the Pope! Come... Sit down... We'll start on the new article... Spinoza's idea of the body... as a potential... like a strength... open to the world... a generosity... something freely given... A wonderful idea, yes? The body, which so many 'wills' makes unknowable! Come here!

FILM-SEQUENCE 2: The FAT WOMAN takes LOUIS (Boy) on her lap and counts the parts of his body.

LOUIS. To think with one's body! - Which so many wills make unknowable!

REPETITION: Replay SEQUENCE IN VARIATION 3 of RED R(W)OMB SEQUENCE in which CHARLEY looks down LOUIS (Boy's) trousers.

YELLOW OUTDOORS
SEQUENCE 2

LOUIS moves into the stage area of the yellow outdoors.

TIME: 1920s.

MUSIC- SCORE: Turn of the century French freedom song of the peasants
LIGHTING: Blue.

VARIATION: White light on the hanging figure of Marx.

ACTION

THE ACTORS form a line and mime scything hay in time to the music. LOUIS (Boy) watches, then he tries to join in. The peasants laugh, make a place for LOUIS in the line. LOUIS slowly gets the hang of the rhythm.

GIRL'S VOICE. (Off-stage.) Pierre! Pierre! Pierre Berger!

LOUIS and PEASANTS work some more, then down tools and stop working. LOUIS looks at his hands.

LOUIS. My hands! Never done work like this.

The PEASANTS laugh.

LOUIS. *(Groaning as he touches.)* Forearms. Shoulders. Thighs. Calves. Stomach. Buttocks. Throat.

Enter GIRL in bathing costume on bicycle.

GIRL. *(Giggling.)* Buttocks! Buttocks! Buttocks!
LOUIS. *(To GIRL showing her his hands.)* Look.
GIRL. Dirty!
LOUIS. Worker's hands!
GIRL. Ugh! You stink!
LOUIS. *(Rolling on the floor in glee.)* The dung. The superb stinking dung! The wild asparagus is... erect! The red cyclamens open like a girl's...

GIRL pours a handful of sand down her bathing costume, lifts her leg to show LOUIS, and lets the sand trickle out of the bottom of her costume. Exit GIRL, on bicycle. LOUIS crosses to the RED ROOM

HELLY. *(Holding his arm.)* You're going too fast for me Louis.

LOUIS. *(Pushing her down on bed.)* And Spinoza's refusal of a theory of knowledge... The glory of it... 'Man thinks - that is all. - Facts as facts without origins.'... There's nothing more materialist than that - thought without origin or end, history without subject and without end - the royal road to Marxism!
HELLY. Theory! Theory!
LOUIS. *(Shaking her violently.)* Idiot! Why don't you understand? I had to make a philosophy of Communism that changed Capitalism now, didn't I? I had to theorise how we put revolution back in the West!- Rethink the class struggle, scientifically!
HELLY. Nowhere... Nowhere...
LOUIS. ...Play Marx against Marx. Unhinge the Party's neat dialectics and frozen certainties...
HELLY. Kick the party up the arse?... **Your** will! What kind of Communist does that make you?
LOUIS. *(Releasing her.)* Didn't Machiavelli say, 'The future lasts a long time'? Didn't Marx say that history has more imagination than we do? We're not finished yet!
CHARLEY'S VOICE. Vautre, vautre, vautre. Wallow, wallow, wallow.
HELLY. Why do you stay in the Party? It betrays me. - It betrays the whole of the working-class!
LOUIS. *(Beginning to massage her neck.)* So you are betraying us? Oh you are so stupid! Stupid. Do you think I'd bother with something that doesn't allow Communist politics to happen?... I don't need you to tell me what to do. I think for myself. And if I have to do it from inside the Party - alone, then...

LOUIS continues to massage HELLY. Telephone rings. It continues to ring. LOUIS falls to his knees, cries out in anguish and fear.

LOUIS. Ah!... Ah!...

BLACKOUT

Telephone continues to ring. LOUIS controls himself. He answers the telephone.

LOUIS. Yes... No, that's quite all right, my dear. No, I don't see why not -
HELLY's VOICE. No, Louis. Please. You're not fit -
LOUIS. Shouldn't take that long... You know my door is always open.

HELLY'S VOICE. Please, Louis... Put her off... I asked her when your medication was -
LOUIS. Yes... Bring it along. We can talk.
HELLY'S VOICE. You're not in a fit state to see anyone! Louis - Listen to me!
LOUIS. *(Replacing receiver.)* There. She's coming. The new student. That's what you wanted. You arranged it. Anyway, I feel quite randy. Do me good. You said so yourself. I won't have you changing your mind. It was good of you to arrange it. I'm grateful. I remember the profile. As you say - angelic, pure. Just my type.
HELLY'S VOICE. Christ!
LOUIS. Poor old girl. Do I frighten you? My love, my little Red Saint... So brave!

Louis goes to the bed, pushes HELLY on to the bed, face upwards. LOUIS begins to massage her.

BLACKOUT

REPETITION: Repeat RED R(W)OMB SEQUENCE I, ACTION I.

BLACKOUT

TIME: 1940s.

MUSIC-SCORE: Post-war songs.

REPETITION: Repeat RED R(W)OMB SEQUENCE, ACTION 1.

WHITE ROOM SEQUENCE
VARIATION 2

Takes place on the white bed.

FRENCH/ENGLISH TAPES:
Louis and Helly are friends.
Helly is visiting Louis.
Louis is studying at the university.
Helly brings Louis a bunch of daffodils.
It is Spring. It is not Winter.
Helly and Louis play some games.

Who will win the games?
Do you like to play games?
I like to play games, too.
Louis likes to learn new games.
Helly will teach him new games.
That is why they are friends.

LOUIS (Young man) poorly dressed in ill-fitting late '40s clothes, bends over HELLY (Younger woman) lying face-up on the bed, unkempt, dressed in black patched '40s dress, her hair loose.

SUBSTITUTION: White light on hanging figure of LUCY.

FILM-SEQUENCE: 1 - The huge white worm pushes out of the top of the cupboard.

LOUIS is being rough with HELLY.

HELLY. Hey! Get off!
LOUIS. I don't know... how to do... it.
HELLY. *(Sitting up.)* Oh my God! How old did you say you were?
LOUIS. You've got to show me. *(Roughing her up a bit.)* Go on. - Show me! Little bitch!
HELLY. Not even in the German POW camp...?
LOUIS. Shut up! I had better things to do. I met Marxists in there. Heroes.
HELLY. I bet you do it to yourself though.

LOUIS shakes her violently.

HELLY. Stop it!... And I'll show you ...My God!

LOUIS tries to make love to her clumsily, violently, but does not know how.

LUCY'S VOICE. Louis. Louis. Louis. Such a pure man...
GIRL 'S VOICE. Pierre, Pierre, Pierre.
LOUIS. Bitch! Bitches and whores! Mothers! All of you.

He gets up, rushes to the basin and is sick. HELLY sits up.

LOUIS. Get out! I never want to see you again.
HELLY. What the hell...
LOUIS. Think you can invade a person's body like that... Swallow him up... Suck him down... I hate... the smell of you.

HELLY moves across to him.

HELLY. I was in the Resistance, you know. In charge. - Took decisions on the torture of prisoners. Russians, too. *(Smiling.)* I have a splinter of ice in my heart.
LOUIS. Oh?
HELLY But I'm a Jew.
LOUIS. A Jew and a Communist. That's good.
HELLY. And you?
LOUIS. I don't know.
HELLY. You don't know who you are? Well! Catholic, Communist - it's all the same to you, then?
LOUIS. How did you know?
HELLY. What?
LOUIS. That I'm Catholic.
HELLY. I was in love with one. In the Resistance. A priest. *(Pause.)* The Nazis shot him. *(Pause.)*
HELLY. What did you say your name was? Louis, wasn't it?
LOUIS. Yes - *lui*. That's 'him'.
HELLY. Come here, Louis. I've got something to show you.

She pulls LOUIS towards her and kisses him.

HELLY. No. Open your mouth. Don't be so... tight. Relax.

LOUIS pulls away from her.

LOUIS. Where did you learn it?
HELLY. Where have you been! You must be at least ... twenty-eight.
LOUIS. Bitch!
HELLY. Shut up, you. That's enough from you, you hear? Who do you think you are? Jesus Christ? Do you or don't you want to know how to do it?

They continue to make love, roughly, awkwardly, with HELEN giving instructions.

HELLY. Slowly. What's your hurry. There's all the time in the world.
LOUIS. *(Taking her hands, examining them.)* Rough hands.
HELLY. I live rough - in the Resistance, and before. Always lived rough. Since my parents died... Cancer - in Paris, both of them and me the nurse. Fourteen. And the doctor visiting, to do the injections. *(Giggles.)* Well, that's not all, of course.
LOUIS. Stay with me.
HELLY. He'd push me back on the bed and...
LOUIS. Stay!

RED R(W)OMB SEQUENCE
VARIATION 6

Louis carries her to the bed, pushes her down and begins to massage her shoulders.

BLACKOUT

TIME: 1980.

LIGHTING: Red.

SUBSTITUTION: Hanging Figure is now Marx.

MUSIC SCORE: Subliminal 'La Marseillaise'.

Enter STUDENT (Older woman) on bicycle, carrying papers. She rings the bell. LOUIS stops massaging HELLY's shoulders. HELLY sits up.

HELLY. Don't answer!

LOUIS takes the key from his pocket, unlocks the door and opens it.

LOUIS. (Closing door.) Welcome! Delighted to see you.
STUDENT. I hope I'm not intruding.
HELLY. Perish the thought!
LOUIS. You know each other.
STUDENT. Oh yes! (To HELLY.) You've been so kind...
HELLY. How refreshing!
LOUIS. You're looking wonderful. (To HELLY.) Isn't she looking wonderful?
HELLY. Superb.

LOUIS. Helly is such a help to me.
STUDENT. And to me.
LOUIS. Is there any coffee?
HELLY. I haven't been shopping much lately.
LOUIS. Hot chocolate?
HELLY. No milk.
STUDENT. Don't worry. *(Pause)* Shall I go?
LOUIS. But you brought the pamphlet for translation?
HELLY. We have some wine... My husband is a gourmet - and a Marxist.
LOUIS. Champagne!
HELLY. Not too much Louis.
LOUIS. You're not my mother.

He finds and opens a bottle of champagne. He pours glasses. They drink.

STUDENT. Delicious.

LOUIS drinks again.

HELLY. So - What are you waiting for?
LOUIS. Shall we get down to it?
STUDENT. I can't wait.

LOUIS takes the typescript and lays it on the desk. He takes the STUDENT in his arms and kisses her. Helly sits at the typewriter and begins to type. LOUIS and the STUDENT continue to make love.

LOUIS. Little angel...
HELLY. ...Hobbes; 'the security of the State - the absolute authority of the State, in a world of conflict, can assure the security of the people'... Cut out repetition of he the word 'state'...
LOUIS. A nose...
HELLY. Then this bit on Rousseau: 'the discovery, by looking at his childhood - on **sex** - that made Rousseau realise that you won't change people by intellectual change'... How true-
LOUIS. ... like an angel...
HELLY. ...Repetition of the word 'change' is ...

As they make love, LOUIS and the STUDENT knock over the red flag, which unrolls.

HELLY. ...clumsy, to say the least.
STUDENT. Please!
LOUIS. Ignore her...
HELLY. *(Frantically typing as LOUIS frantically makes love.)* Hobbes... 'The absolute authority of the state - can assure the security of people - by ending the war of all against all...' Rousseau: 'The illegitimate contract - subterfuge and ruse born in the perverse imagination of the rich - to submit the spirit of the **miserable**...' Machiavelli: like Marx - a radical account of the uncertain factuality... uncertain factuality... uncertain factuality...uncertain factuality...'

LOUIS lies the STUDENT face-up on the bed. Sound of typing continues.

REPETITION: Repeat RED R(W)OMB SEQUENCE I, PART I.

VARIATION

HELLY. *(Anxious, over her shoulder.)* Don't overdo it Louis... Louis! You'll hurt yourself. You are not in control of your mind! *(With rising anxiety.)* Louis - You must stop at once... Too much **sex** and... Louis, for Christ's sake... Don't kill yourself over a piece of skirt... *(Hardly containing herself for terror.)* Listen to me... Listen to your old lady... You'll kill yourself. I can't stand it... Please Louis... No, no...

HELLY paces, moaning, tearing her hair with anguish.

BLACKOUT

ADDITION: SOUND-SCORE: Running feet, bursts of gun-shot, snatches of Marxist slogans, 'La Marseillaise.'

SUBSTITUTION: TIME: 1968, Paris student riots.

LIGHTING: Blue.

Enter, running, STUDENT (Young woman) in '60s dress that is bloodied. She carries the Red flag to the outside of the door, chanting: 'EVERYTHING IS POSSIBLE'... 'THE IMAGINATION TAKES POWER'... 'IT IS FORBIDDEN TO FORBID' ...'LIBERTY IN ACTION'... SEIZE THE CHANCE! *Sound of marching boots becomes louder. She rings frantically. No reply. She knocks, opens door, runs inside, bangs door shut behind her, looks around.*

STUDENT. Anyone here? *(Pause.)* Professor? *(Pause.)* Fuck!

STUDENT takes a large felt-tip pen and writes on the wall: 'LISTEN TO ALTHUSSER' sound of shouting voices, gun-shots closer.

STUDENT. Where exactly the fuck are you Professor? You swore you'd be here. You started this whole bloody revolution... I read all your books on the subject. So just exactly where are you? Just when we need you... What do you expect me to do now?

STUDENT crosses out the slogan she has written and writes underneath it: 'WHAT USE ALTHUSSER' She hesitates and writes above 'ALTHUSSER' the word 'THE PARTY'. Sound-score very loud.

STUDENT. Oh Jesus!

STUDENT crosses herself, drops the Red flag and jumps out of the window. LOUIS climbs out of the cupboard, peers out of the window. He picks up the Red flag, rolls it up and stands it in the corner.

LOUIS. *(To departed STUDENT.)* Oh dear! You'll get hurt! You haven't a clue what the Party's really up to. A true revolution never comes from the rich little daughters of lawyers, my dear! How can you understand? Russia decides these things, not me. You see how we are the mere subjects of history. The historical process is complex. A necessary contingency. Revolution is the exception that disproves this rule.

BLACKOUT
SUBSTITUTION: TIME: 1980.

REPETITION: RED R(W)OMB SEQUENCE, PART I, with LOUIS (Old man) massaging STUDENT (Older woman) on bed. The STUDENT is stripped to the waist.

LOUIS. Mao's the man to go for. I really believed the Russians. - What a splendid life they led - the right to work guaranteed -
HELLY. Planned and guaranteed...
LOUIS. The working-class strong and respected -
HELLY. Police never entering the factories -

LOUIS. No-one shut away in psychiatric hospitals -
HELLY. Only happens here!
LOUIS. My books translated, but hidden away... Then the Hungarian uprisings. - Kruschev at the Twentieth Congress...
HELLY. Mao.

Silence.

VARIATION: LIGHTING: White on HANGING FIGURE OF LUCY.

STUDENT. *(Sitting up, dressing.)* The family -
LOUIS. Ah, now the family is the most criminal of all State institutions... The family is one of the most damaging and controlling tools of fascism ... The family is Capitalism's most effective way of reproducing Capitalism's values.
STUDENT. I don't quite see -
HELLY. The site of the sacred -
LOUIS. Where you come to be constructed -
HELLY. Where Capitalist ideology creeps right in -
LOUIS. ...to the human personality, as it is forming -
HELLY You think you are a free person, making choices...?
STUDENT. Yes...
LOUIS. But you are misrecognizing reality - what you think is real - is all imaginary! It's just your family's ideology which you take as 'natural'.
HELLY. Thinking what is familiar to you, is 'real'!
LOUIS. The family deforms the very self! It's a trap!
HELLY. And made you its own... That's what controls you!
STUDENT. So I am just another 'production' - a commodity of the capitalist State, via my family?
LOUIS. Via its class position.
STUDENT. Not me at all... Not me as an individual?
HELLY. Right! You are its subject .You learn to desire what the family desires.
STUDENT. No room at all for me to form myself?
LOUIS. Quite!

Silence.

STUDENT. I think I'd like to go now.
LOUIS. You see, it's very subtle... It all lies in language... Language, after all, exists before us, so it waits to assign us our place in it.

STUDENT. And words... Surely words release meaning... All sorts of meaning... Meaning that isn't... political?

HELLY and LOUIS laugh. LOUIS pours more champagne.

LOUIS. Champagne?
STUDENT. *(Making for the door.)* I really must be going.
HELLY. *(Removing the champagne.)* Do stay!
LOUIS. You have given me such... energy!
HELLY. Now that is a privilege!
STUDENT. *(Collecting her papers.)* It's been wonderful, but...
LOUIS. *(Pushing student on to bed.)* But... What of history?
HELLY. He can teach you so much more!
STUDENT. Really, I ought...
HELLY. We are merely actors in history!
LOUIS. History is a process without subject.
HELLY. 'History is more imaginative than we are.'
LOUIS. There is no inevitable scheme to history... No inevitable progression. We must think it.
HELLY. It's like getting on a train not knowing where you got on...
LOUIS. ...nor where you will get off!
HELLY. So you see. You are determined by history too!
STUDENT. *(Getting of the bed in a hurry.)* Get off... Get off... Thank you so much professor, but I really must be getting off...

HELLY and LOUIS laugh.

HELLY. Let her go!
LOUIS. Isn't she wonderful. That profile...
HELLY. Wonderful.
LOUIS. Thank you so much for coming. I'm sorry we haven't had time for the translation of your pamphlet into Spanish.
STUDENT. Another time. You have given me so much … er… to think about.
HELLY. Yes, you must come again.
STUDENT. *(Practically running for the door.)* Goodbye!

Exit STUDENT, slamming the door. She leaves in a hurry, on her bicycle.

LOUIS. Poor little thing! Was I cruel?
HELLY. A successful... Prince... must act outside the boundaries of

ordinary ethics.
LOUIS. Machiavelli. Thank you, my dear. Yes, one must know when cruelty is a sensible policy.
HELLY. That barge - rowed by the unions- crossing the Socialist river of shit. - Who controls the galley-workers? - The proles. - And if the galley-workers don't pull their weight?
LOUIS. Punish them, punish them, I say. Or how will the barge ever get to the other shore?
HELLY. 'Where sunny, soft breezes blow...' No more market forces, no more strife... And Beethoven's 'Ode to Joy on the tannoy...
LOUIS. Fruit and flowers in profusion for everyone to gather... You don't think we could be wrong , do you?

Silence.

LOUIS. Forgive me. I am not Louis. I'm an impostor. *(Pause. Anguished.)* I am not truly myself, you see. I'm so ashamed! The terror of it! Having no real identity. Belonging in limbo. No man's land. Do you understand me?
HELLY. Louis! What are you saying?

Silence. LOUIS goes to desk, writes a placard. HELLY sits on the bed.

LOUIS. *(Reading placard aloud.)* 'Do not disturb. Temporarily absent.'
HELLY. You want to provoke me, don't you?
LOUIS. You know I'm right. Tell me. Tell me I'm right. Tell me what an impostor I am.
HELLY. You want to provoke me until I do something awful.
LOUIS. *(Suddenly anguished.)* How can I let myself do it? How can I let myself fool the world like this? Look what that young woman thinks of me! *(Menacing her.)* Why do you let me do it?

LOUIS hangs the notice on the front of the door. He locks the door and pockets the key. He pushes HELLY face - down on the bed.

HELLY. Your books are fine... Original, independent...
LOUIS. How can I live with myself...
HELLY. Oh Louis... Come here... My boy, my poor boy! How we all love you!

LOUIS begins to massage HELLY's shoulders.

RED R(W)OMB SEQUENCE
VARIATION 7

Telephone rings.

LOUIS. Don't answer.
HELLY. *(Answering the telephone.)* Yes... Oh it's you... Yes, we're alone... No, it's difficult to say...
LOUIS. Who is it?
HELLY. Well, as best I can... Exactly! - You've hit the nail on the head. As you know... Not right now... I'm doing my best... Yes, you had better... As soon as possible... Oh, I'll manage until...

LOUIS tries to get the phone away from her. A comic battle ensues with elements of farce.

LOUIS. *(Wresting phone from her.)* Hello... Hello!... Who was it? Damn you, tell me!

LOUIS picks up the rifle and points it at her.

HELLY. Louis! Louis... Put that down.
LOUIS. Who was on the telephone.
HELLY. Pierre. OK? - Our analyst, that's all. Now stop being such a fool and put that thing down!
LOUIS. Our analyst! Our analyst! He's my analyst. You just borrow him occasionally. He speaks to me, do you hear? Me!
HELLY. He belongs to you? You own him?
LOUIS. Oh you're so clever! You think you can spy on me? Think you can use him to control me?
HELLY. What a child you are!
LOUIS. Stay away from him.
HELLY. Louis, I need someone to talk to.
LOUIS. Getting your tentacles on every corner of my life.
HELLY. Paranoia!
LOUIS. Think you can own me?
HELLY. *(Suddenly collapses.)* Either stop pointing that gun at me, or just get it over with. *(She moves to the desk and scoops up some fallen pills, pours some water.)* Come on... Take these. Be a good boy.
LOUIS. What have you been telling him behind my back?

HELLY. Me... It's me we've been talking about.
LOUIS. Think you know everything. Think you know what you're doing? He's a flatterer I tell you. He flatters me. That's what he does. Tells me my books are the only ones on philosophy he can understand. Tells me I'm special - all that crap. A father-figure - that's what he's looking for. I won't be his bloody father-figure! He can go to hell.
HELLY. We were talking about me... Me! About me going to London to abort our child Louis, because you and I don't believe in families. Because for you to be a father...
LOUIS. I forbid you to speak to him.
HELLY. I was telling him about my abandonment -
LOUIS. Cheat!
HELLY. About waiting - raw, crying, crying, crying for my dead child.
LOUIS. Narcissist!
HELLY. About my mother cursing me... About being always on the outside. Always the Jew.
LOUIS. Self-pitying little -
HELLY. About the family doctor who pushed me back on my mother's bed and ...
LOUIS. Leave my analyst alone!
HELLY. You don't own me.
LOUIS. You're mine!
HELLY. I'm leaving.
LOUIS. *(Lowering gun.)* You wouldn't.

HELLY draws a suitcase from under the bed and begins to throw clothes into it.

HELLY. I'm walking straight out of here.
LOUIS. You can't.
HELLY. I've had enough.
LOUIS. I need you.
HELLY. Find my own place. Get some work.

LOUIS takes the door-key from his pocket locks the door and throws the key out of the window. HELLY sits on the bed.

LOUIS. *(Gentle with her.)* You're mine... My little Red saint.

LOUIS pushes HELLY down on the bed and starts to massage her shoulders.

RED R(W)0MB SEQUENCE
VARIATION 8

TIME: 1980
LIGHTING: Red. White lighting on the HANGING FIGURE OF LUCY.

SOUND-SCORE: Subliminal church bells.

FRENCH/ENGLISH tapes:
Louis and Helly are getting married.
Louis has bought an engagement ring.
Helly will wear a wedding dress.
It will be made of lace and satin.
They will be married in church.
Louis' father works in the bank.
Louis' mother is a housewife.
Louis is training to be a teacher.
Helly wants to be a typist in an office.

HELLY. I'm tired.
LOUIS. Rest.
HELLY. An end. Now.
LOUIS. We can work on my papers.
HELLY. An end of it.
LOUIS. We can go south.
HELLY. You can't even swim.
LOUIS. You see - You do care.
HELLY. Too tired.
LOUIS. Courage.
HELLY. Lie here.

LOUIS pulls her up to a sitting position. HELLY flops back again.

LOUIS. Sit up, will you.

There follows a comic struggle.

HELLY. Help me.
LOUIS. I'm helping you.

HELLY. You've been good to me Louis, but you don't listen.
LOUIS. I'm listening.
HELLY. End it.
LOUIS. I ... can't.
HELLY. You know what I mean.

LOUIS begins to tremble.

HELLY. Make it easy for me.

LOUIS trembles more violently.

HELLY. I'm hateful.- Unlovable. An old dog yapping at your heels. Worthless.
LOUIS. Everything to me.
HELLY. They all say it behind my back.
LOUIS. No.
HELLY. Nasty little dog at your door. Aggressive, blood-sucking, quarrelsome.
LOUIS. You keep me alive.
HELLY. I know what they say.
LOUIS. I say no!

Silence. LOUIS still trembles.

HELLY. End it now. I beg you. Won't take much.
LOUIS. Enjoying it?
HELLY. I'll just lie here. Nice and easy. No resistance. I promise.
LOUIS. Stop!
HELLY. I really want it.
LOUIS. You know what you're doing to me.
HELLY. Peaceful. All I want is a bit of peace.
LOUIS. Hell.
HELLY. I don't want anything else.
LOUIS. You can't do this to me.
HELLY. Out of love... I beg you.
LOUIS. The loneliness for me would be... unbearable.
HELLY. I'd make a terrible mess if I did it myself.
LOUIS. For God's sake!
HELLY. You're kind. Gentle. The gentlest of men.
LOUIS. To be without you -

HELLY. Just a tired old woman. No family... We Jews believe in families...
LOUIS. Marry me. Marry me now.

LOUIS pulls a curtain ring from the rail at the window. He places it on her fourth finger and makes the sign of the cross.

HELLY. *(Laughs.)* That's it. Do what you've always wanted to do.
LOUIS. You're mine now.
HELLY. Louis... Be 'lui'.
LOUIS. *(Laying her back on the bed.)* I'll look after you.
HELLY. My neck hurts...

Trembling, LOUIS begins to massage HELLY.

RED R(W)OMB SEQUENCE
VARIATION 9

LOUIS (Older man) massages his mother, LUCY (Young woman) face-up and dressed in 1940s clothes.

LIGHTING: White. White light on the Hanging Figure.

SUBSTITUTION: HELLY is the bleeding Hanging Figure.

SOUND-SCORE:
CHARLEY'S VOICE: 'He'll make 'em happy, happy, happy.'

REPETITION: RED (W)ROMB SEQUENCE, PART 2, until LOUIS runs out of the room.

VARIATION: To LOUIS: 'I think I've strangled my mother.'

BLACKOUT

RED R(W)OMB SEQUENCE
VARIATION 10

LOUIS (Old man) massaging HELLY (Older woman).

SUBSTITUTION: Marx is the Hanging Figure in white light.

FRENCH/ENGLISH TAPES
Louis and Helly are married.
They have moved into their new home.
Louis is teaching History.
Helly is typing.
What is Louis studying?
Louis is studying History.
What is Helly typing?
Helly is typing Louis' History lesson.

Telephone rings.

LOUIS. Damn!

LOUIS answers telephone.

LOUIS. Yes?... Yes, I see... When did you say?... Right... Yes, I've got that. - Wednesday, two-thirty. I'll be there... The usual place. Good-bye.

LOUIS sits on the bed.

HELLY. It's them, isn't it? *(Silence.)*
LOUIS. An advisory meeting, that's all.
HELLY. We know what that means. *(Pause.)* You're going? *(Pause.)* Why?
LOUIS. You know why. *(Silence)*
HELLY. You know, I think you will. You actually will testify against me. I don't trust you!
LOUIS. No, I wouldn't if I were you. *(Pause.)*
HELLY. Why don't you just leave them? Leave the Party. *(Silence.)* You can't leave, can you. What's the matter with you?
LOUIS. It's you - you - they want me to walk out on. It's you they want to throw out for good. *(Silence.)* It's you they're investigating. It's you they don't trust. You and your Resistance work. They want me to confess. They want me to admit I know. They want me to say you did it, say you betrayed the Party in the Resistance. That you got Communists into trouble. That you lost your head. That you were a spy for the Nazi's. That you ordered -
HELLY. Stop! *(Silence)* Shit - I'm glad I'm not a member any more! *(Pause.)* Well? Are you going to?
LOUIS. *(Laughing.)* Stick by you? -

HELLY 'Impeachment of the state officers by the rule of law.'
LOUIS 'Sensible cruelty for the greater good.'
HELLY 'Subterfuge, deception for the wider end.'
LOUIS 'Forget morals... Plan a strategy... Take charge!'
HELLY 'Find the hidden springs of power that control us and manage them carefully - For the benefit of all.'
LOUIS 'Let there be conspiracies... Invasions... Violence - '
HELLY '.... as long as the Party is in control.' *(Silence.)*
LOUIS. They're trying to humiliate you.
HELLY. They're trying to control you. *(Pause.)*
LOUIS. Nobody controls me. I think for myself.
HELLY. *(Laughing.)* My wonderful miraculous boy!
LOUIS. He's a good boy.
HELLY. ' Lui'?
LOUIS. He'll never leave you.

LOUIS yanks the telephone from its socket. He goes to the window and throws it out. He sees something that terrifies him.

LOUIS. *(Wild.)* Who's there? Who are you out there watching me? What do you want? *(Frantically tugging the other curtain shut.)* Bastards! You won't get me...

HELLY approaches him, draws him back to the bed, lies him down.

HELLY. There's no-one there, Louis. You're imagining things, I'm here. I'll look after you.

HELLY leads him to the bed, lies him down face upwards and bends over him, massaging his shoulders.

LIGHTING: The light on HANGING FIGURE OF MARX goes out.

FILM-SEQUENCE 2: The NAKED FAT WOMAN takes LOUIS (Boy) on his knee and counts his body parts.

BLACKOUT

WHITE ROOM SEQUENCE
VARIATION 3

SUBSTITUTION: HELLY is the Hanging Figure.

SOUND-SCORE: Subliminal Beatle songs of late 1960s. Lucy in the Sky with Diamonds

Doctor leads shuffling LOUIS (Younger man) in pyjamas to the white bed, lies LOUIS down, places gag in LOUIS' mouth, places electrodes on either side of LOUIS' forehead, shocks LOUIS, who convulses. Exit Doctor.

BLACKOUT

RED R(W)OMB SEQUENCE
VARIATION 11

LOUIS (Old man), in a trance-like state steps back from HELLY (Old woman.)

LOUIS. *(To himself.)* 'Lui'... What has he done? What has the stupid bastard gone and done? Answer me, you little two-faced swine! What have you done to her? She's not moving - and I love her. I need her. She's mine you know, you bastard! - Posturing and pretending. - Strutting - when you're numb as a block of ice inside. - Watching her like a snake. - I've seen you. Murderous old devil- You've been itching to lay your dirty hands on her all this while! Never show a thing! Cunning! When you know she's the only thing I've got! If she goes, I'm ruined. She's precious to me, do you hear!... Priceless. One in a million... I don't care about the rest. Touch another hair on her head, and you're dead! She's mother and father to me. This place is a tomb without her. So clear off!

LOUIS bends over HELLY and begins to stroke her.

BLACKOUT

REPETITION: RED (W)ROMB SEQUENCE, PART 1 and 2.

BLACKOUT

TIME: 1990.

LIGHTING: Normal daylight.

WHITE ROOM SEQUENCE
VARIATION 4

SOUND-SCORE: Echoing weird cries and sad calls, feet running down a passage. Subliminal announcement on tannoy.

FRENCH/ENGLISH TAPES:
A visit to the Hospital.
A hospital is not a prison but a hospital.
Hospitals sell flowers.
All hospitals are clean and safe.
The doctors and the nurses wear white.
They wear white uniforms to keep clean and to keep you safe.
You may post a letter in a hospital.
Each hospital has a priest.
(Pause.) And a rabbi.

LOUIS (Old man) wearing pyjamas, sits on the small white bed. He is knitting, under the small crucifix on the wall. Enter NURSE with LOUIS' clothes.

NURSE. *(Taking knitting.)* We can put the knitting away now.
LOUIS. Who am I? Do you know who I am?
NURSE. Come along now.

The NURSE deftly injects LOUIS.

LOUIS. I am... *(In a panic.)* You know! You know... Do you know who I am?
NURSE. Louis. Louis. Everyone's heard of you. So you can stop pretending.
LOUIS. Ah, yes. Of course. *Lui*
NURSE. (Dressing him.) Buttocks!... Lift!
LOUIS. You know, all my life I've wanted to be someone else. That hasn't happened to you has it?

NURSE. Arm.
LOUIS. Someone who doesn't have to seduce everyone by pretending he is someone else- so he can breathe, move... live. That would be bliss. Someone who lives in his own body! Imagine...

FILM SEQUENCE 1: White worm comes out of the cupboard.

LOUIS. That feels good.
NURSE. Leg.

FILM SEQUENCE 2: NAKED FAT WOMAN takes him on her lap and counts his body parts.

LOUIS. Careful!
NURSE. Feet.
LOUIS. Do you know, for a while I thought I was losing my body parts - it happened to me when I was a boy.

LIGHTING: We see only LOUIS' head.

LOUIS. This place has made me disappear. It is what institutions do to people.
NURSE. I said 'feet'!
LOUIS. Eyes, ears, oesophagus, intestines, liver, fingers, aorta, spleen - They all went!
NURSE. Back!
LOUIS. Neck.

NURSE hauls LOUIS up and continues to dress his unseen body.

LOUIS. Since she has gone, I feel so light - like I've dumped a lorry-load of sand off my shoulders.
NURSE. Feet.
LOUIS. Now that I've killed myself off...
NURSE. Yourself? Ha!... Toenails!... Scissors
LOUIS. She was the closest thing to 'him'.

NURSE attempts to cut LOUIS' toenails. LOUIS wriggles and giggles.

LOUIS. Nurse! Please... Enough. You'll be the death of me!

NURSE threatens him with scissors.

LOUIS. There are five hundred ways you can commit suicide. You can commit suicide by rope, poison, fire, the window - *(NURSE glares at him.)* Water, knife, gun *(Pause.)* Gun. *(Pause.)* Couldn't do it. Couldn't take my ... own self... I'm so sad... Sad. I'm the saddest person alive.
NURSE. *(Putting on his slipper.)* Foot!
LOUIS. *(To audience.)* Nurse thinks she's so calm, so reasonable. But she's contaminated with state ideology. So she plays this violent game because she's trained to think I'm a criminal. - Mad. She doesn't know I'm lying under a tombstone. Embalmed. Dead to the world. She doesn't even know I'm a reasonable human being. But they have wiped me out! How dare they! They won't even accuse me of murder. *(Whispers.)* Even the law of this country gives me no person, no place. - I am *non-lieu*. *(Shouts.)* I demand to be taken seriously! I demand to be accused of what I've done! Give me my identity, d'you hear? I demand to be a -
NURSE. Other foot.
LOUIS. *(Panicking)* Let me out! Let me out! Please, please, please, please. I'll never get out!
NURSE. Front.
LOUIS. No persona. No being. Why does it matter when I've been in mourning for myself my whole life?
NURSE. *(Knotting his tie.)* Neck.
LOUIS. I killed off myself so that 'he' could live. *Lui.* You know... *(Panic.)* What's-his-name?
NURSE. Louis. The famous Louis. Don't worry, you are honoured - They won't do anything to you.
LOUIS. Yes! Helly is the closest thing to 'him', you know.
NURSE. *(Pulling him up.)* Up!
LOUIS. (*Gripping the NURSE.)* I'm so lonely. Come into this black hole with me...
NURSE. *(Loosening his grip.)* Come on now! Your things...

NURSE pulls suitcase from under the bed, opens it.

NURSE. What have you been hoarding now!

NURSE shovels out handfuls of foodstuff - oranges, biscuits, tea-bags etc. She stuffs as much as she can into her own pocket and mouth.

NURSE. (*Mumbling.)* Slippers.

WHITE ROOM SEQUENCE
VARIATION 5

LOUIS. *(Barefoot, back to nurse and facing audience.)* I've got to talk to you. Why bother. Because - I choose to. I can still choose.
NURSE. No dawdling!
LOUIS. Explain - scientifically, with lucidity - I've read all the news cuttings about it - so I can fill in the gaps can read what I did. I'm perfectly rational. I can order my thoughts. Do you know what I found out today? I discovered what love is. Love is being attentive to others. *(NURSE laughs.)* I'm nearly seventy. I feel young again. I'm alive. Life is beautiful -

LOUIS genuflects to Crucifix. Exit LOUIS and NURSE.
SOUND-SCORE: 1990s Pop Music, very loud. This continues on the workman's radio.

LOUIS old and dishevelled in old hat, coat, and slippers stands in front of the door to the RED R(W)OMB. A WORKMAN bricks up the door. His radio plays loud modern Euro-pop music.

LOUIS. *(Shouting above radio.)* Excuse me...
WORKMAN. Yes?
LOUIS. Well... It's just that... This is my flat.
WORKMAN. That so...
LOUIS. Look, I know I haven't got the key... I threw it away but-
WORKMAN. Oh yes?
LOUIS. Yes. I didn't know what I was doing at the time.
WORKMAN. I'll say!
LOUIS. How are things here?
WORKMAN. Much the same I'd say, guv... Except this place is Mister Blank's... Or is it Blanc?
LOUIS. No, no. That's impossible.
WORKMAN. Come to the wrong place, guv.
LOUIS. Don't tell me, young man! I lived here for thirty years!
WORKMAN. Did you now?
LOUIS. You don't understand...
WORKMAN. I understand who pays me.
LOUIS. There's some mistake.
WORKMAN. It's no use getting at me. Speak to my boss. I'll tell you

where to go...

LOUIS tries to push his way into the room. The WORKMAN bars his way.

WORKMAN. Sorry sir. Orders is orders. No-one comes in here except the workmen.

LOUIS. *(Shouting above the radio.)* Do you know who I am?

WORKMAN. What?... Sorry, can't hear you.

LOUIS. I am... I am...

WORKMAN. Look, piss off will you... I got work to do.

LOUIS shuffles five steps to front-stage.

LOUIS. We are coming to an end.

WORKMAN finishes bricking up the door. He picks up the Red flag, rolls it up puts it under his arm, throws it our of the window. Exit WORKMAN out of the window. LOUIS shuffles five steps to the left, five to the right. Pause.

LOUIS. I must confess... The fact is... I strangled my wife during a state of mental confusion. *(Pause.)* She meant everything to me...

VOICE 1. It's a scandal.

VOICE 2. Everyone in the university clams up.

LOUIS. She loved me so much...

VOICE 1. Didn't even put him in the dock, did they? One set of laws for the likes of them and another for us.

LOUIS. And since she couldn't go on living, she wanted to die...

VOICE 2. Should have brought him to court.

VOICE 3. She's bloody dead isn't she, and he's alive!

VOICE 4. Wasn't in his right mind, that's why.

VOICE 1. Took away all his rights.

VOICE 2. Can't even plead in court?

Enter the STUDENT, holding a baby and some lecture notes. She is talking and laughing into a mobile telephone.

LOUIS. (On his knees.) Helen. Can you hear me? I'm in this terrible place. There is nothing here. I am buried alive. Locked in a tomb. Will this ever end? The future... lasts... a long time.

LOUIS watches the STUDENT. Light darkens.

THE END

THE STRANGE PASSENGER

by

Sonja Linden

My translation of Viktor Ullmann's opera, *The Emperor of Atlantis,* for its London premiere in 1988, sowed the seeds for my play *The Strange Passenger,* first performed in 1995. I was fascinated by this allegorical opera and by the story of its little known creator, a Czech composer of Jewish origins, who was perversely liberated as an artist during his final two years in the ghetto of Terezín/Theresienstadt: 'Theresienstadt.' he wrote, ' has served to enhance and not impede my musical activities... by no means did we sit weeping on the banks of the waters of Babylon - our endeavour with respect to art was commensurate with our will to live.' For a number of years I struggled to find the way tell the story of this complex man - musician, poet, anthrophosophist - and the grim circumstances in which he wrote his remarkable chamber opera, remarkable not only because of its satirical portrait of Hitler, but also because of its presentation of Death as a benign entity to his fellow-inmates of Terezín. In the end I focused on the tension between his drive to compose the opera and his need to meet the demands of those closest to him. The play sets out to deal with the role of art as a redemptive force in times of darkness, while questioning the morality of those who sacrifice the lives of their family on the altar of their art. It has as its back cloth the life in Terezín ghetto, where physical deprivation and spiritual humiliation were combatted by the phenomenal outpouring of artistic and intellectual endeavour in the form of concerts, operas, cabarets, plays and lectures, all put on with the Nazis' cynical blessing as part of their scheme to use 'Paradise Ghetto' as a propaganda showcase.
The Strange Passenger was the title Viktor Ullmann gave to his verse diary, which he named after a character in Ibsen's *Peer Gynt.* The four lines of the exchange between Peer Gynt and The Strange Passenger quoted by Viktor Ullmann on the front page of his diary, have in turn been woven into my play.

The Strange Passenger was first performed in Great Britain at the Plymouth Drum Theatre on 26th September, 1995 as the first stage of a two month national tour by Paines Plough Theatre Company which ended at the Battersea Arts Centre, London.

CAST

VIKTOR ULLMANN	Andrew Normington
HEINO/HEINRICH	Peter Hamilton-Dyer
ELLY ULLMANN/LOTTE	Race Davies
ANNY ULLMANN/LISE	Tina Jones
CELLIST/STRANGE PASSENGER	Julia Marsen

Director	Penny Ciniewicz
Designer	Emma Donovan
Composer/Musical Director	Derek Barnes

The play features original music for solo cello by Derek Barnes, and extracts from Viktor Ullmann's *The Emperor of Atlantis,* arranged by Derek Barnes for cello accompaniment.
All the cabaret songs are set to music by Derek Barnes. The lyrics are by Sonja Linden, with the exception of *'Theresienstadt, Theresienstadt....'* (Act I Scene 3), written in Terezín/Theresienstadt by Leo Strauss and translated by Sonja Linden.
The characters Death (bass) and the Drummer (mezzo soprano) should be able to sing in an operatic style: Lise and Lotte in a cabaret style (as mezzos). Heinrich and Ullmann sing in the final 'Chorale' (as baritones).
The musical underscoring and the accompaniment to the vocal music is played on solo cello.

Derek Barnes writes: 'The extraordinary phenomenon of Victor Ullmann's musical output in Terezin was a great inspiration to me in the writing of the score to *The Strange Passenger.* I have tried to capture the musical influences on Ullmann himself, that is those of Mahler, Schönberg, Zemlinsky and others, and to ensure that the spirit of Ullmann is present in the underscoring of the play.'

NB: A licence to perform, record or broadcast any part of Derek Barnes'score to the play *The Strange Passenger* including the arrangement quotations of Victor Ullmann's music, must be obtained in advance from Derek Barnes, Coryphaeus Music, 56 Further Green Road, London 9E6 1JH.

CHARACTERS

The characters of Viktor, Anny and Elly Ullmann are based on real life characters in real life events. The sixteen characters in total are to be played by five performers as follows:

VIKTOR ULLMANN
HEINO/HEINRICH/Man/Compère
THE STRANGE PASSENGER/DEATH
ANNY/LISE/1st Woman/Klara/GhettoOfficial
ELLY/LOTTE/2ndWoman/Drummer

The characters of Death (bass) and the Drummer (mezzo soprano) should be able to sing in an operatic style, Lise and Lotte in a cabaret style (as mezzos). Heino/Heinrich and Viktor sing in the final 'Chorale' (as baritones).

The musical underscoring of the play, and the accompaniment to the vocal music is played on solo cello.

SETTING

The Strange Passenger takes place in the Czech ghetto of Terezín/ Theresienstadt, 60 miles north of Prague between the years 1942 and 1944.

ACT ONE

Scene 1: Arrival

Terezín. September 8,1942. A vast station- like room swarming with newly arrived inmates of the ghetto pressing forward to be processed or 'ghettoised'. When the new arrivals are not talking among themselves in short exchanges, they are being interviewed by an invisible Jewish ghetto official. When this happens, the actors step forward in turn, each delivering a response from a new character.

MAN. Excuse me!
1ST WOMAN. I think we were next.
2ND WOMAN. Such bad organisation! Typically Jewish!
1ST WOMAN. I can't see what takes so long
2ND WOMAN. Especially when some of us have already booked our accommodation in advance.
MAN. Four and a half hours we've been stuck in this place now.
2ND WOMAN. My husband's not in the best of health as it happens.
MAN. *(To Ghetto Official.)* Rosenfeld. Rudi. January 5, 1886. Newspaper editor. Vienna.
1ST WOMAN. *(To Ghetto Official.)* Judas. Jutta. October 11, 1881. Housewife. Kassel.

2ND WOMAN. *(To Ghetto Official.)* Friedman. Fanny. July 29, 1887. Milliner. Linz.
1st WOMAN. Why do you think they had to take our luggage?
2nd WOMAN. I hope they're not chucking it about. There wasn't a mark on those suitcases you know. I just hope they don't get lost.
MAN. Don't worry, they'll have it all organised. You know how efficient the Germans are.
1st WOMAN. I wonder if Herr Hitler has any idea that former officers of the imperial army are being treated to conditions like this.
2nd WOMAN. *(Starts scrabbling about in her handbag.)* Thank God I put your medals in here and not in the suitcase. Ah! *(She is about to fish them out, to her husband's embarrassment.)*
MAN. Put them away!
2ND WOMAN. Listen, you be pleased I thought of it! If they try and fob us off with inferior accommodation, at least I've got them here at the

ready. (*She has taken out an official piece of paper.*) 'Theresienbad.' It's a pretty name, isn't it.

1ST WOMAN. *(To Ghetto Official.)* I'd like a room with a view.

MAN. *(To Ghetto Official.)* Of the lake.

2ND WOMAN. *(To Ghetto Official.)* South-facing please. With a balcony.

1st WOMAN. I didn't know it was a spa town.

MAN. Oh yes, and there's a lake. I'm going to insist that we get a room overlooking the lake.

2ND WOMAN. Of course, we had to pull a few strings, but then we've always been well connected through my husband's position. We used up all our savings.

MAN. Shhh!

1ST WOMAN. *(To other people in the queue.)* Just think, this lady and her husband purchased a privilege with their life-savings that we're getting for free!

1ST WOMAN. *(To Ghetto Official.)* Lehrer. Lotte. November 30, 1884. Housewife. Leipzig.

2ND WOMAN. *(To Ghetto Official.)* Sauer. Steffi. January 2, 1887. Doctor. Vienna.

MAN. *(To Ghetto Official.)* Hertz. Hermann. April 14, 1872. High Court Judge. Berlin.

1ST WOMAN. I need the ground floor.

2ND WOMAN. No stairs.

MAN. I can't manage stairs since my accident. Is there a lift?

2ND WOMAN. I only packed one evening dress for in here.

1st WOMAN. Well, fifty kilograms is nothing is it. I didn't know what to bring. Whatever my maid doesn't want will just have to rot in the wardrobe.

MAN. Our girl wasn't much good. She was in tears most of the time. I told her we'd be better off once we left the city. No more petty regulations.

2nd WOMAN. The amount of work, the arrangements, the packing - one box schlepped here, another there. Whoever will keep it for you? We have some very good neighbours.

1ST WOMAN. If I'd listened to my son he'd have handed it all over to the Nazis. We already handed in the gramophone and the radio. That's it I said, we have to draw the line somewhere, we need something to come back to, we're not going to let them clean us out completely. The rugs stay!

MAN. *(To Ghetto Official.)* Lipmann. Lorenz. February 12, 1882.

Company Director. Berlin.
1ST WOMAN. *(To Ghetto Official.)* Klein. Klara. June 26, 1866. Schoolteacher. Retired. Vienna.
2ND WOMAN. *(To Ghetto Official.)* Lippman. Liesl. August 17, 1885.Singer... Dressmaker then. Freiburg.
MAN. I don't understand.
2ND WOMAN. But it says on the ticket.
1ST WOMAN. No lake?
2ND WOMAN. It must be a mistake.
VIKTOR. *(To Ghetto Official.)* Ullmann. Viktor. December 31, 1898. Composer....Oh... Toy maker? Prague.
1ST WOMAN. You speak Czech Herr Ullmann, ask them if this is Theresienbad.
MAN. Terezín Spa.
2ND WOMAN. Tell them we booked for a spa.
1ST WOMAN. Look it's written here.
2ND WOMAN. On my ticket.
MAN. Tell them I can't take stairs.
1ST WOMAN. I'm seventy-six years old Herr Ullmann. A widow.
MAN. 'Privileged Resettlement for Elderly Jews'.
2nd WOMAN. 'Protectorate for the Jews of the Reich'
MAN. Board and lodging.
1ST WOMAN. Medical services.
2ND WOMAN. Laundry services.
1ST WOMAN. Set up by the Führer.
MAN. We'll have work to do....
2ND WOMAN. But we'll be left in peace, till the end of the war.
1st WOMAN. 'Paradise ghetto'.
2ND WOMAN. They promised us.
MAN. They said it was a spa with a lake.
2ND WOMAN. We sold everything to buy a place here.
1ST WOMAN. We couldn't bear to go to a concentration camp.
2ND WOMAN. So we paid up.
MAN. 30,000 Reichsmarks we paid.
1ST WOMAN. All their savings.
MAN. It's a mistake Herr Ullmann.
1ST WOMAN. Tell them there's been a mistake.
2ND WOMAN. We must have the best rooms.
1ST WOMAN. My husband was an officer in the imperial army.
2nd WOMAN. Mine fought in the great war.
He got a medal for bravery.

MAN. I lost my leg for the Kaiser.
1st WOMAN. It must be a spa.
2ND WOMAN. Look I brought this specially, for the evenings. (*She removes outer garment to reveal evening dress beneath).* I left all the others for my maid. Black satin and red velvet.
1ST WOMAN. To a peasant from Bukovina!
MAN. *(He undresses to reveal evening suit underneath outer clothes.)* My wife told me to wear it underneath.
2ND WOMAN. We couldn't fit it into the suitcase.
1ST WOMAN. Fifty kilograms is nothing.
MAN. I told her it was ridiculous.
2ND WOMAN. *(She pulls her husband's medals out of her handbag.)* My husband's medals.
MAN. It's a disgrace.
IST WOMAN. What would Herr Hitler say!
MAN. Treating old soldiers like that. Tell them Herr Ullmann!
2ND WOMAN. Show them Herr Ullmann! *(Holding up the medals.)*
1st WOMAN. Help us!
2nd WOMAN. My medals! (*Waving her medals at him.)*
1st WOMAN. My ticket! *(Waving her ticket at him.)*
MAN. My leg! *(Waving his leg at him.)*

Viktor looks at them and then at the invisible official and back again at them. He shrugs helplessly.

MAN. *(Suddenly turns away from Viktor in irritation.)* Ach! what's the use, we won't get anything out of this one!
VIKTOR. I'm sorry.
MAN. That's a lot of help! *(Starts to move to the window.)* Leave it to me ladies, I'll find out what's going on.(*Mumbles to self.*) Someone's got to do something round here. *(He climbs up onto a ledge and looks through a window.)*
1ST WOMAN. Get down! You'll get into trouble!
2ND WOMAN. What is it? Can you see the lake from there?
MAN. It's not a lake, it's a sea!
1ST WOMAN. A sea?
MAN. It's a sea of humanity out there. It's unbelievable!
2ND WOMAN. What is?
MAN. They're like ants!....
1ST WOMAN. It's dangerous up there!
MAN. ....swarming in one direction down one side of the street and in

another down the other side. It's packed!
2ND WOMAN. Anything else, any cars, buses?
1ST WOMAN. I don't walk so good.
MAN. There's something out there on wheels... Can't make it out... It's a hearse and my God, one of the men pulling ... It's my rabbi. - Rabbi Baeck!
1ST WOMAN. Is that all you can tell us about - a funeral!
MAN. There's no coffin though ....

They all turn on Viktor and all their remarks are now addressed to him in increasingly shrill tones.

MAN. It's not a funeral. - It's a delivery.... *(He comes down from the ledge.)*
1ST WOMAN. ... of bread!
2ND WOMAN. Hot from the oven!
MAN. How do you fancy your bread delivered in a hearse Herr Ullmann?
VIKTOR. Don't!
1ST WOMAN. Well Viktor?
2ND WOMAN. What do you say Viki?
MAN. Take a look. Climb up and see. *(He touches him on the arm as though to lead him to the ledge.)*
VIKTOR. Don't!
1ST WOMAN. Go on!
2ND WOMAN. It's your turn!

At this point they all bear down on Viktor so that he backs away and is finally rammed up against a bunk bed that now comes into view.

2ND WOMAN. Up you go!
VIKTOR. Don't make me!
1ST WOMAN. Scared of heights?

The women titter mockingly.

2ND WOMAN. Go on up Herr Ullmann!
1ST WOMAN. That's it Viki!
VIKTOR. (R*eluctantly climbing up onto the bunk bed.)* Why do I have to?
1ST WOMAN. That's more like it. Act like a man!

2ND WOMAN. What you got your eyes shut for?
1ST WOMAN. Your eyes need opening Viktor!
2ND WOMAN. Open your eyes Viki!
VIKTOR. No!
1ST WOMAN. You've got to face it!
VIKTOR. I don't want to!
2ND WOMAN. Open your eyes!
VIKTOR. No!
1ST WOMAN. Open your eyes and see what there is to see!
VIKTOR. *(Screams.)* No!

Viktor's nightmare has now reached its climax. He breaks down sobbing and repeatedly murmuring 'no!'. By this time he is in the middle bunk.

Scene 2: Waking

Viktor's quarters in the ghetto. On-stage is a crude three-tiered bunk. Viktor is half sitting up in the middle bunk, rocking back and forth, his head cradled in his hands. He has been woken by his dream. It is in the early hours of the morning and semi-dark. Everyone else is asleep, save for his neighbour, Heino, in the bottom bunk, who has been roused by Viktor's rocking movements. They speak in whispers so as not to waken the other men in the room.

HEINO. You all right?
VIKTOR. Where am I?
HEINO. Paradise mate, where else?
VIKTOR. *(Confused and half to himself:)* I had a bad dream.
HEINO. We all have nightmares when we first get in here, it's the shock. It's later you start dreaming of home, and food, lovely grub that your mum used to make, plates of steaming goulasch, calves liver, potato dumplings, paprika chicken...
VIKTOR. It was so real. Someone was shouting 'Look that's Leo Baeck, the saintly rabbi.' and they made me look and... *(He breaks off, distressed by the memory.)*
HEINO. Yeah?
VIKTOR. .... he was working like a common labourer, pulling this enormous carriage. This refined man with such a gentle face. You could see the strain. And suddenly I was standing right next to him, and I

could hear him talking to the other men pulling it, and he wasn't complaining, he was talking about Plato.
HEINO. Plato!
VIKTOR. In all that chaos and degradation he was able to discuss Plato.
HEINO. Some say he's a saint. That's a load of shit I say. Saints are dead, aren't they. That's the whole point. You can't keep yourself alive in this dump and stay a saint. Baeck's alive and he's in Terezín. Ergo he can't be a saint. You don't need a degree in philosophy to work that one out, or theology for that matter. Elementary my dear...What's your name?
VIKTOR. Ullmann, Viktor.
HEINO. Elementary my dear Ullmann. I'm Heino. Christened Hendrik, but always known as Heino.
VIKTOR. Christened? I too was....
HEINO. Course I wasn't christened, what do you take me for? I'm a Yid through and through me! No-one needs to trace my blood back to 1800.
VIKTOR. But you just said...
HEINO. Only trying to draw you out Viktor. You'll get used to me. I'm full of surprises. *(Pause.)* Where you from then? *(Silence.)* Not speaking to me now eh? Offended? *(Silence.)* There's a woman in the room?
VIKTOR. Where?
HEINO. That gottcha! Dirty old man. Where you from? *(Silence.)* Ooh, sulking now, are you?
(Silence.)
VIKTOR. I abhor deceit.
HEINO. Only a little joke Vik. OK. I'll pack it in. Pax? *(Silence.)* Pax?
VIKTOR. *(Grudgingly.)* Pax. *(Silence.)*
HEINO. Nullmann's a nice Jewish name though.
VIKTOR. My father was...Oh never mind.
HEINO. It's nothing to be ashamed of. There's loads of people like you in here.
VIKTOR. I don't know what you mean.
HEINO. Jews who've converted.
VIKTOR. What makes you think I......
HEINO. *(Knowingly.)* Ah! *(Pause.)* They've go the worst of all possible worlds I reckon, they're damned if they're Jews and they're damned if they're Christians. Oh what difference. We're all damned in here.
VIKTOR. You don't believe in salvation then, redemption, in the world to come?
HEINO. That's the biggest cheat of all time, that is. - Put up with a bit of suffering now, don't make a fuss, 'cos if you're a good boy and keep

your head down, you'll get rewarded in the world to come! Very convenient that, for the blokes with the sticks if the masses just accept their lot as lousy donkeys. Well I ain't buying it. It's too damn convenient for the pricks on top.

VIKTOR. You have strong views.

HEINO. You gotta be strong in this place, or you'll get to donkey heaven before you can say carrots. In a manner of speaking that is, 'cos of course there ain't no heaven, for donkeys or pricks... Got any grub? My belly's so empty I could eat a camel, humps an' all.

VIKTOR. Well I've got a bit of bread, I was saving for breakfast, here...

HEINO. You donkey! Haven't understood a word I've been telling you, have you? You don't want to give me that! First lesson of survival in here, never, never, give any grub away. You need that bread, Vik, hang on to it. Now give it here, let's have a look at it, come on. *(Viktor, now confused, is reluctant, and half hands Heino a small crust. Heino grabs it.)* Right, just what I thought. Now here comes lesson number two, you got to mark off your bread ration. It's got to last three days, so mark off three divisions when you get it, make it last. Look at this, pathetic, how's this little lot going to last you till Thursday? *(He swallows it and speaks with his mouth full.)* And now you ain't even got that. Lesson number three, don't trust anyone, not even your mates. Best to learn the hard way Vik. No ill feelings, eh?....Vik?....Viktor?

There is no response as Viktor has withdrawn and turned over in his bunk.

Scene 3: The compère *Cabaret (1)*

Spotlight on the compère, in a battered top-hat, addressing the audience in one of the attics used for live peformances in Terezín.

COMPÈRE. Ladies and gentlemen, *dámy á pánové, mine damer og herre, dames en heren,* welcome to the unique, the bittersweet, the indefatigable Terezin cabaret! *(Addressing a late-comer at the back of the audience.)* Ah, another late arrival. One of our more recent guests, I suppose. Come in, come in sir, I'm sure you can manage to squeeze round that door - and if you can't tonight, you'll have no problems doing so in few weeks time, will he ladies and gentlemen! That's it. *Guten Abend, dobrý vecer, godaften, goedavond.* How was your train journey? -

Ah! don't ask! My goodness we're packed tonight, and so we should be, for tonight we have a fabulous new act from two lovely ladies from the cleaning corps, and lots of other goodies besides. Yes sir, you are in the right place, it's surprising what we get up to when the cat's busy licking its paws. Yes, feel free to look around you sir, a little different from what you're used to perhaps, not quite the *Kurfürstendamm*, but a pretty close second I think you'll soon agree. The fact is sir, the people are the same. You only have to look at the bill for tonight to see that. We are privileged to have some of the finest actors and singers brought to us here by special courtesy of our German friends, no expense spared! Even the audiences must surely look familiar to you, look around, don't you feel you've seen these faces before? It's just the surroundings that are different, a little, shall we say, avant-garde, a little...minimalist? I see I've brought a smile to your face sir, can I ask for more! Its' what we're here for. And now, without further ado, let's start the show with a little number containing some valuable advice for our new arrivals. And just in case our hosts should want to pay us a surprise visit, we have Norbert at the ready... *(Cups ear , the klaxon sounds.)* Thank you Norbert! We wouldn't want to offend after all, would we ladies and gentlemen! *(Lise emerges with her travelling rug and carrying a birdcage.)* And here comes Lise, fresh from the country. *(She is joined by Lotte.)* Lotte will soon tell her what's what, won't you Lotte! Ladies and gentlemen -. Lise and Lotte, a big hand!

LISE. *Sings:* As a new girl in this town,
I need help to get around.
No-one else here can advise me,
But I'm sure you'll help me wisely.

LOTTE. *Sings:* At your service, it's my pleasure,
As an old hand from Vienna,
To act like your friendly granny -
I know every nook and cranny!

BOTH. *Sing:* Theresienstadt, Theresienstadt,
Ist das modernste Ghetto, *dass die Welt heut hat,*
The most modern ghetto the world now has,
That's what we've got in Theresienstadt

LISE. *Sings:* Is the climate here OK,
Or do people fade away?

Do they serve you well at table?
Is ill health inevitable?

LOTTE. *Sings:* Food is scarce for biggish eaters,
Sick folk thrive and so do cheaters.
If you want a bit more dinner,
Join the sicklist - be a winner.

BOTH. *Sings:* Theresienstadt, Theresienstadt,
Ist das humanste Ghetto, *dass die Welt heut hat*,
The most humane ghetto the world now has,
That's what we've got in Theresienstadt

LISE. *Sings:* I don't want to dress in rags,
But the trouble is my bags
Have been emptied so I do lack
Basic things which I now need back.

LOTTE *Sings:* What's a bit of petty crime!
You don't want to waste your time!
Even if you found your luggage,
There's no room here for more baggage!

BOTH. *Sing:* Theresienstadt, Theresienstadt,
Ist das kulanteste Ghetto, *dass die Welt heut hat*,
The most obliging ghetto the world now has,
That's what we've got in Theresienstadt.

LISE. *Sings:* Who arranges where to stay?
I'm not fussy I must say,
One or two rooms with a study,
Somewhere clean but nothing fancy.

LOTTE. *Sings:* Dream of rooms from your top bunk,
Though you'll barely have a trunk!
All you need's imagination,
For such fine accommodation!

BOTH. *Sing:* Theresienstadt, Theresienstadt,
Ist das verträumteste Ghetto, *dass die Welt heut hat*,
The dreamiest ghetto the world now has,

That's what we've got in Theresienstadt

LISE. *Sing:* One last thing before I go,
For my friends back home to know,
Something no-one here's made quite clear,
How long are we going to be here?

LOTTE *Sings:* There are always different views,
Take the very latest news,
Which I just heard for example.....
(Music drowns her words.)

BOTH. *Sings:* Theresienstadt, Theresienstadt,
Ist das modernste Ghetto, *dass die Welt heut hat,*
The most modern ghetto the world now has,
That's what we've got in Theresienstadt.

Scene 4: The carrot

Viktor's barrack. On-stage the three-tiered bunk as in Scene 2 and a crude table with a wooden form alongside it. Viktor enters exhausted with a shovel over his shoulder. He sinks onto the bench, in a state of near physical collapse. After a few moments he gets up and goes over to his bunk. He is surprised to find a carrot lying on it. He is in the middle of contemplating it with some stupefaction when Heino appears, as if from nowhere. Heino is wearing a cap.

HEINO. That's gold-dust that is. Aren't you going to eat it. I went to a lot of trouble to get you that. *(Viktor hesitates, on the point of offering some to Heino who gives him a knowing look and a shake of the head at which Viktor tears into the carrot ravenously.)* I organised it for you mate. Felt a bit bad after scoffing your rations last night. (V*iktor stops eating and looks at Heino in astonishment.)* Don't look so surprised. Old Heino isn't all bad you know. Just a bit of a rough diamond. You need building up.Grave-digging takes it out of you. I know, I remember... I'm going to help you Nullmann. I've decided to take you under my wing.
VIKTOR. *(Moved.)* I've misjudged you. *(Grasps Heino's hand.)* You've given me hope - that there is humanity even in hell.
HEINO. (S*haking Viktor's hand.*) Now don't go all high faluting on me. It's a deal isn't it, all for one and one for all? I'll help you and then one day you'll help me right? Let's get down to practicalities. We'll start

with your work category. Fact one: you're a new boy and so your stuck with manual labour for the next few weeks; fact two: you're clearly not cut out for it ; fact three: a little bird tells me you're a famous composer.
VIKTOR. Well... not exactly famous.
HEINO. *(Aggressive.)* What do you mean 'not exactly'? How 'not exactly'?
VIKTOR. Let's say I've had my successes, I've shown promise.
HEINO. What is this a school report! You're famous or you're not famous!
VIKTOR. (*Gradually waxes more and more enthusiastic.)* Well, Herr Schoenberg thought enough of me to take me on as a pupil when I was twenty. Later I studied composition with Alois Haba - you know, the micro-tonalist - and I was assistant conductor to Zemlinsky at the Prague German Opera House for seven years. Alban Berg - we used to correspond - he was always very encouraging, especially when I won the Hertzka prize. - Krenek was one of the judges... (*He breaks off at Heino's stony blankness.)* My music has been played in Geneva, London and New York... (*He trails off* .) The truth is I haven't been able to write for some time. I get these blocks you see. I gave up altogether once. To work full-time for the Rudolf Steiner movement. I gave up my conducting too. I was actually doing rather well. Starting to make a name for myself. It was a regular salary too... It was all a bit of a mistake really.
HEINO. That just about sums you up doesn't it? 'A bit of a mistake'! We're going to have to do something about that. We've got to get you on the map in this place, so from now on, if I say you're a famous composer, you're a famous composer! That way we'll get you a job in the Leisure Department. Yeah! it's a joke innit! The Germans want us to make merry in here - cos' tomorrow... Anyway I've got you an interview with one of the top dogs in here. That's just for starters.
VIKTOR. What do you mean one of the top-dogs?
HEINO. The man at the top, chief top-dog, Jacob Edelstein, King of the Yids! - Till they take his throne away, which could happen any moment, if he doesn't play his cards right.
VIKTOR . The Head of the Jewish Council!
HEINO. For his sins!
VIKTOR. You know him!
HEINO. Yeah, yeah, he's expecting you at eight in his flat. *(Seeing Viktor's look of surprise.)* Yeah, the *crème de la crème* don't have to doss down with the dregs like we do, they get a couple of rooms to live in with their families, lucky bastards - it's not bad that just for handing over a list of names to our German friends from time to time!

VIKTOR. I don't know what to say.
HEINO. Say nothing. I'll do the talking. Just make sure you get there on time.
VIKTOR. Where does he live?
HEINO. Magdeburg Barracks.
VIKTOR. I'm not sure where that is.
HEINO. Well you'd better find out,'cos that's where all the big noises live. Anyone who tells you he lives there's going to be worth cultivating. Sink or swim mate, that's what it's all about in here.
VIKTOR. What if ... someone can't swim?
HEINO. Well you know what they say don't you, the best way to learn is to jump in at the deep end! Don't worry, I'll be there to coach you and we can start right now with lesson number one. Got any snout?
VIKTOR. I don't smoke.
HEINO. That's not the point. Snout's what we use for gelt in here. Today's rate of exchange: ten ciggies for half a loaf.
VIKTOR. But smoking's banned.
HEINO. Yes donkey, but everyone does it and even if they don't smoke, they use fags to get what they want. So, here's your first supply. (*He produces two cigarettes from under his clothes and gives them to Viktor.)* Stick these somewhere safe.
VIKTOR. I don't really want them.
HEINO. That's worth a slice of bread and marge that is.
VIKTOR. *(Hesitates, then*) All right. (*Viktor takes the cigarettes).*
HEINO. Only don't get caught because the punishment's not very pretty - they like to ram a red-hot poker against your lips or make you sit on your hands on a burning hot stove. And you never know when that *mamzer* the commandant's going to pop up, it's one of his hobbies, cruising round on his little bicycle catching people red-handed. *(A bicyle bell is be heard ringing. Urgent.)* Get rid of them.!

Viktor panics, then hides them in his bunk.

Scene 5: Two little scrubbers: *Cabaret (2)*

Lise and Lotte prance on with their hair in scarf-turbans, wearing overalls and twirling mops. They sing the following opening number:

LISE & LOTTE. We are the ladies that do for you.
This is our debut - we hope we'll do!
Folk think we're twins 'cos we're dressed alike
But Liesl's the Yid and I'm the Kike!

Oh we are the girls from the Cleaning Corps
If you like what we've got you can clap some more..
We're two little scrubbers
Complete with our rubbers
(They display their hands in rubber gloves)
We're the girlies from the Cleaning Corps

LISE. Good evening ladies and gentlemen. As you can see we belong to the oldest profession in the world. Even a charming little town like this needs girls like us.
LOTTE. Yes, wherever you go - Berlin, Vienna, Munich, Hamburg they all need us on their pavements.
LISE. On our knees...
LOTTE. Keeping them spotless
LISE. Even in Theresienstadt, they've got us at it...
LOTTE. Come, come Lise, don't exaggerate, not all the pavements in Theresienstadt require cleaning, only those along which certain gentlemen are expected to pass.
LISE. Certain gentlemen?
LOTTE. Yes, you know?
LISE. Do I?
LOTTE. You know the...(*She looks around nervously and takes on a conspiratorial air as she mimes Nazi officers.)*
LISE. Oh them - I thought you said 'gentlemen'...

They quickly break into the chorus of their song to cover up the dangerous nature of their lines.

LISE & LOTTE. Oh we are the girls from the Cleaning Corps.
If you like what we've got you can clap some more.
We're two little scrubbers
Complete with our rubbers -

(They display their hands in rubber gloves.)
We're the girlies from the Cleaning Corps.

LOTTE. Yes ladies and gentlemen, we 'do'.for you - we're the invisible army that transforms this place into the palace that it is, and tonight we'd like to come clean - after all dirt is our business - and tell you what goes on behind the scenes.
LISE. Yes, we char-ladies reach the parts that plebs like you cannot get anywhere near
LOTTE. You see we're allowed into the 'posh' part of Theresienstadt!
LISE. Magdeburg Mansions.
LOTTE. Where the uppercrust live.
LISE. The Elders, the Prominents, the skivers...
LOTTE. Now, now, there you go again. Take a swig of this. *(Hands a huge bottle marked 'anti-septic' to Lise who takes a quick swig, grimaces and then smiles sweetly as though cured.)* Who did we do for yesterday Lise?
LISE. *(Still smiling.)* Listz's granddaughter.
LOTTE. And the day before yesterday, it was Kafka's sister.
LISE. *(Sweetly.)* And don't forget Thomas Mann's sister-in-law.
LOTTE. And the Baroness Thingummy.
LISE. And Count Whatsit.
LOTTE. Oh yes nothing but the *crème de la crème* in here.
LISE. And what do you think ladies and gentlemen?
LOTTE. We made a remarkable discovery, didn't we... One that should keep our socialist friends in the audience happy at any rate.
LISE. Yes, guess what ?- They've all got the same number of bedbugs as you and I - we know, we counted them!
LOTTE. Talking of pets... What's the difference between a crab louse and an ordinary louse?
LISE. I don't know... What is the difference between a crab louse and a head louse?
LOTTE. One gives you an itch in the head, the other gives you an itch for bed. *(She scratches her crotch suggestively.)*
LISE. Oh yes, we all, we all itch in the same places in this little socialist paradise! (*She scratches her crotch. Lotte threatens her with the bottle of anti-septic, Lise waves it away as they break into their song.)*

LISE & LOTTE. Our jokes may be dirty but it's all just clean fun -
We may lack polish but then she ain't a Hun -
(They point to each other.)

All we can hope is that you take a shine
To our little ditties, hers and mine

Oh we are the girls from the Cleaning Corps -
If you like what we've got you can clap some more.
We're two little scrubbers
Complete with our rubbers -
(They display their hands in rubber gloves.)
We're the girlies from the Cleaning Corps.

On the last line they twirl their mops provocatively at the audience and run off stage.

Scene 6: The ghetto

Viktor and Heino are walking through the ghetto.

HEINO. So it went well.
VIKTOR. I'm still in shock from what they told me, and this Edelstein - what a cultivated man, and passionate about music! - Would you believe it he's had his own grand piano sent in from Prague! There are conductors here, choirmasters, singers. From all over Europe, big names from all the major orchestras and opera houses, and here they are all cooped up together in this flea-ridden hole. The Germans among them can't have been allowed to play in public for years, nine years at least. And in Prague it's been three years since we could play. Anyway they want me to organise the new music section - Krása is here and Haas. My God the talent here, it's unbelievable. And there are even some instruments. Somehow they've been smuggled in....
HEINO. They're cunning these Jews!
VIKTOR. You call it cunning, I call it a passion for the higher life, for music which -
HEINO. I call it smart! And it suits the Germans to have us fiddling away while Rome... For some *meshuggenah*, twisted, German, crazy reason they want the world to think they're being nice to their Jews in Terezín. Suits us too!
VIKTOR. Well I didn't think they were doing it out of the kindness of their hearts.
HEINO. Glad to hear you say that Vik. I like to hear some healthy

cynicism. Gives me hope for you.
VIKTOR. Cynicism? I call it realism. We all have our darker side.
HEINO. What, even you?
VIKTOR. Especially me.

Klara Klein, one of the women interviewed in Scene 1, comes up to Viktor.

KLARA. Please sir, a piece of bread sir for an old lady. I'm seventy-six years old, a widow.

Viktor looks at Heino who shakes his head.

HEINO. *(Without lowering his voice.)* Tell her she gets the same rations as everyone else. *(Viktor is embarrassed even though it is clear that Klara can neither see nor hear Heino.)* There's no reason why you should give up your ration because she's too greedy to hold on to her bread for more than half a day.
VIKTOR. My dear lady we are all in the same boat, we all have to survive on the same meagre rations. Is it fair to ask me -
KLARA. Forgive me sir, but you are young and strong...
VIKTOR. Hardly dear lady I'm forty-four years old and -
KLARA. We cannot live on what they allow us, sir. It's the young and healthy who get the most because they can work. We have no value here so we must starve and grow weaker.
VIKTOR. Nazi bastards! (*He fishes into his pockets for some bread, and finding none beckons urgently to Heino to give him some.*)
HEINO. Tell the old bag to clear off, she's filling my nostrils with her stink. *(Viktor winces.)*
KLARA. *(To Viktor)*. Oh no sir you don't understand, it's the Jewish Council that decides how to allocate the rations...
HEINO. *(Hisses.)* Your nice, cultivated Herr Edelstein!
KLARA. *(Shuffling off)*... and it makes sense of course, who can blame them. The young must survive. So sorry for the indignity sir, so sorry.

Klara shuffles off. Viktor looks after her, moved.

VIKTOR. I was so wrapped up in myself I didn't even notice them. Look they're everywhere Heino.
HEINO. You don't want to look. Just walk straight past them. Best thing. Think of your new job.

VIKTOR. *(Angry.)* How can I? Look at them, shuffling along, bent, emaciated, dribbling, wretched.
HEINO. There's just no pleasing some people is there. You should be cockahoop - and grateful.
VIKTOR . *(Ignoring him.)* They all look so hopeless.
HEINO. They're not going to make it, that's why. He'll be dead within a week, and she hasn't much time left either. Typhus, starvation, dysentery - it'll be one of them, or maybe the whole lot. Look at that!
VIKTOR. It's disgusting!
HEINO. But what a will to survive! Look - straight in her mouth!
VIKTOR. Straight from the rubbish tip! It's not even proper food. - It looks like potato peelings. And they've gone off. I can smell the stench from here.
HEINO. They can't get enough of it!
VIKTOR. I can't bear to watch them. The humiliation.
HEINO. No, it's to stay alive! They'll go to any lengths and they're right to. Two fingers to dignity and airs and graces. It's down to the bare essentials for us in here. Belly first. Then marbles *(He taps his head.)* Then *shmekel. (He taps his penis.)* In that order. You've had the first two attended to so far, so now you need... *(Viktor still watching the wretched elderly, suddenly can bear it no longer. He abruptly covers his face with his hands.)*You need a woman's soft arms around you. Ten ciggies and I can get you -
VIKTOR. I need to see Elly
HEINO. You need a pair of breasts pressed up against you. I know just the right -
VIKTOR. I need to see my wife! I'm late as it is. *(The music from the cafe is suddenly audible. Viktor is completely overwhelmed by the unexpected sound of music.)* Where's the music coming from? My God music, real music, can you hear it Heino, it's music! After three years of desert. My God!
HEINO. *(Very matter of fact.)* It's only the coffee-house. They have music every afternoon and evening. It's a real hole, that place. The old crocks pile in from the minute it's opened. They close their eyes - and they're in Berlin, on the Kurfürstendamm, or in Vienna in the Hotel Sacher, they're in elegant cafés in Prague and Budapest, they're anywhere but here. The saddest coffee house in the world, they call it. The *alte kackers* listen to the music and they weep.
VIKTOR. *(Urgent.)* Take me there.

The cafe comes into focus.

HEINO. There aren't any seats. It's always packed.
VIKTOR. They all look so sad.
HEINO. What did I tell you - they've all got their eyes shut.
VIKTOR. Transported.
HEINO. They will be, most of them.
VIKTOR. No, no, now - look the music is transporting them. I'm going in.
HEINO. Got your ticket have you?
VIKTOR. What ticket?
HEINO. Come on, or we'll get moved on in a minute. You can't get into the cafe without a ticket, and people sell the coats off their backs to get hold of one. A ticket lets you have two hours in the place. And it's two months before you can go again. It would be mobbed otherwise. Come on, don't let's hang around.
VIKTOR. This changes everything. Don't you see - music, art can break down the walls of this fortress! *(To Heino.)* I'm talking about transcendence Heino! Breaking through to the other side!
HEINO. And I'm telling you there's no getting to the other side without your little piece of green card. Let's go and find your little wifey. She must be missing you.
VIKTOR. Oh I know, I know, my darling is finding this separation so difficult. We've only been married two years and fate has wrenched us so cruelly apart.
HEINO. You talk like a novel sometimes you know, or a character straight out of a play.
VIKTOR. Oh that's what my second wife said, she's very down to earth, it got on her nerves in the end. And then I met Elly, who loved me for what I was. She's artistic herself, she understands. *(Pause.)* She needs me. *(He looks up at Dresden barracks, then at his watch.)* It's too early. We're not allowed in yet. It's another half an hour.
HEINO. Stuff that! A man's got to do what a man's got to do!
VIKTOR. It's not like that... Anyway we can't, it's too risky. If we're caught.
HEINO. Caught, schmaught, a man's entitled to a bit of female comfort even in this place - especially in this place, and these things can't just be done to schedule.
VIKTOR. Look you've got the wrong idea...

Elly appears, a striking, distraught-looking woman of great intensity. She falls on Viktor, hysterical.

ELLY. Viktor! Oh Viky, thank God it's you and not one of those Czech bitches.
HEINO. Don't worry about me. I'll just make myself invisible.
ELLY. *(Pours forth a stream of distress.)* There are nine of them and only two of us. They won't even give us the time of day. If I move my bed-roll one centimetre, they pounce on me. They argue over every centimetre of floor space, even amongst themselves - spiteful cats. Five centimetres apart, the Room Elder (she's a bitch too), has decided our bedrolls should be. They're so hostile to us, it's unbelievable. What do they think we are - Nazis? I've got to get my room changed Viktor, you've got to help me, I'll go mad in here, my nerves are in shreds, Viki, I can't take much more, and I finished my bread ration last night, I couldn't sleep for hunger. I'm so starving Viki and I'm so miserable. Oh Viki. *(She breaks down and sobs. Speaking through her tears.)* And the work. I can't bear it, digging up potatoes. My hands, look at my lovely hands, you loved my hands Viki. *(Viktor hold s up one of her hands tenderly and puts it to his lips. He strokes her hair gently, more like a father.)* I have to get out of here. You've got to come every evening, Viki, take me somewhere, anywhere. It's really getting to me in here. Promise you'll come straight here after your evening meal tomorrow. I'll be waiting for you. Come as soon as you can. I have to get in the queue now. Yesterday, the soup was cold by the time it was my turn. I keep thinking about food, Viki. I know I shouldn't but I can't bear it, I must go now. It's crazy to look forward to it. It's always the same, disgusting greasy swill with a lump of rotten horse meat. Not even that yesterday, just half a mouldy turnip. What kind of a world are we living in Viktor. Tell me it's a dream. Tell me we're going to wake up soon, under our nice soft featherbeds, ready to ring for hot chocolate and brioche... Oh it's too much for a soul to bear! *(Exits)*

Viktor hovers in the vicinity of the coffee-house, where a concert is in progress, before reluctantly going to join the outdoor soup queue in one of the courtyards.

Scene 7: Meeting

Viktor is queuing for his evening meal, bowl and spoon in hand. He does not notice the figure of a man, the Strange Passenger, watching him with curious intensity throughout this scene, his hat pulled down over his eyes, his bulk shrouded in a large overcoat. This half-seen presence in the shadows is reminiscent of Harry Lime in the film 'The Third Man '. The woman serving the soup addresses Viktor.

ANNY. *(Quietly.)* I've been waiting for you to show up.
VIKTOR. *(Makes an effort at recognition and then is visibly shocked.)* Anny ! I hardly recognise you. How are you? How's Max?
ANNY. He's all right.
VIKTOR. You're so thin now. *(She shrugs.)* And so pale. What happened to my rosy-cheeked Annitschke!
ANNY. *(Stiffens.)* Don't!
VIKTOR. Where can I find Max?
ANNY. He's in the children's home. They're wonderful to them in there.
VIKTOR. When can I see him.
ANNY. It'll only mess him up.
VIKTOR. Please Anny, just tell me when and where.
ANNY. He doesn't need you. He's managing to forget.
VIKTOR. Anny please, stop this now. *(Pause.)* Annitschke, remember it's me, not some devil! I've made mistakes, Anny, but I still love the boy.
ANNY. *(Softening.)* All right. But it can't be before tomorrow, tomorrow night. Come to Hamburg barracks, block three. I'll send him down to you at seven.
VIKTOR. Seven? Can't it be earlier?.... It's the only time I can see Elly, I can't let her down at such short notice. She's in a bad way.
ANNY. That's the only time he's allowed. But I shouldn't worry about it, Max will understand, I'm sure if you can't make it.
VIKTOR. Anny! What's happened to you!
ANNY. Let's say a few too many knocks.
VIKTOR. It's been hard for you... in here.
ANNY. You could say that.
VIKTOR. If you can't find the light, Annitschke, what hope is there for me, your man of shadows?
ANNY. Oh you'll be all right. You're selfish enough to manage in here. Other people may be taken in by your mournful looks, but I know you better. You're not quite the frail artist everyone takes you for.
VIKTOR. You sound so bitter. Have you no feelings left for me? *(Silence.)* I've thought of you often. Fondly. So fondly. *(Silence. Then quietly.)* I've missed you.

ANNY. What have you missed? My linzertorte? My potato dumplings? The way I polished your shoes for you and made sure you looked well turned out for your lady friends?
VIKTOR. Oh Anny, that's nonsense.
ANNY. Oh it's nonsense. You didn't like my linzertorte then?
VIKTOR. Of course I did but that's not..
ANNY. And it's nonsense that without me you'd have gone out of the house looking like a wreck?
VIKTOR. Yes, yes I know I...
ANNY. And that wouldn't have done you much good with your lady friends.
VIKTOR. I didn't have lady friends, you know that.
ANNY. And what was Elisabeth then, a whore?
VIKTOR. Anny, please! Elly was just a friend, a fellow artist.... a soul-mate. And when things with us didn't...
ANNY. Oh blame me. Blame me for your lust for Elisabeth!
VIKTOR. It wasn't like that! It happened... for all sorts of complex reasons.
ANNY. Is that what you told your first wife?
VIKTOR. Look at the way we were living, with your parents...
ANNY. Whose fault was that? Why couldn't you earn some money!
VIKTOR. No-one could earn a living. Even your father couldn't get patients any more.
ANNY. I'm talking about earlier. Giving it all up to go to Stuttgart!
VIKTOR. Anny we had these conversations! All right it didn't work out but working for the Rudolf Steiner movement, immersing myself in his teachings, it was more important even than my music then. Running their book shop seemed like such an opportunity for me then. I had to grasp it.
ANNY. Yes but you dropped something in the process Viktor. When you were reaching out for this 'jewel', you dropped us.
VIKTOR. You were my jewels too.
ANNY. Huh!
VIKTOR. Look it was complex, you know it was.
ANNY. You're the one that's complex.
VIKTOR. The whole situation was complex. Look at the strain we've all been under in the last few years, it would have tested the most harmonious of families. And then, sending away the two little ones, all on their own. That was terrible.
ANNY. But I thank God for that, I thank God every night. I thank God that we got them out at least, that they are both with English families.

(Pause.) I dreamt of them again last night. There's no news is there?
VIKTOR. No. And they're in the best place, I promise you, a long way from all this.
ANNY. I hope so. I hope they're going to be all right.*(Pause.)* I must go. I'll tell Max to expect you at seven.
VIKTOR But...
ANNY. *(She has turned way from him.)* Priorities, Viktor, remember?.

Scene 8: The saddest coffee-house in the world.

Viktor is drawn back to the coffee-house, even though he can't go in. He needs the solace of music. An old person approaches him and in a silent exchange offers Viktor a ticket in exchange for his soup. Viktor hesitates then accepts the deal. He enters the crowded cafe, where the piano concert is still in progress. He sits down and closes his eyes, immeasurably moved to be once more bathed in music, however incongruous the setting. The café is largely filled with old, very decrepit-looking men and women, some with heads bandaged, some with silent tears pouring down their faces. Heino materialises by his side.

HEINO. How did you worm your way in here you crafty bastard! What did you have to shell out then?
VIKTOR. Oh, just my soup.
HEINO. *Schmock.* What did I tell you, belly comes first. You've gotta keep your strength up. Still, folks have traded a lot more than a bit of soup to get what their heart desires. This is it, isn't it? This is where you're real heart is. It wouldn't be for me, I like a bit of flesh, the softer the better, but it takes all sorts. Artists like you go for the higher life as you put it. And whose to say you've got your priorities wrong. *(Peers closely at Viktor.)* You been crying? Music been getting to you eh? Dangerous business that. That's when the memories come back. Look at them all, sitting there *stumm*, staring into space, their eyes all wet.
VIKTOR. Shhh! *(Tries to listen to the music.)*
HEINO. I keep telling you it's the future that counts, not the past. Like that meeting I set up for you with Elder Eppstein. You have't forgotten!
VIKTOR. Not now Heino, please!
HEINO. Look mate, I arse-licked to set up this meeting for you. Running the New Music section's all very well, but Epstein draws up the

transport lists - I told you you've got to cultivate the right people in here.
VIKTOR. I've only got *(Consults his watch.)* another thirty seven minutes before my ticket runs out! Let me just listen, please!
HEINO. Lessons with his precious son start tomorrow night.
VIKTOR. *(Impatient.)* Fine.
HEINO. Half an hour a week to start off with.
VIKTOR. *(Impatient.)* Right.
HEINO. But he wants to meet you first.
VIKTOR. Please Heino! Can we talk about this later!
HEINO. *(Exiting.)* Priorities Viktor, priorities.

Viktor closes his eyes and enters a state of reverie. A scene from the past is evoked, triggered by his recent meeting with Anny.

Scene 9: Parting

It is 1939 and Viktor and Anny are standing on a Prague railway platform looking up at a train window at their two youngest children aged three and five. Anny is addressing a teenage girl who is accompanying them and speaking quickly and loudly over the sounds of the station and the crowds.

ANNY. We can't thank you enough, my husband and I, really, it's been such a worry, they're so little you see. See how lucky you are darlings, going on a big holiday...
VIKTOR. Anny!
ANNY .... with this nice young lady and on a lovely puffer train, just like I said. And soon... and soon we'll be able to come too. *(Her voice breaks and she turns to Viktor who doesn't react it. She stifles a sob.)* Oh!... Now you listen to Miss Helga. She's going to keep an eye on you. She's going all the way with you, and on the ship too, but she's a big girl so she can look after you. *(Still looking up at the train window.)* Wipe your noses both of you. Here. *(She hands up a hanky.)* Oh would you, thanks.They've both got summer colds I'm afraid. I hope they don't give them to you. *(The guard's whistle sounds.)* Viktor the suitcase! For God's sake! *(Viktor hastily hands one of two suitcases on board. Anny speaking increasingly fast.)* Mamma and Babba will see you soon... as soon as we possibly can, and Maxie and Opa and Oma... (T*he whistle sounds for the train to depart. Shouting above the sound of steam.)* The leberwurst

sandwiches are on the top ... Bye!
VIKTOR. *(Releasing a sudden anguished wail.)* Oh my darlings, my little sparrow and my little treasure. (*He covers his eyes with his hands.)*
ANNY. They're going Viktor! *(Shouts.)* It's all right, Babba's only got something in his eye. Bye bye! Big smiles now. *(To self.)* Oh my God, they're going. *(To children.)* Bye. Bye. Bye.
VIKTOR. Bye.

Anny and Viktor stare after the departing train. After it has disappeared they suddenly cling to each other.

ANNY. It's better for them isn't it Vik. It's for the best?
VIKTOR. Anny, Anny, of course it is.

They straighten up.

ANNY. They're so little. Did you see Licia's face? Her eyes!
VIKTOR. *(Sobs.)* Like a wounded deer.
ANNY. Don't! *(Silence.)* They've got each other. *(Viktor nods trying to compose himself.)* And that nice young girl - she seemed nice didn't she. She's only sixteen but she seemed sensible don't you think? And there are all the other children.
VIKTOR. Yes *(Silence.)* Do you want me to take you back to the flat first?
ANNY. You're not still going to see Herr Baum, are you?
VIKTOR. Listen it was you who said I should take him on. And you were right, we need every penny now. Your parents can't always...
ANNY. It's a bit late, isn't it, to worry about sponging on my parents! Couldn't you cancel? Just tonight? Please Viky. For Maxie's sake. For mine.
VIKTOR. *(Hesitates.)* I don't like to let Herr Baum down. I've hardly any pupils left.
ANNY. My God Viktor he'll understand! You've just said goodbye to your children! Put them on a train that's going to take them thousands of miles away! We don't even know when we're going to see them again! *(Pause.)* Or is it Frau Elisabeth you're thinking of seeing?
VIKTOR. Really Annie. Your insane jealousy. Elly and I are friends, that's all.
ANNY. She's after you Viktor. She's... *(Breaks down.)* How will they manage?
VIKTOR. (*Softens and embraces her.)* They'll be all right. Anny,

they're going to a safe place.
ANNY. That grey island!
VIKTOR. That grey island is a highly civilised country and it's offering them asylum, and maybe soon, who knows, us too.

SCENE 10: Inspiration

Viktor's quarters in the ghetto in the early hours of the morning. Viktor wakes up from another bad dream . His neighbour Heinrich looks down from the top bunk.

HEINRICH. There, there Herr Ullmann.
VIKTOR. Who's that?
HEINRICH. I'm in the bunk above you.
VIKTOR. Did I wake you? I'm sorry.
HEINRICH. Oh, it's I that am sorry - a fine man like you weeping into the night.
VIKTOR. You know my name.
HEINRICH. I've been following your fortunes for quite some time now.
VIKTOR. What here?
HEINRICH. Here and there.
VIKTOR. I don't understand.
HEINRICH. You're an artist Herr Ullmann
VIKTOR. I was.
HEINRICH. You cannot shake off your responsibility so lightly. *(Silence.)* I think you understand what I mean. *(Silence.)* If you cease to make art now that you're in here, well then, Victor, they've won.
HEINRICH. Exactly. It's a battle, a heroic battle against the forces of evil. But it's a battle that must be won, must, at all costs.
VIKTOR. Are you a poet?
HEINRICH. They have cast us into a dungeon, we are in chains, death hangs over us and so we look to you. Only art can break down the walls of this fortress.
VIKTOR. Why do you say that? Who are you?
HEINRICH. Don't shirk your duty.
VIKTOR. I have more than one.
HEIRICH. That's where you're wrong. You know yourself that there is a higher duty, which cuts across all other responsibilities, for it reaches far beyond the petty networks of one's immediate circle, and speaks to the

whole of humanity. Art is God's champion.
VIKTOR. Why are you telling me all this in the middle of the night?
HEINRICH. It is at night that we have our greatest struggles, when our unconscious wrestles with all the opposing forces within us. You are an artist, Herr Ullmann, and the struggle between art and life which besets every artist is one that now has to be definitively won. I think you understand what I am saying.
VIKTOR. Who are you? What is your name?
HEINRICH. Heinrich. At your service. *(He proffers his hand for Viktor to shake.)*
VIKTOR (*Shaking his hand.*) Viktor. Thank you.
HEINRICH. Very pleased to make your acquaintance at last. Goodnight.
VIKTOR. Goodnight.

Heinrich settles down to sleep. After a few moments, Viktor gets up and makes his way first to his belongings then to the table. Dawn is now breaking and he can just about see. He stares at a piece of paper he has just fetched and after some thought begins to write. Heinrich looks over the side of his bunk and smiles contentedly.

ACT TWO

Scene 1: 'Asrael'

Viktor is sitting at his table, composing, unaware that Heinrich is watching him. He writes some music, pauses, then reads it through. He goes through these stages repeatedly, each time altering the music slightly.

HEINRICH. *(Unctuous.)* Fascinating! To see the act of creation in progress! It's an honour Herr Ullmann. Oh! I'm so sorry. I seem to have brought the process to a halt.
VIKTOR. It's all right. It's just that I thought that I was quite alone.

Viktor writes some more music, then reads it through again and once more we hear the music being played.

HEINRICH. Ah! 'Diabolus in musica'! That interval is so enigmatic.

VIKTOR. That's right, you can't tell where it's going...
HEINRICH. As in life Herr Ullmann, we don't know how it's going to turn out or when it's going to be resolved.
VIKTOR. Exactly, exactly Heinrich, tension and resolution, tension and resolution, in music as in life, the eternal conflict. Look at this for example. *(He jots down some more music and shows it to Heinrich.)* You recognise it?

We hear the 'death' motif played.

HEINRICH. Of course, the death motif from Suk's 'Asrael'. - Everyone in here knows that - well the Czechs among us certainly do. What have you got in mind Herr Ullmann? I can tell you're excited about something. You seem quite different from the last time we spoke.
VIKTOR. I've had an idea! (*He starts to write again and we hear the music.Heinrich interrupts and the music stops.)*
HEINRICH. Not a requiem please Herr Ullmann, we need something uplifting!
VIKTOR. Something uplifting. Exactly - so, I've had an idea for an opera... about death. It's something you said the other day, about art being the only means to reality. I don't know, it set me spinning! *(We hear music as Viktor continues to writes music. He stops suddenly.)* I'm very grateful to you Heinrich.
HEINRICH. Please! It is I that feel privileged. *(Pause.)* Herr Ullmann? May I ask you something? You may call it foolish
VIKTOR. No, do.
HEINRICH. How exactly... does one compose?
VIKTOR. *(Laughs.)* Mahler was always being asked that. You know what he once answered?
HEINRICH. No.
VIKTOR. He said, 'Do you know how to make a trumpet? You take a hole and throw some brass round it!' He also said, and here I agree with him, one doesn't compose, one **is** composed, one fuses with the music. When he was composing the funeral march of the second symphony, he actually saw himself lying on a bier covered in wreaths of flowers. *(He shudders.)*.
HEINRICH. You feel very close to Mahler.
VIKTOR. Oh yes, of all the composers, he is the one! I know him you see, through his music. I know him. He didn't just hear his music, he saw it! He was a visionary.

HEINRICH. A man of vision Herr Ullmann, that's what I admire above all.

Scene 2: The potato peeling room

The potato peeling room.

ELLY. Is this the potato peeling room?
ANNY. What does it look like!
ELLY. Sorry. Yes of course.

Anny waves a knife at her and indicates a pile of potatoes.they peel potatoes in silence for a bit.

ANNY. You don't look as if you've ever peeled a potato in your life!
ELLY. Well, I...
ANNY. Don't worry, we're all learning to do things we never did before. Hold the knife like this..no like this and then... that's better. I was twenty-four before I peeled my first potato. We couldn't afford a maid, my husband and I. We lived abroad when we were first married, so it was all down to me. Later we lived with my parents, back in Prague, so of course we had a cook and a maid then. That seems like a different world now.
ELLY. I know. My first husband always use to joke to our guests that I had never been into our kitchen. He wasn't far wrong.
ANNY. *(Laughs.)*And look at us now! Look, you've got to be more careful - you're taking off half the potato. - Mind you, the old folk will appreciate that when they ferret around the trash pile, but we need as much as we can scrape off, for the soup. They're already hanging about like vultures out there, waiting for us to throw this lot out.
ELLY. My God! But half the stuff's rotten. Look at this one it's covered in mould. Ugh, it stinks. *(She's chucks it away.)*
ANNY. *(Snatches it from the rubbish pile and cuts into it.)* We can use some of it at least, look this is all the potatoes we've got for the day.

They continue to peel in silence for a bit.

ELLY. Oh well, I suppose this is an improvement. Peeling potatoes must be better than digging them up.

ANNY. At least you'll be in the warm now the weather's changed. It's no joke working outside in the winter.
ELLY. As long as I get the job. I'm only on trial still.
ANNY. I'll put in a good word for you.
ELLY. Oh would you? How kind. You're the first Czech who has spoken to me like a human being.
ANNY. Oh all that's a lot of ignorant nonsense. I won't have anything to do with those sort of attitudes. *(She watches Elly's clumsy attempts at peeling.)* You'll have to improve your technique, though. *(She fishes some of Elly's rejected peel from a bucket.)* There's a whole load of potato still left on that.
ELLY. Oh sorry. You're... you must think I'm pretty useless.
ANNY. Pretty, yes. And useless. *(Laughs.)* You'll have to get used to my sense of humour -it's blunt and it's dry, English style. I hope my kids don't have too tough a time with the dry English.
ELLY. They're in England?
ANNY. Fortunately. And unfortunately -it's terrible not knowing anything, having no contact. They were only three and five, when they left. That was three years ago. *(She wipes her eyes.).*
ELLY. At least you know they're safe.
ANNY. (Sniffs.) That's true. And my eldest is here with me. Not that I see much of him. He spends all his time with the other children.
ELLY. Nice for him.
ANNY. Not so nice. It's getting him into some bad habits. They're teaching him to become a thief. I caught him with three cigarettes in his pocket, and some margarine. And last night he brought me a piece like this of bread.
ELLY. Clever boy!
ANNY. I don't like it.
ELLY. But you ate the bread?

Anny nods her head.

ANNY. I told him it's got to stop.
ELLY. You see you're a good mother. You have principles.
ANNY. He won't listen to me though
ELLY. But at least you told him. I probably would have turned a blind eye.I would have taken the bread and asked no questions. I'm not good like you. (*She drops her head and starts to sob silently.)* I...I... don't know where mine are or what's happened to them. And the worst of it is, I sometimes even forget to think of them. I'm not a good mother you see,

I'm not like you. And now I've lost them. I don't know what's happened to them or anything....It's all my fault. I... *(She breaks into sobs again.)*

Anny comes over to her and puts her arms round her.

ANNY. There. *(She fishes in her pocket for a handkerchief and holds it out to Elly.)* Not freshly laundered I'm afraid, or smelling of lavender. *(Calls out.)* Otto, me and the new girl are taking our break.

She guides Elly outside into the courtyard, removes a half cigarette from a pocket lights it, puffs, the hands it to Elly. They continue to hand the cigarette back and forth between then as they speak.

ANNY. You can't help everything. We've all lived in hell these past few years, and nobody's perfect. I'm sure you're not a bad mother, you just blame yourself because you feel helpless.
ELLY. Oh, but you're wrong. I... I'm the worst mother in the world... I left them you see. I left my little girls. I left their father and he... *(Whispers)* He tried to kill himself. It was all so terrible. I had to leave you see. It was impossible. I was dying there, I was crushed. But I couldn't take them with me. Not then, and by the time I could, Hitler finished us off. And then those bitches in my room - that's why I asked to be moved - Those Czech bitches - sorry - they talk about 'my' Herr Hitler. - It's so insensitive. (*She breaks off to cry.)* And now I'm in here, in this terrible place, and I find it all so frightening, I'm just not very good at coping on my own you see, I'm pathetic like that. I'm not strong like you seem to be.
ANNY. Oh, I wasn't always like this. It's just that I had a weak husband so I had to learn early how to cope by myself.
ELLY. Mine at least is not that. He's strong but...
ANNY. You're lucky. There aren't many men like that around. You want to hang on to him. Don't lose him to some bitch like I did. Actually I'm glad I came in here without a husband. What's the point? You can't be with him anyway. You only spend half your time worrying how he is or...
ELLY. Or what he's up to. You're right.
ANNY. Men are basically selfish. I've always thought that and in here, I've become even more convinced. Women help each other. I mean I've never liked women but I see their strengths. Men on their own are pretty helpless. Look what they're like in here mostly. It's sad, really.
ELLY. They need us.

ANNY. Yes but we don't need them.
ELLY. Right.
ANNY. They're a pathetic lot. They want to do their own thing and when they can't manage, they come running.
ELLY. Pathetic. You can have this back now. Thanks. I feel better. *(Holds out the hanky.)*
OTTO. *(Calls from the kitchen)* Frau Ullmann.
ELLY. Yes.
ANNY. Yes.

They look at each other in disbelief, Elly inadvertently retaining the handkerchief.

OTTO. Inside now. And get rid of that cigarette!

Sound of bicycle bell. The two women move inside stung by the revelation of their mutual identity.

Scene 3: Hello! Hello!

Viktor is looking up at a window of Hamburg barracks, talking to his son Max, who is invisible to the audience. It's a cold November evening. The Strange Passenger is lurking in the shadows in this scene. At one point Viktor's gaze seems to rest on him and he raises his hat to Viktor.

VIKTOR. *(Sings.)* 'Hello! Hello!' That's how it starts Max, with a trumpet call and the character I told you about calling out 'Hello, hello' like that. This character's called the Loudspeaker, you know, like the one they have here in the ghetto. That was Peter's brilliant idea. The Loudspeaker. He's a bit like a compère - do you know what that is? Like a circus ringmaster. He says what's going to happen next. I think you're really going to like this opera Maxie, maybe even be proud of your Babba, when you see it. *The Emperor of Atlantis* by Viktor Ullmann. I told you about Atlantis didn't I, about the race of giants who got too big for their boots, so their whole civilisation had to be destroyed by water. Just think, a whole continent sinking beneath the ocean. They're choosing the best pieces for when the Red Cross Commission come for their inspection. That means we'll be in the gymnasium - they've got a stage in there. We'll have a full production, set, costumes everything, can you imagine! We've got the orchestra all lined up. The gym seats a hundred and fifty, and you'll be in the front row. And when they see it, they'll know, they'll know what the real struggle is, between the forces of light and the forces of darkness. They'll see it all, our Swiss friends, they'll see why the Emperor has to die! *(Pause.)* You still don't want to come down do you? Maxie, don't look so sad, you'll break my heart. Look, this is a song I wrote specially for you. *(He holds up a piece of paper.)* Come down and I'll show you. *(He reads from the paper.)* It says 'To My Son Max' and it's called *(He chokes)* 'First Meeting'. I can sing it to you. *(Pause.)* It's getting cold here Max, *(Coughs.)* Hurry up and come down. *(Pause. Starts to sing.)* 'I have seen you long ago, seen you smiling even so, with your enigmatic -' *(Enter Anny, making for the door of her barracks. She listens and observes unnoticed by Viktor.)* '... smile.' *(Pause.)* You used to smile at me like that. Isn't it nice to see your Babba again? *(Coughs.)* Maxie, now really, now this is going too far. I want you to come down this minute, it's very cold out here and Babba's got a bad cough. *(Pause. Viktor coughs vigorously.*) Oh all right, if you don't love your Babba, he'll just have to go. *(He turns way from the window ready to leave and starts as he sees Anny. To Anny.)* What have you been saying to him? He won't come down. Is this your doing, some sort of revenge. *(He bends over, coughing furiously.)*

ANNY. Why are you so surprised? The boy's been hurt by you. I can count on my hand the number of times he saw you before we came in here.

VIKTOR. *(Coughs again.)* Look can we go inside for a minute we can't talk like this.

ANNY. *(Barring the entrance to the barracks)* Husbands only!

VIKTOR. Well it was just that... Anny, I've started composing again. The first time for - I suddenly became inspired again, Anny can you believe it, in that drab, depressing, freezing room, stinking of sweat. Right in the middle of all that, something happened. The music suddenly came back to me. You understand Anny. You used to. Nothing else mattered. I wasn't cold, I wasn't hungry, I wasn't frightened, I swear I didn't even cough, or if I did, I didn't notice. I was somewhere else.

ANNY. You always were, Viktor. (*She turns to enter the barracks.*) By the way, next time you find time to visit your son, and you want to bring him something, make it something he can eat.

Viktor looks at the piece of music which has become crumpled in his hands, then looks up, his attention suddenly arrested by something.

VIKTOR. My God that's - *(Shouts.)* Martha! Martha... Oh! *(His voice fades as he realises he's mistaken. To Anny.)* I was sure it was her. I recognised her coat. Martha in here!.

ANNY. You'd like to have all three of us in here wouldn't you, then you could agonise between us, telling us all that you really still love us.

VIKTOR. But I do... I don't understand it. I know it was her coat.

ANNY. You're sure.

VIKTOR. Absolutely.

ANNY. Ah!

VIKTOR. What? Tell me!

ANNY. Martha **was** here, Viky, and is no longer. There was a transport last week, remember.

VIKTOR. Yes.

ANNY. That's how her clothes must have ended up in the store - and on to that lady's back. It happens all the time.

VIKTOR. So she's dead.

ANNY. *(Moves to console him.)* Not necessarily. She's gone east.

VIKTOR. *(Outburst.)* She's dead. That dear sweet girl is dead. *(Anny allows him to weep silently on her bosom.)* You must stay alive Anny, you and Max.

Anny strokes his head. His piece of music is completely crumpled up in his hands.

ANNY. We'll do our best.

Scene 4: Beautification. *Cabaret* (3)

Lotte, wearing a scarf-turban and overalls, is up a ladder attempting to hang some lace curtains. She is humming. Enter Lise similarly clad. They speak with the exaggerated diction of a stage double-act.

LOTTE. Don't just stand there, give me a hand Lise.

LISE. What are you doing Lotte?

LOTTE. I'm putting up lace curtains Lise.

LISE. I can see that. Why are you putting up lace curtains, Lotte?

LOTTE. Because Uncle said so Lise. Uncle said the Elders have to have curtains from now on, and the Danes of course. I mean, what will people

think if they come here and there aren't even curtains up? We can't have the place looking like a slum, can we Lise? That's what Uncle said, Lise.
LISE. Which uncle would that be Lotte?
LOTTE. Oh Uncle Rahm of course. All young people will have to call the new commandant, whoops, the new principal 'Uncle' on the big day. Didn't you know that Lise? I thought I'd get in some practice so that I don't pass out when I hear it.
LISE. That wouldn't do Lotte.
LOTTE. No it wouldn't do at all Lise.We have to get it right for when our visitors come .
LISE. Oh most definitely.
LOTTE. And we mustn't use the 'G' word when they come either Lise.
LISE. The 'G' word Lotte?
LOTTE. Yes, Lise. *(Pauses and looks around nervously.)* When the Red Cross team are around we must never use the word *(Whispers)* 'ghetto'.
LISE. Ghetto, Lotte?
LOTTE. Shhhh! No, Lise, it's not a - *(Whispers)* 'ghetto' any more. It's a 'Jewish Settlement.'
LISE. A Jewish Settlement. Oh that sounds much nicer Lotte.
LOTTE. Yes, that's what I thought Lise.
LISE. A place where Jews have settled .
LOTTE. Exactly
LISE. A sort of - Zion.
LOTTE. Yes.
LISE. Where everything's Jewish.
LOTTE. Right.
LISE. Jewish cockroaches, Jewish fleas..
LOTTE. Oh very Jewish - full of Jewish gestures.
LISE. Jewish style furniture - 40s style - Jewish Bauhaus, no frills, just simple, elegant...
LOTTE. Nothing vulgar.
LISE. Jewish cuisine.
LOTTE. A slimming version.
LISE. I begin to see what you mean. It is very Jewish in here. I mean even the inmates...
LOTTE. Shh. 'Settlers'.
LISE. They're all a bit 'Jewish', aren't they. Of course some are more Jewish than others.
LOTTE. Naturally.
LISE. I've only got a Jewish grandfather myself.
LOTTE. Ah, never mind, I won't crow just because I've got two Jewish

grandparents. On my mother's side.
LISE. Lucky! Is that why you've got half a star and I've only got a quarter?
LOTTE. Yes love, sorry. It doesn't seem fair does it, that some people are handed out gold stars just like that, where others have to struggle for them. *(Lise's attention has been drawn to a list on the wall.)* So what have they got on today? They're a very highbrow lot in here. It's all Molière or Gogol.
LISE. Or Shakespeare of Hoffmansthal. *(She starts to snigger at the list in front of her.)*
LOTTE. What are you laughing at Lise?
LISE. How do you fancy a lecture on 'The World of Papyrus' or 'A Hundred Everyday Technical Problems'?
LOTTE. *(Joins her and reads the list over her shoulder.)* Or 'Undiscovered Holland' or 'Ethical living in Terezín.'
LISE. What about: 'Prague in the 19th century'...
LOTTE. Useful!
LISE. Or 'Basic Physics' or 'The Value and Meaning of Money' or -
LOTTE. This one: 'Nietsche's Zarathustra'.
LISE. Or 'Genetic Diseases'.
LOTTE. 'The Berlin Aquarium'
LISE. 'Optimism in Judaism'.

As they go through the list of lecture titles their mirth increases so that by the time they reach the end they are doubled up with manic laughter.

LOTTE. Whoever heard of a cabaret in a potato peeling room!
LISE. Oh well, what's in a name. Ugh. *(She holds up a bit of rotting peel she has just found on the floor)*
LOTTE. I think name's are very important nowadays actually. I mean when they do their shows in here, they can't exactly say, 'Ladies and Gentlemen, welcome to the potato peeling room', now can they?
LISE. I'm not with you.
LOTTE. Well part of the programme is giving everything fresh names, more beautiful names, like they're doing with the street names. You must have noticed.
LISE. I couldn't exactly miss it, could I, with all those new street signs popping up: Seestrasse, Badstrasse, Bergstrasse...
LOTTE. They give a nice impression, don't they. I mean it would be nice to have a lake, or a spa, or some mountains.

LISE. Still they're pretty names.
LOTTE. Exactly. So we can't welcome our audience to the potato peeling room. It's not impressive enough.
LISE. How about....the Vegetable Depilation centre.
LOTTE. Perfect!
LISE. Ladies and Gentlemen, welcome to the Terezín VD Centre!

(They break into their song.)
We are the ladies that do for you -
Don't think we're char ladies, 'cos that won't do!
We're 'Hygiene Officials' what scour this place,
Since beauty's the in-word and dirt's a disgrace.
CHORUS:
Oh we are the girls from the Cleaning Corps -
If you like what we've got you can clap some more.
We're two little scrubbers
Complete with our rubbers -
(They display their hands in rubber gloves.)
We're the girlies from the Cleaning Corps.
(They run off with their mops and buckets.)

COMPÈRE A big hand ladies and gentlemen for those indefatigable ladies from the.... so sorry, for those officers of the Hygiene Corps.

Scene 5: Flight.

Viktor is at his table in his room. He's sitting with his head in his hands. His music spread out in front of him. Heino is pacing about.

HEINO. I'm telling you, you don't owe Anny anything. And Max is fine with all those other kids.
VIKTOR. He won't talk to me. And Elly needs me.
HEINO. Elly's an adult. She's got to learn to fend for herself. I don't buy all that hysteria anyway. She's tough enough under all that. And it's no use letting Anny play on your guilt strings. Marriages take two - to prosper and to fail.
VIKTOR. But I fell in love with Elisabeth. She was so exciting. So..
HEINO. She was a sexy piece, Vik and you'd just turned forty. Dangerous age for a man. Some say men get wiser as they get older. You can't get to study the kabbalah unless you're forty and married, did you know

that? They say you have to be stable before you can to enter the unknown. But I reckon that's not the real reason. They knew a thing or two those old rabbis.- They knew blokes are ripe for new experiences at that age, hungry for them. And studying the kabbalah doesn't break up the happy home.

Viktor starts assembling his papers.

What's that you're working on? Not that opera thing. I'm warning you, no good will come of it. You'd do much better to involve yourself more with the Ghetto Council. Go to some meetings. Put yourself about a bit. This isn't going to do you any good, it's too dark. People want something to cheer them up a bit, they don't want to see an opera about a character called Death And it'll never get past the censor with all that stuff about the Emperor. They'll see through that all right.It'll end in tears, you mark my words.
VIKTOR. Listen Heino, I've been hesitant all my life, leaping forward and then pulling back. Now is the moment. What have I got to lose.
HEINO. Only your life.
VIKTOR. Exactly
HEINO. And what have you got to gain?
VIKTOR. Victory - over them. It's a message to everybody in here - good will triumph in the end. Even Hitlers have to surrender to death one day. Everyone does. It's not just a political message, it's a philosophical one. It's about mortality. Death, when it comes, is not to be feared.
HEINO. It's not to be welcomed with open arms though is it. Keep it at bay I say, for as long as possible. Isn't that the whole point of living? Survival, living, that's the thing. I can't believe you Vik, I dedicate the last year to teaching you all the tricks of survival, and you're prepared to throw the whole lot away for a piece of make-believe. That's gratitude!
VIKTOR. Heino, don't think I'm ungrateful. I know I couldn't have come this far without you, your maxim, 'belly first, then marbles' has been spot on. But you left something out.
HEINO. *Schmokol* I told you, it ranks third, but it's there.
VIKTOR. For you maybe but for me - it's the spiritual dimension, its' where my music comes from, it's hard to describe, it's up there somewhere .
HEINO. It's from up there, isn't it ? (*He indicates the top bunk.*) Ever since you met that Heinrich, you've been living in cloud-cuckoo land
VIKTOR. He makes me feel good about myself.

HEINO. He's given you an inflated view of your abilities.
VIKTOR. He respects my work, he thinks I'm good. He... he helps me to fly.
HEIN0. Oh yes, flight's his game all right. Flight from any responsibility. For once I find myself agreeing with Anny. She thinks you're risking Max's life with this. He's officially protected here as your child and with your special status working for the Ghetto Administration. If you go, he's on his own. She's got no clout without you.
VIKTOR. That's a ridiculous argument. It's preposterous to try and gag me like this. I have a -
HEINO. Mission. Yeah, yeah, that's what Heinrich says isn't it. Well what about me then. Remember our agreement? You owe me you know. What happens to me if you get carted off? You're my only hope, don't you realise that. Everybody has someone to protect them in this hell-hole, and I've got you.
VIKTOR. Well of course I'll always try to put in a good word for you Heino...
HEINO. You patronising snake!
VIKTOR. I mean it. We're friends.
HEINO. You're not my friend! We can't stand each other. I can't stand you. Never could. You're a namby pamby little mother's boy, running off to his wives every five minutes.
VIKTOR. I haven't seen Anny for weeks now. And Martha's...
HEINO. Oh yes, you weren't much good for your first wife were you - she got shipped east within months. So maybe I've made a big mistaking cultivating you like this, setting you up in the establishment, getting you immunity in the hope that some of it will rub off on me.
VIKTOR. I see.
HEINO. Don't act hurt. I'm not a member of your family you know, it won't wash with me.
VIKTOR. I am hurt, to think you were only using me.
HEINO. Haven't I managed to teach you anything? We all use each other. That's how we survive, in here, out there, everywhere. You can't afford to be sentimental. You've got to look after number one. Other people - they're just props.
VIKTOR. Even your own family, even your children?
HEINO. Especially them. - They suck you dry given half a chance.
VIKTOR. You've shown your true colours now.
HEINO. I never hid them from you. - Only you didn't want to see them.
VIKTOR. Heinrich was right.
HEINO. Been bitching behind my back has he.

VIKTOR. He said you were the Anti-Christ
HEINO. Come off it, I'm a Yid, me.
VIKTOR. You represent everything I despise.
HEINO. I represent survival.
VIKTOR. At what cost.
HEINO. Any cost.
VIKTOR. *(Shouts.)* No! Get away from me!

Heino looks at him then gives an exaggerated shrug and exits. Within seconds Heinrich appears with mysterious haste. He is triumphant.

HEINRICH. Congratulations Viktor, you finally saw through him. I've been waiting for this moment. He was after your soul, a lover of ease, mean-spirited, a materialist, trying to clip your wings when you were born to fly. You've cleared the decks now, all obstacles have been removed one by one and now you are ready to soar! The artist must soar, nothing, no-one can be allowed to drag on his wings. It is the fate of the little man to be so bound up with his own small life that he fails to see the bigger picture. But it falls to the artist to roam about in the night, far from the comfort of a hearth, it's his task to shine a torch, to light up the sky, to find a path, to lead the way. So now is the time - to spread your wings. It's time to make for the light and soar!

Scene 6: The Visit

Anny appears from the shadows of Elly's room where she has been waiting for her. Elly is changing, she is removing her dress over her head when Anny speaks.

ANNY. Frau Ullmann.
ELLY. *(Muffled.)* Yes. *(She removes the dress to reveal an elegant slip beneath, in sharp contrast to Anny's appearance. Cold.)* Oh, it's you.
ANNY. You took some finding. You seemed to have changed rooms quite a bit. *(Silence. Then slowly.)* I've come to ask you a favour.
ELLY. Me?
ANNY. I want you to do something for me.
ELLY. Why should I?
ANNY. It's in your interest too. *(Silence.)* It's about Viktor.
ELLY. You surprise me!

ANNY. I want you to stop him going ahead with this opera. You know the SS are coming to the Dress Rehearsal to vet it. Only you can persuade him there's still time to pull out.
ELLY. Viki told me about you, how you always tried to put the reins on, whenever he had anything good going, anything that was a bit different. And now's his big chance to make a name for himself and you want to interfere!
ANNY. This is unbelievable! I would have thought you of all people would see sense. There are implications for you too, you know.
ELLY. Oh yes I can see them now - I try and persuade Viki to finish with his opera and he finishes with me.
ANNY. You stupid woman! Don't you see what he's risking by putting himself in the limelight like this?
ELLY. Sour grapes, that's what it is. He wasn't making it when he was married to you, and he is making it now he's married to me . It's his big chance, don't you see that, his musical breakthrough, a chance for his reputation to spread. He's going to be famous after all, and you can't take it! He is going to be famous.
ANNY. Not before his death, and yours and Maxie's. *(She starts to cry.)* He's only ten. I beg you for Maxie's sake, don't let him go ahead with it. It's too dangerous.
ELLY. It's only an opera for God's sake. The SS aren't going to bother with opera. What do they know!
ANNY. The SS aren't fools. They'll see that it's a satire on Hitler and that will be the end of your Viki, and without him there's no protection for any of us. For God's sake woman, you're only protected from the transports because he's a member of the Leisure Department. And so is Maxie. He's worth more alive than dead, you of all people should see that. His special status dies with him. That's what you've got to tell him. *(Cries again.)* For Maxie's sake I beg you.

Scene 7. The Emperor's aria

Viktor is pacing up and down in a rage.

VIKTOR. How can he do this to me!
HEINRICH. He's young. He's arrogant.
VIKTOR. But to walk out! When we're near the end! When so much work has gone into it. And when he knows how much this piece means

to me. You know he's threatened to take his name off it.
HEINRICH. So?
VIKTOR. Well it's so...foolish.
HEINRICH. Then call him back.
VIKTOR. And then what? That final aria is the key to the whole piece...It's supposed to be sublime this aria, a moment of ennoblement. *(He indicates a page of the libretto)* these are the lines of a cynic! It's bleak, bleak.
HEINRICH. I told you that you had talent enough to write the words yourself and then none of this would have ever happened.
VIKTOR. You're right, you're right, I've been too... God, it's insufferable! The dress rehearsal's coming up and now we have no 'Farewell Aria'.
HEINRICH. You write poetry, you could do it. This piece speaks of you Viktor anyway, it's not a young man's piece, it's visionary.
VIKTOR. The Emperor **must** transform utterly! I see him stepping forward at the end, ready to take the hand of Death, ready to face his own mortality: 'As I reach the edge of time, of time eternal...'
HEINRICH. *(Proffering his hand to Viktor who takes it.)* '... as your hand still rests in mine, so my warm life can feel the warmth of yours. This **is** the moment, this is the final moment, for now I go in peace - I leave this world behind and I yearn for the grave's repose.' And then the vision of the world to come. *(He starts to type as Viktor continues to speak.)*
VIKTOR. 'There will be rivers flowing and mountains all around, and flowers in full bloom exposed to sun and wind in high pastures. I long to see this land of summer's rain, of softly falling summer rain. This is the place for me, this is the place for me. Imagine a child, playing by a fountain, while a horse stands waiting for the village blacksmith, then imagine me released from sorrow. For it's not the other side that we need fear, but rather this world that is veiled in darkest shade, in darkest sorrow.'
HEINRICH. *(Typing.)* Yes, yes!
VIKTOR. Death then takes the Emperor gently by the hand and leads him off through the mirror.
HEINRICH. *(Claps.)* Bravo! Bravo Maestro!
VIKTOR. *(Taking a mock bow, then clapping for Heinrich.)* Maestro! *(Heinrich now takes a mock bow.)*
ELLY. *(Bursts in.)* Vikichen! What are you doing talking to yourself like that.
VIKTOR. Elly! Are you crazy coming in here.

ELLY. I had to come and see you. I was just hoping no-one would see me coming in.
VIKTOR. It's so dangerous! Why aren't you at work?
ELLY. I've been changing rooms Viki, remember you promised to help me. I've had to move everything myself, the Room Elder wouldn't let me wait any longer for you. Viktorchen! Why are you neglecting me? You never have any time for me. Don't you love me any more? You don't look well. Something's wrong isn't it? What is it? Your eyes are so shiny, do you have a temperature, here let me... *(She goes to feel his forehead.)*
HEINRICH. Kindly escort the fine lady out of here Viktor we have work to do and we can't waste our valuable time on this feminine nonsense.

Viktor stiffens away from Elly's attempt at feeling his brow.

ELLY. There is something wrong. You're hiding something from me. I can always tell. What's that, a letter? That's not music is it, music I can accept as my rival, I believe in you Viktor as a composer, you know that, I encourage you, you used to even say I was your muse - but another woman...
HEINRICH. What would you want with another woman?
VIKTOR. What would I want with another woman?
ELLY. Well perhaps not another woman - **the** other woman, there is only one now that your first wife has been transported!
HEINRICH. She's being hysterical
VIKTOR. You're being hysterical
ELLY. Don't tell me it's your composing that takes up all your spare time. - You're visiting that precious second wife of yours instead aren't you, holding hands and playing happy families!
HEINRICH. She's got to go, she's affecting your equilibrium. This is not good for you Viktor, you're an artist.
VIKTOR. You've got to go, you're affecting my equilibrium, it's not good for me, I'm... (*He looks at Heinrich who nods.)*... an artist.
ELLY. We know you're an artist! But what about my equilibrium!. I'm dying in here, can't you see, dying. It's too ugly for me all this. I need to share another world - with you. I can't play happy families with anyone. You're the only family I've got now, you know that. I gave up my family for you, for God's sake. You owe me Viki, you must see that. Make your music, yes, but make it for me, like you used to. Come and tell **me** about it - play it out on my thighs, Viktorle, remember?

HEINRICH. I'm very sorry but you have to attend to your work. You must finish it. You'll see her out before she gets caught in here.
VIKTOR. I'm very sorry, but I have to attend to my work. I'll see you out before you get caught in here.
ELLY. *(Snatches the paper from Viktor's table.)* Let me see.
VIKTOR. *(Makes a grab for it.)* Give it back! *(It tears.)* Now look what you've done you damn woman! *(Heinrich smiles. Elly, horrified, rushes to the door.)*
ELLY. I don't know you any more Viktor. *(Exits.)*

Viktor stares after her, then takes up his seat. Heinrich stands over him as he continues to write. Viktor suddenly breaks off his writing and rushes outside.

Scene 8: The Strange Passenger

Outside in one of the courtyards. Viktor is pacing about in a highly disturbed state. It is evening. The Strange Passenger is once more observing him from the shadows, his hat pulled well down over his face. Suddenly for the first time, Viktor notices him. The Strange Passenger raises his hat in Viktor's direction in acknowledgement of this.

S.P. Good evening.
VIKTOR. Who exactly are you?
S.P. With respect - your fellow passenger.
VIKTOR. I thought I was quite alone.
S.P. A tiny error - now undone.
VIKTOR. Have you been here all the time? I didn't notice.
S.P. I'm always around, but not everybody wants to know me. You've looked right through me on a number of occasions.
VIKTOR. Have I? I'm sorry.
S.P. Can I help? You seem upset.
VIKTOR. That's very kind, but it's not something I could expect a stranger to help me with.
S.P. Who better?
VIKTOR. I have to decide something that's all. And time is running out.
S.P. *(Softly agreeing.)* Yes.

VIKTOR. Don't I know you? There's something about your voice. It seems so familiar. Why did you say you were my fellow passenger, we're not on a journey.
S.P. You know what they say Herr Ullmann. Life is a journey and to travel hopelessly...
VITKOR. Hopefully, to travel hopefully you mean.
S.P. The secret, Herr Ullmann, is to travel without hope.
VIKTOR. That's terrible! Who can do that?
S.P. Most of us travel through life seeing only what we want to see. How else could we cope? But we miss out on the truth.
VIKTOR. That it's all hopeless?
S.P. That's not what I said.
VIKTOR. I don't understand why you seem so familiar to me.
S.P. I told you, I've been around. It's just that you've always been too preoccupied to notice me, and now....
VIKTOR. Yes?
S.P. *(Pause.)* I think you understand. As you say, time is running out.*(He glances at his watch.)* I must be off. Goodnight Herr Ullmann.
VIKTOR. Goodnight. Perhaps we'll meet again.
S.P. I'm sure we will.

Scene 9: The dress rehearsal

The dress rehearsal of Viktor's opera. Viktor is putting the Drummer through her paces.
DRUMMER. *(Sings to the tune of 'Deutschland über Alles'.)* 'By the grace of God, we Überall...'
VIKTOR. No, no start again. Remember: breathe, and tempo.
DRUMMER. *(Sings.)* 'By the grace of God we Überall, the glorious pride of the fatherland, blessing to mankind, ruler of both Indies, Emperor of Atlantis...' *(Enter woman Ghetto Official.)*
VIKTOR. Much better!
WOMAN. You'll have us all in trouble Herr Ullmann! They're not stupid the SS. They can spot *Deutschland Über Alles* whatever you do to the words!
VIKTOR. They're stupid enough to have typed the whole libretto out for me last week.That little one, Schmidt, didn't bat an eyelid! This is his typing - look. *(He hands her the typed libretto.)* Not even spelling mistakes.

WOMAN. (*Looks at the typescript and on handing it back turns it over.)* They don't like to waste paper, do they, the Germans. Look what he's typed it on - *(Viktor looks but doesn't really register.)* The back of death forms!

DRUMMER. *(Sings.)* '... in our flawless, truly perfect, all-penetrating wisdom, decided to declare throughout all our lands, total, all-out, holy war! Each against the other! No survivors!'

VIKTOR. Better, Hilde, better!

WOMAN. I'm looking for Herr Schulz. Ah, there you are. *(Speaks out to the auditorium)* Right now Herr Schulz, you shouldn't still be here...

VIKTOR. He's our stage manager!

WOMAN. I know but he's needed in the Recreation Hall. He's got to look as though he's having a lovely time playing chess. *(Out to the audience.)* Yes, I know you can't play, Herr Schulz, but I've told you, all you have to do is sit there and look like a *maven.* Just move the pieces around a bit. Sorry Herr Ullmann, everybody has to be in their places for the final rehearsal of this charade. They don't just want to see the performances they want the whole Red Cross visit rehearsed today. And the timing has go to be a hundred percent, you know what they're like. *(The Drummer has been doing a series of elaborate bows and muttering to herself.)* What are you doing?

DRUMMER *(Bowing with an elaborate flourish.*) This way your excellencies... Practising. *(Bows again.)* This way your reverences. *(Bows again.)* This way gentlemen. No, no sir, that's strictly off- limits, this is the way, just follow the smell of fresh paint!

WOMAN. You're not going to say that!

DRUMMER. Why not?

WOMAN. You're crazy! You know what they'd do to you!

DRUMMER. *(Increasingly hysterical.)* **I'm** crazy? **I'm** crazy You're telling me **I'm** crazy - when you're running round trying to keep this place as neat as a pin so that the Germans can convince our Swiss friends that we're in some kind of a holiday camp! Tell me Herr Ullmann - who's the crazy one here?

VIKTOR. Calm down Hilde, calm down. In an insane world it's the sane who appear mad, remember!

WOMAN. That's too deep for me, Herr Ullmann, I've no time for philosophising now. Just promise me Fräulein, that you won't say anything like that again. After all I expect you have a mother here.

DRUMMER. *(Cowed.)* Yes.

WOMAN. Exactly, so have I, so give a thought to her. *(Softening.)* And besides, who knows, the Red Cross Commission might...

DRUMMER. Might what? They're not going to **see** anything, are they? It's all been 'beautified'!

VIKTOR. They may **hear** something though. And anyway, the Swiss are a sophisticated race. They're not fools. *(Looks at his watch.)* Where's the Loudspeaker? For God's sake! And the Emperor! The Emperor's not here yet!

DRUMMER. Still scrubbing down the crematorium, I imagine.

WOMAN. *(To Drummer.)* Which bit of the afternoon shift are you doing?

DRUMMER. I'm on at the bandstand.

WOMAN. Right,well it's a good job I found you, then. Trudi Feingold was supposed to be doing it with you, but - *(Drops her voice.)* She's been sent on a long journey. She didn't have to go, but she chose to go with her elderly parents. *(Sighs.)* Now do you know what to do?

DRUMMER. *(Doing a bob curtsey.)* This way your excellencies...

WOMAN. No, no after that. Look I'll be the SS and Herr Ullmann will be one of the Red Cross Officials..

VIKTOR. Please! Don't involve **me** in your nonsense. Really we have no time for this.

WOMAN. *(Angry.)* This is not 'my nonsense'. I didn't choose to be part of their games any more than you did Herr Ullmann, but now that we're in them, it's in our interest to play by their rules!

VIKTOR. But there's no time! They're coming here this morning and we're still not ready!

WOMAN. *(Almost hysterical with tension.)* We have to get it right!

VIKTOR. All right, all right, two minutes then!

WOMAN. Right. *(To the Drummer.)* I'm the SS. I'll give you your cues. *(Speaks in a heavy German accent.)* 'So, what do we have here?'

DRUMMER. *(Speaking mechanically and addressing Viktor.)* 'This, your excellencies, is the band-stand. We have concerts here everyday. The music is of a very high standard.'

WOMAN. 'Our Jews are very fond of music, are you not?'

DRUMMER. 'Oh yes, sir...'

WOMAN. Not 'sir' - they want it relaxed.

DRUMMER. 'Oh yes, indeed, as you can hear, we even have a Jazz Group, the Ghetto Swingers, since this is only place in the Reich where decadent music can be played. Oh yes, we like it hot, we Jews - the hotter the better!'

WOMAN. *(Snaps.)* Who told you to say that?

DRUMMER. Nobody, I just...

WOMAN. Leave it out then.

VIKTOR. *(To woman.)* All right, all right, can we get back to our dress-rehearsal now, Fräulein? We have precious little time left.
WOMAN. Certainly Herr Ullmann, if you'll just let me remind everyone in this gymnasium of the procedure. Once the SS have passed through the hall, stay in your seats for a few minutes only, then get out of here as quick as you can and make for the town hall. The SS want you to be in your chairs ready to play audience for the next concert before the Red Cross get there. We have to check the timing today.
VIKTOR . *(Cuts in.)* We know this Fräulein, we know it, now please! *(Speaking out to the audience)*. Will the cast get into your positions, and the orchestra? We'll pick up from the end of scene three. I'll read the part of the Loudspeaker:'Now that Death has refused to make people die, the Emperor is forced to witness the total breakdown of society. The sick are so terrified that their pain and suffering will go on forever, they are almost driven frantic. But Death is prepared to return to mankind on one condition only - that the Emperor is the first to undergo the new death. The Emperor of Atlantis agrees, and newly delivered mankind welcomes the return of Death.' Cue.
HEINO. *(Sings.)* 'Death's bound to arrive any moment now.'
WOMAN. (*Looking out of a window. Urgently.*) The SS are here! There are two of them.
HEINO. *(Sings.)* 'Death's bound to arrive any moment now.'
VIKTOR. Right, now remember, when I raise my baton, you begin.
WOMAN. *(Looking out of the door.)* Quick, they're on the stairs!
HEINO (*Sings.)* 'Death's bound to arrive any moment now.'
VIKTOR. Lights!
DRUMMER. They'll be coming through the back, any moment - now!
VIKTOR. 'The Emperor walks up to the mirror covered with a cloth. He pulls the cloth away and jumps back when he sees the figure of Death. He pulls out his pistol, so...' (*Viktor now acts out the role of the Emperor coming face to face with the character of Death, who has now appeared on the scene.)*
DEATH. 'Don't waste your bullets Emperor Überall. I've been in the state you'd like to put me in for millions of years already!'
EMPEROR. Who are you?

DEATH. *(Sings.)* My name is Death, the gardener Death,
Who sows the seeds of sleep in pain-filled furrows.
My name is Death, the gardener Death,
Who root's up wilting weeds life's worn out fellows.
They call me Death, the gardener Death,

Who harvests ripened corn of suffering from your meadows.
I'm he that frees you from the plague,
I'm not the plague.
I'm he that brings relief from pain,
Not he that causes pain.
I am that lovely, cosy nest to which you persecuted mortals fly.
I am the greatest freedom feast,
I am the final lullaby.

Scene 10: Banned

In Viktor's barracks.

VIKTOR. Banned?
HEINO. You heard. Come on Nullmann what did you expect. You've got to work with the enemy, not set their teeth on edge. I told you time and time again it was on the cards. Those two SS bastards weren't going to let that pass. Nah, it's curtains for the Emperor of Atlantis, always knew it would be. *(Tuts and shakes his head in mock commiseration.)* All that work down the drain! But I did warn you, *(Viktor turns round and Heino's eyes fix on the call-up slip in Viktor's hands)* I did tell you it would end in tears. Catching a train, eh? I suppose they told you you're being sent off somewhere to build a new labour camp, and that you only need light luggage, a change of linen and food for twenty four hours! That's what they told me. It's a good one that is. Everyone's got their call up papers. Did you know that? Elly, Anny, Max, all your singers and musicians. Nice one Vik. They've got you to thank for that.
VIKTOR. It's not true. That's a wicked lie! Heinrich said we'd all have been sent east anyway. The opera had nothing to do with it. It's just a coincidence. You're just twisting everything like you always do.
HEINO. You believe that, you're even more of a donkey than I thought you were. But I can see you'll want to start packing, so I'll leave you in peace. Cheers Nullman.... You never know, we may meet again.
VIKTOR. *(Shouts.)* The name's Ullmann!

Viktor turns his back on Heino and starts to get his things together. Unknown to Viktor, however, Heino does not leave at this point but stays in position, taking on the voice and persona of Heinrich. Throughout the following exchange Viktor has his back to

Heino/Heinrich.

HEINRICH. My commiseration Viktor!
VIKTOR. *(He is starting to pack.)* Thank you Heinrich.
HEINRICH. To fly so high, and then to fall, *(Viktor continues packing.)* I think I have some understanding of how that feels. But 'courage!' - the work at least has been completed, it's had its first airing and we know it is magnificent! I was at dress rehearsal - it was a triumph!
VIKTOR. Lines on paper. No-one will hear it now.
HEINRICH. Uh, uh! You say that, but can you be sure? There may come a time, twenty, thirty, fifty years from now when your opera is recognised for the work of inspiration it is! The name of Viktor Ullmann will ring out!
VIKTOR. A hollow ring, Heinrich, hollow.
HEINRICH. Not at all, my dear fellow, this is surely what you struggled for, it is for this you performed the act of creation, pushed yourself to your limits. - Posterity will be you final reward!
VIKTOR. But I am mortal, Heinrich, I will not be there to claim my reward.
HEINRICH. Viktor, this is the remark of a small man. You! You are a giant!
VIKTOR. No, Heinrich, I'm no giant, I'm as mean and stunted as the rest.
HEINRICH. Come, come, this is no way to regard yourself after your shining hour. You are no ordinary man, Viktor. What is it to you whether you live one day more or less? Your work is done, enough of it to feel you've acquitted yourself and thus you will live on!
VIKTOR. A friend of mine, a business associate, would only have one word to say about that: carrots. *(Viktor spins round on this word and approaches Heinrich, removing Heino's cap from his pocket and thus revealing that they, Heino and Heinrich are one. He places the cap on Heino/Heinrich's head.)* I suspected for a little while time that you two were in league against me, one with your sharp practice and one with your smooth tongue. I don't need either of you now. I've learned from both of you, I won't deny it, but now I'm ready to be myself *(Heino/ Heinrich doffs his cap, bows and backs away in a gesture of defeat.)* I didn't write this opera for posterity. Oh all right, part of me did, perhaps, that part of me that you, Heinrich, understand so well. I admit I got caught up in the megalomania, the Emperor's megalomania. I wanted to soar, but - and this neither of you will understand - in the end, the most important thing for me was to have it performed here and now, in

Terezín! I'm not a fighting man, I'm not like my father, I'm weak, I know that. I avoid confrontation at all cost. But this was my stand! It was for me and for all of us in here. That's what finally drove me. You know, Mahler said something I never really understood before. He said it's our works that are the mortals of this world, they are the fleeting things, but it is what man makes of himself, what he becomes as a result of his ceaseless striving and living - that is what is lasting.

Viktor completes his packing. As he does so, we hear the Emperor's farewell aria.

'You may have charmed the gods, throughout your life,
But even they cannot prevent - a man's departing.
As I reach the edge of time, of time eternal,
As your hand still rests in mine,
so my warm life can feel the warmth of yours.
This is the moment, this is the final moment,
For now I go in peace, for now I go in peace -
I leave this world behind
And I yearn for the grave's repose.
There will be rivers flowing and mountains all around
And flowers in full bloom exposed to sun and wind
In high pastures. I long to see this land
Of summer rain, of softly falling summer rain.
This is the place for me, this is the place for me.
Imagine a child playing by a fountain, while a horse
Stands waiting for the village blacksmith,
Then imagine me released from sorrow.
For it's not the other side that we need fear.
But rather this world that is veiled in darkest shade,
In darkest shadow.'

Epilogue: Departure.

Elly and Anny appear on stage, both with suitcases in their hands.

Viktor, Heino/Heinrich, Elly and Anny walk towards the audience then freeze before singing the final chorale from 'The Emperor of Atlantis' straight out to the audience before exiting through the auditorium.

CHORALE

Come death and be our honoured guest,
Our hearts for you are waiting.
Free us from life's tormenting tests,
Lead us to rest from all our suffering.

Teach us never to ignore
The yearnings of our brothers.
Teach us to keep your holiest law:
Thou shalt not use the name of Death
In vain now and forever.

THE END

No.10 - Scene Link and Cabaret II

CUE:-

Heino: ***......And you never know when that mamzer, the commandant's going to pop up, it's one of his hobbies, cruising round on his little bicycle catching people red handed.***
(A bicycle bell can be heard ringing.)

Heino: ***Get rid of them.*** (The music starts.)

Lise & Lotte
Cello
clap some more We're two lit - tle scrub - bers Complete with our rub bers
We're two lit - tle scrub - bers We're the girl - ies from the Clean - ing Corps
Mop March I
La la la la la La la la la
la La La La La La La La la la la
la La la la la la la la
La la la la la la la la la la la la la la la la la la la La la la la
Lise: Good evening ladies and gentlemen. As you can see we belong to the oldest profession in the world. Even a charming little town like this needs girls like us.
Lotte: Yes, wherever you go - Berlin, Vienna, Munich, Hamburg - they all need us on their pavements.
la
(repeat continuously under dialogue)

THE ELEVENTH COMMANDMENT

by

David Schneider

With statistics indicating more than half of American Jews marrying outside the faith and the Anglo-Jewish community heading the same way, *The Eleventh Commandment* looks at continuity, tradition and the Holocaust through the eyes of a young, assimilated Jew. Danny, the son of a Holocaust survivor, is a model Jewish son, even if his desk in the estate agent's office is a little too close to the door for his mother's liking. His only crime is that, at the age of thirty, he is still resolutely single. Then along comes Christina, an Ulster Protestant and not at all the sort of girlfriend Danny's mother had in mind. Broad comedy and Jewish tradition, Woody Allen and Kafka, Moses and Abraham, all jostle together in this examination of the modern Anglo-Jewish psyche.

CHARACTERS

DANNY
INSPECTOR
ANGEL
ABRAHAM
DANNY'S MUM
DANNY'S DAD
DETECTIVE
CHRISTINA
ISAAC
SAM
QUIZMASTER
MESSIAH
GREAT-GRANDFATHER
GHOST
MOSES

The Eleventh Commandment was commissioned by Hampstead Theatre, where it was first performed on 28th November 1996.

CAST

INSPECTOR	Nicholas Ball
DETECTIVE	James Clyde
CHRISTINA	Tracey Lynch
DANIEL	David Schneider
ABRAHAM/DAD/MOSES	Jeffrey Segal
MUM	Sheila Steafel

Director	Atthew Lloyd
Designer	Les Brotherston
Lighting Designer	Paul Russell
Sound	Scott Myers

ACT ONE

Lights up on Danny, looking miserable and holding a prison slate with his number on it. The stage is bare except for a wooden table with a chair behind it and a door frame, suggesting a front door.

INSPECTOR. *(Off)* Name?
DANNY. Daniel Feinman.
INSPECTOR. Age?
DANNY. Thirty
INSPECTOR. Occupation
DANNY Estate Agent.
INSPECTOR. Crime?
DANNY. Single.

There is a bright flash, as if a flashbulb had gone off. Danny winces. 'Tradition' from 'Fiddler on the Roof' bursts in as the scene changes. A travelling salesman/angel goes up to the front door and we hear it ring. The music cuts and Abraham goes to answer it.

ANGEL. Abraham?
ABRAHAM. Yes.
ANGEL. Abraham, son of Terach?
ABRAHAM. Yes.
ANGEL. Abraham, son of Terach, son of Nahor?
ABRAHAM. Yes, that's me.
ANGEL. Oh, hello. I represent God in Heaven.
ABRAHAM. *(Trying to shut the door on him.)* I'm sorry, I'm very busy.
ANGEL. From all the people in the Mesopotamia area, God Himself has chosen you to…
ABRAHAM. Look, I had all this with the Homecare shopping catalogue and I'm not going to fall for it again.
ANGEL. No, this is different. This is from God.
ABRAHAM. I'm not interested.
ANGEL God says that within a year you and your wife Sarah will have a child.
ABRAHAM. A child! What are you talking about? I'm ninety-nine, my

wife's ninety, we can't even have a coherent conversation nowadays, let alone children.
ANGEL. Look, I know it sounds strange, but, believe it or not, your wife Sarah's going to get pregnant.
ABRAHAM. The only thing Sarah's going to get is a telegram from the Queen.
ANGEL. If you agree to do what God wants, God guarantees you a son and heir, and, what's more, he promises that your descendants will be as numerous as the stars in the sky or the grains of sand in the desert.
ABRAHAM. *(Thinks about it.)* That's over a hundred, isn't it? *(The angel nods.)* OK. So what do I have to do?
ANGEL. Simple. Just agree to worship the one God, that's all. And a couple of minor cosmetic changes.
ABRAHAM. Such as?
ANGEL. Circumcising yourself...
ABRAHAM. But I'm ninety-nine years old!
ANGEL. ... And all the males in your household – servants, shepherds, the lot.
ABRAHAM. I can't do that. There are laws against that sort of thing.
ANGEL. Not yet.
ABRAHAM. What about quality? These descendants, will they be famous? Will people like them?
ANGEL. Well, there might be some... teething problems over the first two, three thousand years and over the next two, three thousand years... *(Abraham looks suspicious.)*...
but they will make an enormous contribution to the world and eventually they'll have more than their fair share of doctors, lawyers, estate agents...
ABRAHAM. *(Impressed.)* Doctors and lawyers, eh? Not sure about estate agents, but... yes, OK. Why not? I mean, after all, to have a son, to keep the race going, that's the most important thing anyone can do.
ANGEL. Good, it's a deal then.
ABRAHAM Yeah. I'll start on the old cosmetic changes. I think I've got a fishbone somewhere, that should do the trick.
ANGEL. Great. And I'll go and tell God the good news. *(He starts to go.)* Oh, I forgot to say. A couple of minor details about your descendants. All the males will be short-sighted. Is that OK?
ABRAHAM. Yes, that's fine.
ANGEL. And they'll be hopeless at horse-riding and loft insulation.
ABRAHAM. Fine, no problems! *(The angel leaves.)* I'm going to have a son! All the sacrifices, all the hard work, it's all been worthwhile!

'Tradition' starts up again. The stage is gradually transformed into Danny's parents' home. Everywhere, typical Jewish objects – the candlesticks, Minorah, the Chagall, the model Rabbi, the picture of the Western Wall, the barmitzvah photo, the graduation photo etc. The table becomes the dining table. Danny's dad sits at it, quietly slumped after a hard day's work. Danny opens the front door and enters. The music cuts.

DANNY. Hi! It's me! Hi, dad!
MUM. *(Off.)* I'll be with you in a moment. Don't wait! Sit down! Eat!

Danny takes off his coat and goes to put it over the back of the chair.

MUM. *(Off.)* Coat!

He gets up and goes and hangs it by the front door.

MUM. *(Off.)* Don't know why you insist on wearing that. It's got more holes in it than a golf course.

Danny comes back through and sits down. He is followed by his mum with some tupperware boxes.

MUM. Why not take a risk, Daniel? Live dangerously, buy yourself a new coat.
DANNY. Yes, yes.
MUM. Here's the food for you to take home. Don't forget it. Susie not with you?
DANNY. No.
MUM. She coming on later, then?
DANNY. I'm not sure she can make it. *(Tasting the food on the plate.)* Mmm. Good.
MUM. Can't make it too salty because of your father. Pass me my pills, would you, darling? *(He does so.)* Bless you, sweetheart. Not that they're doing any good. I'm still not sleeping, and I sweat like an overweight pig – if you can have such a thing as an overweight pig. I've

lost another two pounds. But the doctor says don't worry, so I won't worry. *(They eat some more.)* How's your day been?

DANNY. OK, yeah. And you?

MUM. Ach! Nothing but bad news – this one's not getting any better, that one's got to go in for another check-up. I don't want to think about it. *(She sees he's finished and offers him the food she has prepared for Susie.)* Want some more?

DANNY. No, thanks. It was lovely, but…

MUM. Sure? *(He nods. She passes the plate to Dad who quietly accepts it.)* We saw Susie's parents last night at the bridge club.

DANNY. Oh.

MUM. They slaughtered us. Nice people. We're looking forward to getting to know them better.

DANNY. Really.

MUM. They say they haven't seen you for a week or so.

DANNY. Yes…

MUM. Are you not seeing Susie anymore?

DANNY. No.

MUM. Daniel!

DANNY. We're still friends, I'll still see her…

MUM. Why didn't you tell me?

DANNY. Mummy, please. Don't make a thing about it.

MUM. I don't understand. You seemed to be getting on so well. Such a lovely girl, a quiet, polite, yiddishe girl – that's unusual…

DANNY. Are we talking about the same person?

MUM. So what was the problem, the sex?

DANNY. No!

MUM. I'm just asking.

DANNY. You always put everything down to 'the sex'. That wasn't the problem, OK?

MUM. Did you have an argument or something?

DANNY. No.

MUM. Well, did you do something stupid? Did you go off with someone else?

DANNY. No.

MUM. So what's the problem?

DANNY. It just wasn't working out.

MUM. What do you mean 'wasn't working out'?

DANNY. I don't know… there wasn't any chemistry between us.

MUM. Chemistry? Do you thing there's ever been any chemistry between me and your father? You need chemistry to make a bomb, not a

marriage.
DANNY. Can we talk about something else?
MUM. This is what worries me about you, Daniel. You never stick at anything. You're a luftmentsh[1], a drifter. How many years have you been at that firm? Four, five? And you're still the closest to the door.
DANNY. I told you. It doesn't matter who's closest to the door.
MUM. Of course it does. The one closest to the door is the one who has to deal with the public the most. The further away from your desk the closer you are to management...
DANNY. It's not like that....
MUM. I saw a documentary about it on the television.
DANNY. Can we change the subject.
MUM. That's my Daniel: 'Let's change the subject'. *(She addresses the audience.)* You know what he is. He's a fool to himself. He could have been anything he wanted to be, anything...
DANNY. Please, don't start...
MUM. Switch the lights off. Go on!

> *Danny grudgingly gets up and switches off the lights. Mum picks up a remote control for a slide projector and begins her 'lecture' to the audience with a slide of Danny's graduation photo.*

MUM. He got a two-one, almost a first, with honours, from a proper university, he could have done anything... *(She brings up a slide of Danny's grinning face superimposed on a judge.)*... Lord Justice Feinman... *(Then on a surgeon.)* My son, the doctor – I wish!... *(Then on Mrs Thatcher going into Number ten with Denis after an election victory.)*... Prime Minister, why not? And instead, what is he doing? Wasting his time as an estate agent's assistant, with his desk so close to the door it's practically outside on the pavement. He's got no ambition, you see. At least, if he became a manager, tried to make a go of things...
DANNY. But I don't want to.
MUM. So you keep saying. But what do you want?
DANNY. I don't know.
MUM. 'I don't know.' *(To the audience.)* If there was a Nobel Prize for not knowing, my son would have won it. We want to see him settled and happy before it's too late. Is that such a crime?... *(A quick burst of slides showing Danny standing under the wedding canopy with suitable brides. First with Maureen Lipman.)*... Could be someone like Maureen... *(Then with Barbra Streisland.)*... Barbra... *(Then Edwina*

Currie)... Edwina... Yes, she's Jewish, didn't you know? He's thirty years old. And we're not getting any younger. None of us are. Come, Daniel.

Danny switches the lights back on and returns to his seat.

MUM. We tried so hard to have you – the thermometers, the charts – now, that's chemistry! Phone her, Daniel. See if you can't patch it up.
DANNY. Maybe.
MUM. Good boy.

She goes into the kitchen.

DANNY. So, how are you dad?
MUM. *(Shouting from off.)* He's worried.

* * * * * * * * * *

'Sunrise, Sunset' from 'Fiddler on the Roof' plays as the scene changes to an empty flat, one of Danny's properties. After a few bars the music merges into the theme from 'Mission Impossible'. The detective and the inspector burst into the room. The music stops and they settle into their surveillance positions. The detective – young, but already going to seed – sits down and begins eating one of those Mullerrice yoghurts. The inspector – a Morse/Taggart type, plagued by a cold, blocked nose and related symptoms – gazes absent-mindedly out of a window (towards the audience.) He is older and clearly not a happy man.

DETECTIVE. You know what I hate. It's people who pour all the nuts into the yoghurt section in one go. See, your connoisseur mixes them in bit by bit, tries to judge exactly when to add a few more. Yes, I know! That can be disappointing if you get it wrong, but if you get it right... *(He eats the yoghurt demonstrating his connoisseur-like ability to judge when to add more nuts.)* Finished! Or have I? *(He produces the lid with a flourish.)* A triangle of sheer semi-congealed pleasure. *(He starts to lick it.)* Want some? Boss? What's up, boss?
INSPECTOR. *(Taking some nasal spray.)* I think Jean's going to leave me.

DETECTIVE. What! No, never. She can't manage on her own.
INSPECTOR. Well, obviously she thinks she can. Unless she's not going to be on her own.
DETECTIVE. No, not Jean, no way.
INSPECTOR. I don't know what I've done, Dave. I mean, OK – sex has never been easy, what with my injury and everything. But she won't even watch the videos now. And the things she's said to me over the past few weeks. I don't know what she's so upset about.
DETECTIVE. Maybe it's the job, boss. You know – late nights, the danger. It gets to them.
INSPECTOR. Yes, maybe it's the job. Or the booze, I suppose. Or the gambling. Or it could be the affairs. Or the pornography… I just don't understand what's got into her.

A pause.

DETECTIVE. What are we going to do with him, boss? Are we going to have a word?
INSPECTOR. Chocolates. Or flowers.
DETECTIVE. Flowers?
INSPECTOR. Maybe flowers would help? I mean, picture the scene, Dave: Jean, in her wheelchair, in a room full of flowers.
DETECTIVE. She's allergic to them.
INSPECTOR. Oh, yeah.

Another pause.

DETECTIVE. Still no sign of them?
INSPECTOR. What?
DETECTIVE. No sign?
INSPECTOR. Oh, no.
DETECTIVE. They'll be here.
INSPECTOR. How do you know?
DETECTIVE. A little bird told me.
INSPECTOR. What do you mean a little bird told you?
DETECTIVE. It's just an expression. 'A little bird told me.'
INSPECTOR. Oh, not like a parrot, a mynah bird, a bird that can talk.
DETECTIVE. No.
INSPECTOR. It doesn't mean anything. He's just an estate agent showing her round some properties. That's his job.

We hear Danny and Christina off-stage. The two policemen hide: the inspector off-stage, on the opposite side, the detective under the table. In his panic he leaves his Mullerrice pot on top of the table.

DANNY. *(Off.)* If he doesn't sell it soon, he's going to convert the utility room into a bathroom.
CHRISTINA. *(Off.)* Another one! That'll be...
DANNY. *(Off.)* Four bathrooms. Four bathrooms and two bedrooms!
CHRISTINA. *(Off.)* That's ridiculous!
DANNY. And the thing is, I don't know if you noticed but that man has a bit of a body odour problem.
CHRISTINA. *(Off.)* Yes, I know.
DANNY. *(Off.)* With all those bathrooms you'd think he'd have at least one bath once a month! Anyway...

They enter.

DANNY. This is the main reception area. As you can see it's quite spacious. *(He walks to the audience/window, struggling to generate some enthusiasm)*, and it does have a nice view over... *(He looks out of the window. He is not impressed.)* There aren't really any period features left, but some people quite like that. Do you like that? You don't, do you?
CHRISTINA. No.
DANNY. It's horrible, isn't it? I don't know who converted it, but
CHRISTINA. Someone with a chain saw and blurred vision. Still, it's better than the last one.
DANNY. What? Huggy Bear Mansions?
CHRISTINA. That is the first time I have seen leopard-skin wallpaper.
DANNY. And that bedroom! How could anyone sleep in it?
CHRISTINA. I don't think it was for sleeping in.
DANNY. Oh.
CHRISTINA. Have you ever managed to sell a property?
DANNY. What do you mean?
CHRISTINA. You're too honest.
DANNY. Am I?
CHRISTINA. You didn't have to point out those structural problems on Cazenove Road.
DANNY. I know... I just can't... I'd've felt guilty.
CHRISTINA. Guilty?
DANNY. Yes. All you need is one visit from the Big Bad Wolf, huff!,

puff! There goes your house! *(They laugh.)* Can I be deeply embarrassing?
CHRISTINA. Uh-oh!
DANNY. Are you on telly?
CHRISTINA. Afraid so.
DANNY. I thought so. News Room, South East. You're that reporter.
CHRISTINA. What are you doing watching News Room, South East.
DANNY. It's when I eat my tea. Teatime: News Room, South East.
CHRISTINA. What do you do on Saturdays and Sundays?
DANNY. No tea. You sound different on the telly.
CHRISTINA. That's my news voice.
DANNY. Oh.
CHRISTINA. They're not so keen on strong Ulster accents.
DANNY. Is that where you're from?
CHRISTINA. 'Fraid so. So. Where should I live then?
DANNY. It's up to you.
CHRISTINA. Well, if you were going to move, which one would you go for?
DANNY. OK. Let's have a look.

Danny takes the bits of paper with the housing details off her and looks through them.

DANNY. That's rubbish. Terrible. Death-trap. Oh, this is quite a good one. Mountview. Yes, it's nice. I wouldn't mind moving in there – not that we're going to be moving in together.
CHRISTINA. I hadn't planned it.
DANNY. Sorry, I don't know why I said that... yes... Mountview, yes...you could probably get at least £10,000 off the asking price, maybe fifteen – though I didn't tell you that.

The inspector sneezes.

DANNY. Did you hear something?
CHRISTINA. No.
DANNY. Maybe a cat or something. Rats, probably. *(Half whispers to her.)* They've had problems.

He goes off and has a quick look.

CHRISTINA. Did you always want to be an estate agent?

DANNY. *(Off.)* Pardon?
CHRISTINA. Did you always want to be an estate agent?
DANNY. *(Coming back.)* No-one wants to be an estate agent. You just put in an offer of, say, barrister, then life puts its bid of bank clerk, and then you both sort of settle on estate agent.
CHRISTINA. So what do you want to be?
DANNY. God, you are a journalist!
CHRISTINA. Sorry.
DANNY. No, it's better than talking about knock-through lounges and quiet residential areas. Actually, I always wanted to be a writer.
CHRISTINA. Oh, yes? What sort?
DANNY. Fiction. Crime, really. Detective fiction – I love all that stuff. It's people at their extremes: the psychology of the policemen, the psychology of the criminals. And the situations: the tension of the interview room, even... *(he notices the Mullerrice bowl that's been left on the table)*... the tedium of surveillance – I find it all so absorbing. I'm always having ideas.
CHRISTINA. Have you published anything?
DANNY. No. It's just an estate agent's daydream.
CHRISTINA. Have you written anything down?
DANNY. Not really... bits. I had this idea about a detective who eats too much and a miserable inspector... *(the detective snatches the Mullerrice away. Danny double-takes)* ...but it's nothing serious. Listen, I thing we ought to get on to the next one.
CHRISTINA. Is it worth seeing?
DANNY. No.
CHRISTINA. I know. There's a café we passed on the way in. Why don't we have a look round that instead?
DANNY. OK.
CHRISTINA. Come on then.

She exits. He reaches into his briefcase, searches around a bit and pulls out a little bottle of homeopathic medicine. He squirts a couple of drops into his mouth.

CHRISTINA. *(Off.)* Are you coming?
DANNY. Yes. Just coming.

Danny rushes out. The inspector comes out of his hiding place.

INSPECTOR. All clear?

DETECTIVE. *(Emerging with a mouldy, half-eaten piece of cake.)* Look what I found, boss. A bit of cake – Dundee, I think. Someone must have dropped it. *(He takes a bite.)* Not bad. INSPECTOR. See where they're off to, Dave. I think that little bird you spoke to might have been chirping up the right tree. I'll dig around in the files, see what I can find.

* * * * * * * * * * *

A brief burst of news style music. Christina in News Room, South East mode. She uses standard English.

CHRISTINA. The past few days have seen remarkable developments in the life of London estate agent Daniel Feinman. In an unprecedented departure from form, he succeeded in asking news reporter Christina Lawson out on what can only be described as a date. Described by neighbours as 'a quiet man who keeps himself to himself', Feinman was seen to be quite nervous in the run-up to his evening's date, and although Ms. Lawson herself was unavailable for comment, sources close to her indicate that she probably does quite fancy him, she has been single for a while and he seems like a decent enough bloke so why the hell not. After all, it's not a commitment or anything, it's just a date, for God's sake, let's not make a big thing out of it, OK? This is Christina Lawson for News Room, South East.

* * * * * * * * * * *

The lights come up on the rest of the stage, revealing Danny's flat. Some of its features are similar to his parent's place: the little model Rabbi is there, a picture of the western wall etc. There is also a load of detective novels, a sofa and in one corner, a pile of tupperware boxes and plastic bags similar to those handed to Danny by his mum in the earlier scene. This pile stays throughout the play and gradually gets bigger and bigger.

When the lights come up, Christina immediately becomes part of the new scene. They have clearly just come back from their date. Danny is off-stage, getting the coffee.

CHRISTINA. *(Looking around.)* No, it's interesting. 'Tastefully decorated throughout'.
DANNY. *(Off.)* What is this? *Parlez-vous* Real Estate?
CHRISTINA. *(Looking at the model Rabbi.)* 'With distinctive features'.
DANNY. *(Coming in with the coffee.)* You know what they say: there are lies, damned lies and housing lists. *Café, madame*?
CHRISTINA. *Madamoiselle*, please.
DANNY. And *des biscuites*.
CHRISTINA. Merci.
DANNY. Ah? *Tu parles francais*?
CHRISTINA. *Oui. Et toi?*
DANNY. *Non.*

There is a suspended moment in which they measure each other up, deciding where to sit. Finally they opt for the sofa. Christina spots a picture of Danny's mum, possibly out in the audience.

CHRISTINA. Is that your mum in the picture? *(Danny hangs his head in shame.)* Did it have to be so big?
DANNY. I know. She put it there. Look at her. Sometimes I worry it's like one of those pictures on the wall in Thunderbirds and that any moment now the eyes will start blinking and then next thing you know, it's come to life and it's talking to me. It could happen.
CHRISTINA. I think you could be right. Do you see her often?
DANNY. I'm a nice Jewish boy. You know how it is. We never quite cut ourselves off. We're what they call umbilically challenged. *(Another suspended moment. They measure each other up and adopt slightly more intimate positions.)* So you've not got a picture of your mum in the living room?
CHRISTINA. No. I've got one in the bedroom, but not quite as prominent as that.
DANNY. Do you get on well?
CHRISTINA. My mum's dead. Cancer.
DANNY. Oh, sorry.
CHRISTINA. Don't worry. Not your fault.
DANNY. What about your dad?
CHRISTINA. What about my dad?
DANNY. He's still alive.
CHRISTINA. Yes.
DANNY. Are you close?

CHRISTINA. No. We don't get on. He's a total die-hard drum-bashing Unionist – put it this way, if he got a mobile phone it would have to be Orange. Still, it's amazing what it can do for your relationship, living hundreds of miles apart.
DANNY. I know what you mean. Sometimes I'm so glad that my parents live over a hundred yards away.

They readjust positions again. They're getting quite close now.

DANNY. So you're Protestant then?
CHRISTINA. Didn't you know?
DANNY. I thought so, but I didn't like to ask. Dangerous area.
CHRISTINA. You're very Jewish, aren't you?
DANNY. I'll take that as a compliment.
CHRISTINA. It was meant as one. Are you religious?
DANNY. Not really. I go to synagogue, but it's more a cultural thing. I love all the traditions, the learning. It's just such a rich heritage. It was great when I was growing up. I felt there was so much to be proud of: the raid on Entebbe; Uri Geller; Israel won the Eurovision Song Contest twice. Not once, twice. First there was 'Abanibi' – that was brilliant – then there was 'Hallelujah' – I didn't like that so much; Jaffa Oranges – they're the juiciest. I got so into being Jewish. I even wanted to be a Rabbi. Really wanted to, right up till my teens, but my mum thought it wasn't really the right sort of job for a nice Jewish boy.
CHRISTINA. Really?
DANNY. Oh, yeah. Doctor, lawyer – that's fine. But a Rabbi – it's looked down on. Not quite kosher.
CHRISTINA. And what about nice Jewish girls?

She puts her hand on his knee. We see his panicky thoughts externalised momentarily, then he returns to the reality of the scene.

DANNY. Jewish girls?
CHRISTINA. Shouldn't you be married to a nice Jewish girl instead of sitting here with a ... what's the word... a *shiksa*?
DANNY. How did you know?
CHRISTINA. I had a friend who got married to a Jewish fella.
DANNY. Oh right.
CHRISTINA. You wouldn't believe it, but his mother actually refused to come to the wedding.

DANNY. Oh, I'd believe it alright.
CHRISTINA. Anyway, they begged and begged her and in the end she came… wearing black. *(He laughs.)* So what are you doing here with a *shiksa*?
DANNY. Did you know the word *shiksa* comes from the Yiddish *Shik zi* meaning 'send her', because they have a… *(he struggles to avoid the word)*… non-Jewish woman to do the errands on the Sabbath and they'd day 'shik zi aher, shik zi ahin', 'send her there, send her here'…
CHRISTINA. I think you're trying to avoid the question.
DANNY. I think you're probably right, Mr Paxman!
CHRISTINA. He's Jewish, isn't he?

They kiss.

DANNY. I don't think so.

They kiss some more. 'Abanibi' starts playing. The sofa turns into a bed. We are in the bedroom. The lights are dimmed. More kissing etc. Clothes are removed. Danny breaks off from the embrace. Abanini' stops.

DANNY. I better take my lenses out.
CHRISTINA. Why? Danny?
DANNY. I better, just in case we you know… fall asleep.

He switches on the light and gets out of bed. He goes over to a dresser and starts removing his lenses.

CHRISTINA. Will you still be able to see me?
DANNY. Yes.
CHRISTINA. I went to a lot of trouble, you know. Washed my hair and everything.
DANNY. It's just if I fall asleep in them my eyes get all gunged up and covered in green stuff…
CHRISTINA. Oh! You're such a romantic.
DANNY. Won't be a second. *(He takes them out.)* There. That's better. *(He gropes for some small bottles in his toilet bag.)* Now just one more thing then I'm all yours. *(He takes a couple of drops.)*
CHRISTINA. Is this some sort of traditional courtship ritual?
DANNY. It's a homeopathic remedy. They're very good if you feel ill or anxious or anything. I take them all the time. *(He goes over to show*

her.) Like there's the basic Rescue Remedy for 'comfort', 'oak' – that's 'anxiety', 'limeflower' for 'memory'. All sorts of things.
CHRISTINA. So what have you just taken?
DANNY. 'Elm and hibiscus' – 'courage'. Want some?
CHRISTINA. Put them away.

He does so. They kiss. She turns the light off.

DANNY. Hold on.

He turns the lights back on and gets out of bed.

CHRISTINA. What?
DANNY. I'm just getting the – you know – condoms. I keep them here somewhere.

He rolls back the mattress from one corner, so that Christina is almost pushed out of bed.

CHRISTINA. No-one could say your foreplay wasn't original.
DANNY. I have to hide them in case my mum finds them. She's always tidying up, prowling around.

He finds the packet, gets back into bed and turns the light off. They resume kissing. She takes the condoms off him and disappears under the bedclothes to put one on him. Things seem to be going better. She works her way back up his body, but when she emerges from underneath the sheets she has become his mum. Danny sits up, terrified, and moves to the other side of the bed.

DANNY. Mummy! What are you doing here?
MUM. What am I doing here? What are you doing here, more to the point?
DANNY. I'm...you know...
MUM. You're having sex with a *shiksa*, Danny. That's what you're doing!

Danny is petrified Christina might hear.

DANNY. Mummy, please... don't say that... look, it's not serious, OK?

MUM. It's not serious? Not serious! I know how these things develop, Daniel. You start off having sex with her, one thing leads to another, next thing you know you actually like her.
DANNY. Mummy,... look, it won't come to that.
MUM. *Az der klayne shteyt, der seykhl geyt* – When the little one stands, good sense goes out the window.
DANNY. Please...

He pushes her back down under the duvet.

CHRISTINA. *(Reappearing.)* Are you OK?
DANNY. Sure... *(looking around for his mother)* kiss me...

They start kissing again. Mum resurfaces and lies behind Daniel watching.

MUM. What am I going to do with you, Danielik?

He signals her to keep quiet and tries to carry on as best he can, hoping Christina won't notice.

MUM. She's a *shiksa*, Daniel. She's not Jewish. Look at you!
DANNY. Go away!
CHRISTINA. You OK?

Danny murmurs his assent. Christina takes the initiative and climbs on top of Danny.

MUM. Oy! From bad to worse.
DANNY. Oh! Mummy!
CHRISTINA. What's the matter, Danny?
DANNY. I'm fine. Just give me a moment.
MUM. I'm not leaving.
DANNY. Please!
CHRISTINA. Do you want me to stop?
MUM. Don't start what you can't finish.
DANNY. OK. I give up. I'm sorry.
MUM. That's better. Right, I'll be off then. *(She gives him a kiss.)* See you tomorrow evening. Oh, I almost forgot. *(She reaches under the bedclothes and pulls out a thermos in a plastic bag.)* I made you some borsht. *(She gives him another kiss.)* *Zay mir gezunt.*[2]

She leaves.

DANNY. I'm sorry.
CHRISTINA. It's OK.
DANNY. I don't know what happens.
CHRISTINA. It doesn't matter.

He reaches into his bag of bottles.

CHRISTINA. What are you looking for?
DANNY. I don't know. Here.
CHRISTINA. What's that.
DANNY. Larch: 'disappointment'.

He gives her the bottle.

CHRISTINA. Danny! So, does this happen a lot?
DANNY. Yes and no.
CHRISTINA. Would you rather not talk about it?
DANNY. No, it's OK. I can get going and everything, but I can never really… get to the end, if you see what I mean.
CHRISTINA. What never?
DANNY. Well, yes… but only when… you know…
CHRISTINA. …What?…
DANNY. Only when I'm… Oh, God! When I'm not with a partner.
CHRISTINA. Oh. I see. Have you ever managed to get to the end with a partner?
DANNY. Believe me, this is a result. It's just that I've only been with Jewish girls before and every time it's just been so traumatic. I'd be lying there and I'd look at them in the half-light and they'd just look like my mum, or my Auntie Gerda… or me! It's just not that pleasant. It's like incest.
CHRISTINA. But how can you sleep with them if you don't fancy them?
DANNY. You have to.
CHRISTINA. No, you don't.
DANNY. All my friends are pairing off, they're getting married, having children, and, call me traditional, but that's what I want. I want to get married in a synagogue, smash the glass, be carried around in a chair at the reception and then get on with raising some children. And that means finding a Jewish partner whether I like it or not.

CHRISTINA. So what am I doing here?
DANNY. I like you.
CHRISTINA. Do you mind if I smoke?
DANNY. Do you smoke?
CHRISTINA. Only when I fancy a cigarette. Do you mind?
DANNY. Well… It's just that my mum doesn't really like it in here…
CHRISTINA. Oh, it doesn't matter…
DANNY. No! Fuck it! Have a cigarette! Have several! It's my flat, we can do what we want!
CHRISTINA. Alright! *(She lights up.)*
DANNY. So have you had a lot of relationships?
CHRISTINA. Not a lot. But varied. If you lined up my ex's they'd look like an advert for the United Colours of Benetton – Africans, Chinese, Italians – not a good Ulster Protestant among them.
DANNY. Doesn't it make you feel guilt?
CHRISTINA. Better any devil at all than the devil you know.
DANNY. But you must have felt bad about it at some point?
CHRISTINA. Sure! Is the Pope Catholic?
DANNY. So he says.
CHRISTINA Well, so was my first boyfriend. You can imagine how that went down.

She puts out the cigarette. They start kissing again. Danny turns off the light

DANNY. Do that voice like you do on the telly.
CHRISTINA. My news voice?
DANNY. Yeah.
CHRISTINA. No, I feel stupid.
DANNY. Please.
CHRISTINA. *(News voice.)* It was at this point that things started to become interesting for the two participants…

They giggle.

* * * * * * * * * *

The lights suddenly come up on one corner of the stage. The detective is peering at Danny and Christina through binoculars whilst munching on some doughnuts. The cold-ridden inspector is sitting down holding a ransom note put together from newspaper letters.

INSPECTOR. Oh, no!
DETECTIVE. What?
INSPECTOR. It's my youngest.
DETECTIVE. Peter?
INSPECTOR. Yes. Those extremists have kidnapped him again.
DETECTIVE. You're joking? What are you going to do?
INSPECTOR. I don't know.
DETECTIVE. Well, what does Jean think?
INSPECTOR. How should I bloody know? She's left me, hasn't she?
DETECTIVE. What! Who's going to look after her?
INSPECTOR. Her bloody fancy woman, that's who!
DETECTIVE. Yes. Seems Jean's ...you know. She's been lying to me all these years.
INSPECTOR. Christ! I don't know what to say.
DETECTIVE. They want me to cut off one of my ears and send it to them.
DETECTIVE. Who? Jean and her...
INSPECTOR. No. The kidnappers. Peter's kidnappers.
DETECTIVE. Oh. Shouldn't it be the other way round? Shouldn't they be sending you one of his ears?
INSPECTOR. That's what I thought.
DETECTIVE. You going to do it?
INSPECTOR. No way. Give these people an ear, and next they'll be wanting an elbow or something. No. *(He takes the binoculars from the detective.)* I want to get moving on old Danny boy. I want to know everything. Past loves, interests, background, the lot.
DETECTIVE. Right, boss.
INSPECTOR. If someone like him marries out, then – God help us! - soon they'll all be at it.

The Detective is grabbing a few final bites of food.

INSPECTOR. Well, go on then.
DETECTIVE. Right, boss.

The detective nods and exits, leaving the inspector looking through the binoculars. He puts them down, then changes his mind and has another look. In the darkness, Danny and

Christina are reaching a crescendo. We hear Danny's voice especially as he reaches his climax.

DANNY. Oh, God! Oh, God! Ah!... Jesus!!... Jesus!
CHRISTINA. Did you say 'Jesus'?

* * * * * * * * * * *

'Wonder of Wonders' from 'Fiddler on the Roof' is heard. The scene changes. Abraham and Isaac at the altar. The music fades out.

ABRAHAM. Isaac! Come on!

Abraham, unsure of himself, starts to bind Isaac and places him on the altar.

ISAAC. Daddy! Why are you doing this?
ABRAHAM. Because God has asked me to.
ISAAC. But I'm your son. Your chosen son. The future of our race. Why would God want that?
ISAAC. I don't know, my child. It's a test. Sometimes we can't understand why God wants something. We might not like it, it might cause us pain and suffering and sacrifice, but it's out duty as Jews to do as he says. Daddy know best. *(He raises a knife, gets ready to plunge it in.)* I love you!
ISAAC. No! Dad! Look!

An angel has appeared, wearing a fake beard.

ANGEL. Abraham! Stop! The Lord commands you to stop!
ABRAHAM. Who are you?
ANGEL. I am an angel of the Lord, and I command you in the name of the Lord to release Isaac from his bondage.
ABRAHAM. What? Who did you say you were?
ANGEL. I am an angel of the Lord!
ABRAHAM. An angel of the Lord?
ANGEL. Release Isaac from his bondage!
ABRAHAM. Hold on a moment! I know who you are. You're... you're

whatsisname, aren't you? You're that bloke off the telly. *(The angel removes his beard and starts laughing. He thrusts a microphone in Abraham's face and points to the hidden camera.)* I don't believe it! I don't [fucking] believe it! *(A bleep covers the swear words, as it would on TV.)* You [bastard]! All this test thing's a wind-up! You didn't want me to kill him at all… I don't believe it! *(He notices Isaac laughing.)* Were you in on this? Did you know about this? You [bastard]! I… Blimey!

* * * * * * * * * *

The scene changes to the parental abode. Mum addresses the audience. Dad, as ever, is quietly slumped at the table. Danny, once dressed, joins them.

MUM. I've just seen 'The Sound of Music'… again. Good musical. I can't sing a note, me.

She says, rather than sings, the following lines.

Some fresh baked *challah* I bought at a bargain,
Chopped chicken liver, with chopped egg and onion,
Rakusen's matzos, all crispy and thin,
These are a few of his favourite things.
Soup made from guess what, it's our penicillin,
Cabbage and spinach to have with your chicken,
Stuffed chicken neck, oh, so carefully done,
All special things I've prepared for my son.
Have some herring! Have some *latkes*!
Then some *lokshen* pud!
And when you have finished, my own special boy,
I'll bring you some seconds…

DANNY. …Mmm…Good.

The meal is drawing to a close. Danny's mum is busy eating her food. Danny has finished his.

DANNY. Mmm. Good.

MUM. Glad you like it. I made it specially. They're keeping him on, you know?
DANNY. Who?
MUM. That new Rabbi. They're not going to get rid of him.
DANNY. Why should they?
MUM. He's a disaster.
DANNY. He's not.
MUM. He's a dwarf, Daniel.
DANNY. So? That's got nothing to do with his job. Anyway, he's not a dwarf...
MUM. He's a dwarf, I tell you. Look at him.
DANNY. He's just short...
MUM. He's a dwarf.
DANNY. He's perfectly proportioned...
MUM. Alright, he's a midget then. Whatever you call him, it's just not right. A Jewish midget. He can't even reach the handles of the ark properly, the children can't stop giggling. It's not dignified. The only thing about him that isn't short, more's the pity, are his sermons.

Christina appears and waves to Danny. Only he can see her.

DANNY. What are you doing here?
MUM. If he had a bit of *seykhl*[3], a bit of charm, I might forgive him, but the man's a dummy.
DANNY. *(To Christina.)* I'll see you later OK?
CHRISTINA. I'm not leaving.
DANNY. *(To mum.)* You're just upset because he's being strict about what you cook for the pensioners.
MUM. He belongs in a circus, not at south Finchley synagogue.
DANNY. Mummy!
CHRISTINA. Mummy!!
DANNY. *(To mum.)* He gave a really good sermon last week. You should have heard it, it was all about not judging people by appearances.
MUM. What a surprise he picked on that subject!
DANNY. That's what the *sedra*[4] was about! '*Lo ta'asu ovel bamishpot* – You shall do no unrighteousness in judgement'.
MUM. *(She gets up with the dishes.)* Feh!
DANNY. You're so hard on him.
MUM. *(On way out.)* Well, it's embarrassing. Imagine what your uncle would say if he saw we had Wayne Sleep for a Rabbi. *(She goes.)*
CHRISTINA. Have you told them yet?

DANNY. Not yet.
CHRISTINA. Come on, Danny. It's been three months.
DANNY. OK, OK.

He gets out one of his bottles from his pocket.

CHRISTINA. What's that?
DANNY. Courage.

He drops in a couple of drops. Mum returns with some tea and cake.

DANNY. Can I talk to you about something?
MUM. How's Rebecca? We still haven't met her yet.
DANNY. That's what I wanted to talk to you about.
CHRISTINA. Who's Rebecca?
DANNY. *(To Christina.)* Later.
CHRISTINA. Who's Rebecca?
MUM. *(Handing Danny a cup.)* Pass this to your father.
CHRISTINA. Danny!

Danny realises he's going to have to deal with Christina.

DANNY. I told her I had a girlfriend last week, but I didn't tell her your name.
CHRISTINA. What?
DANNY. She wasn't ready for it.
CHRISTINA. Wasn't ready for it?
DANNY. Yeah – it was just easier. I know it was wrong, I'm sorry. I wish I hadn't…

Mum passes Danny a bit of cake to pass to his dad.

CHRISTINA. So you told her I was called Rebecca?
DANNY. If I say Christina, all she'll hear is Christ-ina. As far as she's concerned you might as well be called Pogrom, or Pork. *(Mum passes Danny a cup of tea.)* Thanks.
CHRISTINA. Rebecca!
DANNY. *(To Christina.)* I'm sorry.
CHRISTINA. Do I have a surname?
DANNY. Yes. I made something up.

CHRISTINA. Well?
MUM. Cake?
DANNY. Erm… Cohen, I think.
MUM. Cake?!
CHRISTINA. Cohen!
DANNY. Yes! *(To mum.)* No!
MUM. Yes or no?
DANNY. *(To mum.)* Yes!
CHRISTINA. Rebecca Cohen?
DANNY. Yes!
CHRISTINA. Oh, very original.
DANNY. Mummy…
CHRISTINA. Rebecca Cohen!
DANNY. *(To Christina.)* Ssh!
MUM. What?
DANNY. It's about Rebecca. She's not actually called Rebecca. She's called Christina and she's not Jewish.
MUM. Oh.
DANNY. I didn't tell you because I though you'd be upset.
MUM. That's alright.
DANNY. You're not angry?
MUM. You're an adult now. You're old enough to make your own choices. As long as she makes you happy that's fine by us.
DANNY. Oh, mummy. I don't believe it! Oh, thank you! *(He gets up and embraces him mum.)* Thank you!
MUM. Daniel! What are you doing? Well? Let's hear this earth-shattering news?

Danny looks around at Christina, but she has disappeared. He realises that his triumph was imaginary.

DANNY. Er… Rebecca, my girlfriend…
MUM. …Yes, when are we going to meet her?
DANNY. That's not her real name.
MUM. What to you mean?
DANNY. She's… she's not Jewish.
MUM. What? A girl called Rebecca Cohen? Not Jewish?
DANNY. She's not called Rebecca Cohen. Her name's Christina Lawson, she's Irish.
MUM. I don't understand. What happened to Rebecca? You were getting on so well.

DANNY. There never was a Rebecca. My girlfriend's called Christina. I didn't tell you because she's not Jewish.
MUM. You lied to us?
DANNY. I thought it was for the best…
MUM. You lied to us? Is that how we've brought you up?
DANNY. I'm sorry.
MUM. 'Christina'.
DANNY. Yes.
MUM. *(To dad.)* You hear that? 'Christina'. *(To Danny.)* Well, I suppose a young man has to have a bit of sex. I understand that.
DANNY. I'd like you to meet her.
MUM. I don't think that's such a good idea.
DANNY. We've been together for a while now, I think you ought to…
MUM. There's no need. I'm sure she'll understand.
DANNY. I just want you to meet her that's all. She's very important to me…
MUM. They're all very important to you at first.
DANNY. No, mummy. She's special, she's different…
MUM. That's right, Daniel! She is different. You know how we feel about this. We've talked about it enough times. There are plenty of eligible Jewish girls out there…
DANNY. But I've tried all the eligible Jewish girls. Suzie and Naomi and Kathy and…
MUM. And what was so wrong with them?
DANNY. We just didn't get on.
MUM. What about Corinne? She was a lovely girl.
DANNY. You never saw her eat.
MUM. Very funny. She was wonderful, charming. What has this girl got that she hasn't?
DANNY. Christina? She's intelligent, witty, she cares about me – she's encouraging me to write.
MUM. Not that *mishigas*[5] again!
DANNY. It's not a *mishigas!* It's what I want to do.
MUM. Get yourself a desk further from the door! That's what you should do.
DANNY. Why don't you just meet her?
MUM. I'm sorry, Daniel.
DANNY. But you'd meet her if she was Jewish. You'd meet her if she was just a friend.
MUM. But that's the whole point, Daniel. She's not Jewish and she's not just a friend. Other people may be able to marry who they want, but

we Jews cannot.
DANNY. Who's talking about marriage?
MUM. I thought she was special.
DANNY. She is.
MUM. Either she is, or she isn't.
DANNY. She is. She's very special.
MUM. Your grandfather, ***dir tsu lengere yorn***[6], he would have torn his clothes, he would have sat *shiva*[7] for you. Even to be seen with a ***shiksa***. You would be dead to him...
DANNY. ... Mummy, don't...
MUM. ... You know what happened to him, Daniel. And you know what happened to me. I've never made a secret of it...
DANNY. ... I'm just asking you to meet her...
MUM. ... By some miracle, by some unforeseen miracle, I escaped. And for what? For this?
DANNY. ... Please, I don't want to get into this.
MUM. You can't avoid it, Daniel. You were born into it. Remember that. Hitler wanted to get rid of us all, every single one of us. But he didn't quite succeed. Some of us got away. And now you come along, you and all the others, and you finish off what he started.
DANNY. That's ridiculous.
MUM. My father, *olevasholem*[8], would turn in his grave. His own grandson! His own flesh and blood! Remember the eleventh commandment, Daniel: thou shalt not give any posthumous victims to Hitler. That's what you're doing, Daniel, you're finishing Hitler's work for him.
DANNY. I'm just asking you to meet her...
MUM. I'm sorry, I'm sure she's a lovely girl – everything you say she is. But I simply cannot see it any other way. And please don't expect me to. Not after all that I've been through! Please!

She rushes off, distressed. Danny looks at his dad. The doorbell rings. No-one moves to get it. It rings again. Danny goes to answer it.

MUM. Leave it, Daniel. Alright. I'm coming!

She crosses from off-stage to answer the door. The inspector and the detective are there. The inspector has a bandage over one ear.

INSPECTOR. Mrs Feinman? Detective Inspector Richardson, this is D.C. Turner.
MUM. Come in, come in!

They come through to where Danny and his dad are. No-one pays any attention to Danny.

INSPECTOR. *(To the dad.)* Mr Feinman.
DETECTIVE. Evening!

They sit down.

MUM. I'm glad you're here. I'm so worried.
INSPECTOR. Of course.
MUM. He's making such a big mistake, I wish I could make him realise that.
INSPECTOR. I understand, Mrs Feinman.
MUM. He's never been out with a non-Jew before.
INSPECTOR. I know. A kiss here, a cuddle there, maybe, but nothing more. I've got a list.

She fetches a booklet.

DANNY. A list of what?
MUM. All his past girlfriends are here, such as they are: there's dates, what they did, when we met them, how long it lasted. It's all there. I thought it might be useful.

She hands it to the inspector. Danny looks at it over the inspector's shoulder.

DANNY. I don't believe it!
INSPECTOR. It's very kind of you to go to all that effort.
MUM. It was no effort. I keep a record anyway. *(Danny takes the book.)* The Jewish ones are in capitals. It's just that Daniel's always been so Jewish. Jewish friends, Jewish activities. Always going to the synagogue.
DANNY. … How did you know about Patricia?…
MUM. … He wanted to be a Rabbi, you know!…
DANNY. … It was a college disco. I was away, I was at college…
MUM. But that's Daniel for you – a *luftmentsh*! Head in the clouds!…

DANNY. … We hardly even kissed… *(He looks at the door.)*
MUM. … No direction…
DANNY. 'Four to five minutes, kissing only'. How could you know that?…
MUM. Even as a child he was always so interested in Jewish things. He used to spend hours writing funny little sketches about the Bible. I keep them here if you want to have a look.

She goes and gets an old school exercise book and is about to pass it to the inspector.

DANNY. Oh, no you don't!

The inspector sneezes. Danny intercepts the book.

MUM. *Gezunterheit*! *(To the detective who is eyeing up the food.)* Please. Have some cake.
DETECTIVE. Don't mind if I do.

He helps himself and spends the rest of the scene munching his way through them.

MUM. I think she's turned his head. You see, they have an awful lot of sex.
DANNY. How do you know?
INSPECTOR. How do you know?
MUM. I know where he keeps his condoms.
DANNY. Bugger!
MUM. And besides, I read his sheets.
INSPECTOR. You read his sheets?
DETECTIVE. These are delicious.
MUM. Thank you. Yes, like the Chinamen who used to read the Emperor's toilet. I've got the key to his flat. I let myself in, tidy up and I do his laundry once a week, so I read his sheets.
DANNY. …Read my sheets!
INSPECTOR. You hear that, Dave? A sheet-reader! We've never had one of those before! You'll do us out of a job Mrs Feinman.
MUM. They must be having sex all the time. Which is surprising given my Daniel's libido. He didn't start masturbating till he was sixteen.
DANNY. Woah!

The inspector sneezes again.

MUM. Let me give you something for that cold, inspector. Would you like something to drink, detective?
DETECTIVE. *(His mouth full.)* No, I'm fine. Thank you. *(About the cakes.)* Lovely.
MUM. Eat up! There's plenty more.

She goes out to the kitchen, leaving an awkward pause caused by the dad's presence. The inspector takes a sniff of nasal spray.

INSPECTOR. *(To the detective.)* She says she can prove paternity. She's taking it to court.
DETECTIVE. Don't worry about that. She's just some girl trying to get something for nothing.
INSPECTOR. Super says I'm off the squad if it's proved. I don't know, Dave. Peter's been charged with attempted murder, Joanne's on hunger strike, says she'll only end it if I become a scientologist or whatever they're called, and now this girls claiming paternity. Oh... and guess what? Jean...
DETECTIVE. What? Jean who left you...
INSPECTOR. Jean is walking!
DETECTIVE. What!
INSPECTOR. Walked right up to me in the high street.
DETECTIVE. But what about the wheelchair? I thought...
INSPECTOR. Yes, well, it seems she was just pretending.
DETECTIVE. Why?
INSPECTOR. She says I'm a terrible dancer and she didn't want to dance with me so she faked the accident. *(A pause; the detective is horrified.)* Do you think I'm a terrible dancer, Dave?
DETECTIVE. No, boss. No. You're great. You are a great dancer.
INSPECTOR. I'm going to take lessons, Dave. I'm going to crack this one.

Mum returns with a drink for the inspector and some cheese-cake.

MUM. *(To the inspector.)* Honey and lemon. My grandmother swore by them. And... *(to the detective)*... I brought you some cheesecake. Would you like to have a look at some photos. I keep them in some trunks...

INSPECTOR. *(Slightly horrified by the prospect.)* Thank you, but we have to get going.
DETECTIVE. *(Clearly disappointed.)* Oh!
DANNY. Thank God.
MUM. Are you sure?
INSPECTOR. Yes, thank you. You've been most helpful. Dave!

They get up to go.

MUM. Wait a minute, inspector. What do you think's going to happen?
INSPECTOR. I wouldn't worry about it just yet, Mrs Feinman. Most of these affairs come to nothing.
MUM. What do you mean? They say it'll soon be as bad here as in America.
INSPECTOR. I'm sure it won't come to that.
MUM. One in two Jews marrying out. What'll happen to us then, inspector? Where will we be?
INSPECTOR. Don't worry, Mrs Feinman. Danny's a sensible lad. And we'll make sure things don't get out of hand. That's what we're here for.
MUM. But what if they do get out of hand? What'll you do then?
DETECTIVE. We move in. Great cheesecake.

She opens the door for them.

INSPECTOR. We'll be in touch.

She shuts the door behind them. Danny gets up to go.

MUM. Think about what I've said, Daniel. Think about it. *(He opens the door to leave.)* Don't forget the food!

Danny picks up a couple of tupperware boxes which have been left for him by the door.

DANNY. I'll be in touch.

Danny places the bags and boxes on the pile. In a corner of the stage, 'Sam' from 'Casablanca' sits playing the piano. Danny walks over to 'Sam' at the piano.

DANNY/BOGIE. Of all the bars in the world, she had to walk into this

one. Play it, Sam. Play it like you used to.
SAM. Which one, Mr Rick?
BOGIE. You know the one I mean, Sam. I couldn't hear it without thinking of her.
SAM. I don't know if I can remember it, Mr Rick.
BOGIE. Of course you can, Sam. Play it. Play it, like you used to.

Sam turns to the piano and starts playing and singing 'A Yiddishe Mama'.

SAM. My yiddishe mama. Oh, what I'd give to see her now!
My yiddishe mama. Oh, how I miss her wrinkled brow!
Oh, how bright and joyful is the home when mama is around.
How sad, how dark it is...

As Sam sings the song, the scene changes to Danny's flat. The model Rabbi and the picture of the Western Wall are slightly less central. It's Friday night. Danny gets out a couple of sabbath candlesticks, some Palwins wine and some challah bread. He covers his head with a skullcap.

DANNY. Ready!

'Sam' stops singing. Christina enters and sits at the table.

DANNY. We ought to stand really. *(She does so.)* 'Borukh ato adonoy...' I feel a bit shy.
CHRISTINA. Go on. Don't be silly.
DANNY. OK. *'Borukh ato adonoy eloheynu melekh ho'olom, asher kidishanu b'mitzvosov v'tsivonu lehadlik ner shel shabes. Omeyn'.*

He lights the candles.

CHRISTINA. Which means?
DANNY. 'Blessed are you, Lord our God, King of the Universe, who has sanctified us with his commandments and commanded us to light the lights of the sabbath.' It should really be a woman doing this...
CHRISTINA. Diplomatic immunity.
DANNY. Feels a bit weird.
CHRISTINA. Go for it!

He waves his hands over the candles in the ritual manner.

DANNY. OK. (He picks up the wine goblet.) *'Borukh ato adonoy eloheynu melekh ho'olom, borey peri hagofen. Omeyn'* - 'Blessed are you, Lord our God, King of the Universe, who has created the fruit of the vine'. *L'khaim!*

He has a swig then passes it to her. She drinks.

CHRISTINA. Ooh! So sweet.
DANNY. I told you, it's an acquired taste. That's why Jews don't follow Jesus. We're not impressed by someone turning water into wine. We're waiting for someone who can turn this into wine.
CHRISTINA. Well, you'll be waiting a long time. Luckily I brought my own. *(She gets up and goes to fetch it.)*
DANNY. Hold on, one more.
CHRISTINA. Oops! Sorry!
DANNY. *'Borukh ato adonoy eloheynu melekh ho'olom, hamoysti lekhem min ho'oretz. Omeyn'*. 'Blessed are you, Lord our God, King of the Universe, who brings forth bread from the earth'.

He breaks off a bit of challah, adds some salt and passes it to Christina, then takes some for himself.

CHRISTINA. Mmm.
DANNY. Good, isn't it?
CHRISTINA. Delicious.
DANNY. *'Tam ganeydn'*[9] - tastes like manna from heaven, *(he adopts a comedy voice)* 'which indeed it symbolises'.
CHRISTINA. It's lovely. Is that it?
DANNY. Uh-huh.
CHRISTINA. OK. I'll get the Chinese.

She exits to the kitchen.

DANNY. Yes! '*Hamoytsi lekhem min ha*-Gate of the Orient! *Omeyn!*'
CHRISTINA. *(Off.)* What?
DANNY. I was just blessing the Gate of the Orient.
CHRISTINA. *(Returning with the Chinese.)* You sure you don't want some of your mum's borsht?
DANNY. *(With a dismissive gesture towards the pile.)* No, no! God

forbid! This is liberty! This is freedom! Friday night and we can eat what we want. *(They start getting the food ready and eating it.)* I'm so pleased we're doing this. It just feels so right.
CHRISTINA. You're not upset about your mum?
DANNY. No. Maybe a bit at first: withdrawal symptoms. But now I feel great: no phone-calls, no surprise visits at the office, I don't have to go round every other night. It's great. It's like a weight has been lifted from my shoulders. And this feels so positive. Maybe next week I'll invite some other people round, make a thing of it...
CHRISTINA. Yes, but you'll have to see your mum sometime. You can't just pretend she doesn't exist.
DANNY. Yeah, I know. Let's not talk about it now. I'll end up back on the remedies.
CHRISTINA. I don't want you to get all bitter about it and end up blaming me.
DANNY. OK.
CHRISTINA. Did you get any writing done yesterday?
DANNY. Yes, I was quite pleased. You really... you thought that stuff I gave you was OK?
CHRISTINA. Yes, it was brilliant. I told you.
DANNY. Sorry, sorry. I'm just trying to find out different ways to get you to say the same thing. Oh! That reminds me. A letter came for you today.
CHRISTINA. A letter for me? Here?
DANNY. Yes.

He goes to get it.

CHRISTINA. That's strange.

He gives it to her. She opens it.

CHRISTINA. It's from your office.
DANNY. What's it say?
CHRISTINA. 'Dear Ms Lawson. We understand that you have still not located a suitable property and have just been notified of a two-bedroom maisonette flat in the Muswell Hill area which you might find of interest. It is in excellent condition, recently refurbished to a high standard with period features, fully fitted kitchen etc. etc.'
DANNY. Sounds alright.
CHRISTINA. 'The owner has specifically asked us to approach you

about the property. He feels that you would be the ideal person to share it with him within the context of a loving, caring relationship. Please address your reply to Daniel Feinman care of our office at your earliest convenience.' *(She goes over to him and kisses him.)* Let me think about it, OK?

DANNY. Sure. Take your time.

CHRISTINA. OK. I'll move in.

DANNY. What?

CHRISTINA. I'll move in.

DANNY. Oh, Chrissie. Do you mean it?

CHRISTINA. No. I just like raising people's hopes only to cruelly dash them the next moment. Course I mean it.

They kiss.

DANNY. Let me say a '*Shekheyonu*'.

CHRISTINA. A what?

DANNY. A '*Shekheyonu*'. It's a blessing you say over anything new or special.

CHRISTINA. OK

DANNY. '*Borukh ato adonoy eloheynu melekh ha'olam shekheyonu v'kimonu v'higionu lazmen hazeh. Omeyn* - Blessed are you, Lord our God, King of the Universe, who has protected us and kept us and brought us in health to this season. Amen'. I love you, Chrissie.

CHRISTINA. I love you too. *(They kiss.)* Better not get too carried away. Not in front of the candles

DANNY. Well, you know what the Talmud says. '*V'shihu okhlin shum va'ash m'shum oneh*'[10].

CHRISTINA. Oh, yes? And what does that mean?

DANNY. You have to shag on Friday nights.

CHRISTINA. I think you're confusing the Talmud with 'Men Only'. Can I finish my Beef and Black Bean first?

DANNY. OK. *(They separate.)* You know, if we're going to do this on Friday nights, we should do something to celebrate your culture. We should do something Irish as well - well, Ulster, Orange, whatever.

CHRISTINA. Sure. We could recreate the Battle of the Boyne when we wopped the Finean traitors. I don't think so.

DANNY. You don't like talking about your background, do you?

CHRISTINA. No.

DANNY. When was the last time you went back?

CHRISTINA. My brother's wedding a couple of years ago. I could have

stayed. ITN offered me the Belfast post about the same time.
DANNY. Really?
CHRISTINA. It would have been promotion, network TV. But I don't belong there any more. I'm an ex-pat now. That's official. *(They eat.)* You haven't been to synagogue for a while.
DANNY. I know.
CHRISTINA. It's because of me, isn't it?
DANNY. Sort of.
CHRISTINA. Because they wouldn't approve?
DANNY. They're very traditional there. They'd find it hard to accept. I was thinking I might look around for a reform *shul* or a liberal one. They'd have less of a problem.
CHRISTINA. I could come with you one week. See what it's like.
DANNY. Yes, that'd be good.

He seems thoughtful.

CHRISTINA. What's the matter?
DANNY. It's just that I've been going to that *shul* since I was a boy. I don't see why I should be isolated like this: no *shul,* no family...
CHRISTINA. Maybe you should give your folks a ring.

During the next speech there is a gradual lighting change. Danny stands and starts addressing the audience, as if at some political rally.

DANNY. We may be from different backgrounds, we may be from different tribes, but with every barrier overcome, our love can only deepen. We are strengthened by our difference, we are nourished by diversity and out of our mingling, out of the merging of our two experiences, a new strength and compassion shall come about. Our trust, our love shall conquer the differences, the barriers and the obstacles, and our two cultures shall merge through us in harmony, joy and triumph - our story, of all stories, will have the most joyous of conclusions. It will have a happy ending.
SAMSON's MUM. *(Off.)* Samson! She's here again to see you. That bloody Delilah woman!
DANNY. Oh, great!

ACT TWO

Danny's cell/interrogation room as in the opening scene. The piles of food are still there, ever expanding. Danny sits in a chair with a heavy spotlight on him. We are in Mastermind pastiche territory.

QUIZMASTER. Name?
CONTESTANT. Diego Perez.
QUIZMASTER. Occupation?
CONTESTANT. Christian.
QUIZMASTER. Occupation?
CONTESTANT. Sorry. Er... Blacksmith.
QUIZMASTER. Just to remind you that at the end of the first round of questioning you were suspected of being a marrano, that is someone who secretly holds the Jewish faith whilst professing to be a true Christian. Your target is to avoid the penalty of death for you and your family, and your inquisition starts...now! On what day did our Lord Jesus Christ enter Jerusalem?
CONTESTANT. Palm Sunday.
QUIZMASTER. Correct. Who was Our Lady's Mother?
CONTESTANT. St. Anne.
QUIZMASTER. Correct. What does the doctrine of malum ex homine expound?
CONTESTANT. That mankind brought evil into the world through the original sin of our father Adam.
QUIZMASTER. Correct. Can you identify the following people?

We see a slide showing a picture of Jesus.

CONTESTANT *(Crosses himself.)* Our Lord and Saviour Jesus Christ.
QUIZMASTER. Correct.

We see a slide showing a picture of Saint Blaise or some other Martyr.

CONTESTANT. The Holy Martyr Saint Blaise, martyred by the Emperor Licinius in the year of our Lord 316.
QUIZMASTER. Correct.

We see a slide showing a brutal stereotypical picture of a Jew.

CONTESTANT. The hated betrayer and Christ-killer, the Jew.
QUIZMASTER. What is the task... *(the whistle blows)*... I've started so I'll finish... What is the task of every good Christian as regards the Christ-killer?
CONTESTANT. To banish them to Hell through chastisement and death in order to hasten the second coming of our Lord Jesus Christ.
QUIZMASTER. Correct. And at the end of that round you have scored maximum points and no passes. So congratulations, Mr Perez, you are clearly a good and faithful follower of the Father, the Son and the Holy Spirit. You are free to go.
CONTESTANT. *(Extremely relieved.)* Ah, *mazel tov! (He realises his mistake.)*
QUIZMASTER. Seize him!

* * * * * * * * * * *

The lighting opens up to reveal the parental abode. The detective sits surrounded by monitoring equipment in one corner of the stage - long-range cameras, headphones and listening equipment, as well as a pizza and a box of cream cakes to keep him going. He remains slightly lit throughout the following scene. Danny and his parents take their position around the table. Whilst all this is going on, Christina steps out and addresses the audience in her news voice.

CHRISTINA. Just a week ago, it seemed that such a summit meeting would be impossible. Mrs Feinman had up till recently stipulated that a full and complete cessation of the relationship would be necessary before all parties could come together around a table, but it seems that after intense diplomatic pressure from her son, she may now have agreed to meet face to face with Ms Lawson. So some progress is being made, although Mr Feinman and Ms Lawson have agreed to postpone discussions of the substantive territorial issue of them having moved in together until a later date, otherwise the whole thing could be a total nightmare, which it probably will be anyway. Still, can't just bury our heads in the sand and hope it goes away, more's the pity. To tell the truth, I'm not really sure why I'm going in the first place - I must be out of my tree. This is Christina Lawson from a position of nervous anticipation for News Room, Southeast.

Christina joins the others around the dinner table. They are at the desert stage. They eat for a while in silence.

DETECTIVE. *(Of his food.)* Mmm... Good.
DANNY. *(Of his food.* Mmm... Good.
CHRISTINA. Yes, it's very tasty.
MUM. Thank you. *(To Danny.)* Oh, Daniel, the information's come through about the survivor's weekend. They've got a lot more activities for children of survivors this year. *(To Christina.)* Daniel normally comes with me. It's important to keep the contact. *(To Danny.)* Naomi's going and Susie and Corinne...
DANNY. I'm not sure I can make it, actually.
MUM. I've got a form for you to fill in. Remind me to give it to you. *(A pause. She addresses Christina.)* What did you say your father did?
CHRISTINA. He's a builder. He runs his own business.
MUM. That's nice. *(It obviously isn't. She collects up the plates.)* Tea? Coffee?
DANNY. Tea, please.
CHRISTINA. Me too. White, no sugar.
MUM. I'm afraid it'll have to be black. We've just had meat, you see.
CHRISTINA. Oh, of course.
MUM. Don't worry about it, darling. I didn't expect you to know.
DANNY. Since when have you not had milk after meat?
MUM. These things become more important as you get older.

Mum goes out to the kitchen. There is a difficult pause.

CHRISTINA. *(To Dad.)* Nice pudding.

No reply.

DANNY. *(Quietly, to Christina.)* He's tired. Works very hard.

Danny reaches into his pocket, pulls out a homeopathic bottle and takes a couple of drops. He is about to put it away when Christina takes it off him and swigs a whole load directly from the bottle. She hands it back to him and he puts it away. Mum returns with some plastic bags, tupperware boxes and some Y-fronts.

MUM. Here's the food for you to take home. *(She hands them to Daniel.)* And I brought you some underwear.
DANNY. Mummy!
MUM. Ach! It gives me pleasure.

She goes back out again. Christina points to her watch and mouths 'let's not stay long'. Danny agrees.

DANNY. Did you see the football last night, Dad?

Mum returns.

MUM. It's too late for him. He's too exhausted. *(She hands out the teas.)* Here we are. Did you bring any washing, Daniel?
DANNY. No. I didn't.
MUM. Oh, don't worry. I'll pop in tomorrow and get it.
DANNY. No, it's alright. There's no need...
MUM. It's no problem. I'm passing that way...
DANNY. Honestly, it doesn't matter...
MUM. I'll get it tomorrow...
DANNY. I'd really rather you didn't...
MUM. Don't be silly...
DANNY. I'm not being silly...
MUM. It's no problem...
DANNY. No! I don't want you to!

Things have suddenly got out of hand. There is an awkward pause.

DANNY. Christina and I are moving in together. *(He waits to see the effect of his bombshell. Mum remains silent.)* We've been going out for quite a while now. We get on really well and I want Christina to move in with me. *(Silence.)* We just wanted you to know, that's all. (Silence.) Aren't you going to say anything?
MUM. What do you want me to say? *Mazel tov*?

DANNY. I know it's not what you would have wanted...
MUM. No, it's not what I would have wanted.
DANNY. Mummy, Chrissie and I really want to...
MUM. Excuse me.

She goes into the kitchen. Danny and Christina look at each other. He decides to follow, leaving Christina to talk to his dad.

CHRISTINA. I know you had probably hoped Danny would settle down with a Jewish woman. But we do feel very strongly for each other. And I want you to know that Danny's Jewishness is very important to me.

No reply. Christina is saved by Danny's return, followed by his mum.

CHRISTINA. *(To Danny.)* Maybe we ought to go.
DANNY. No.
CHRISTINA. Danny!
DANNY. No! I want to sort this out.

Everyone sits down.

MUM. Daniel feels it would be good for us to talk openly. Maybe he's right. You're an intelligent girl, Christina. I won't try and insult you by being anything less than honest. As you know, Daniel is our only son. Sometimes he's disappointed us, but whatever he's done we've always supported him. However, as Jewish parents, there is one thing which we cannot condone, one thing which for us, is absolutely beyond the pale and that is that he marries outside the faith.
DANNY. OK...
MUM. Please, you wanted me to talk so let me finish. *(To Christina.)* It's nothing personal to you. I don't know you, I know very little about you. What I've seen, I like, but that's not the issue here. I wish it were as simple as that. You know what we Jews have been through in our long history, the number of times we've been threatened with extinction. In my own lifetime, we've had to endure the Holocaust, when millions of Jews were killed just for being Jews. I myself lost all of my family and was lucky to come out alive. I'm not telling you this to get your sympathy, I'm just trying to get you to see why we feel that it's so important to make sure that our line continues, to make sure we don't marry out.
CHRISTINA. I understand what you're saying, but...

DANNY. Chrissie and I have talked about this a lot...
MUM. Are you planning to get married?
DANNY. No.
MUM. Why not?
DANNY. Well, one thing at a time.
MUM. So what is this, then? A fling?
DANNY. No.
CHRISTINA. It's a serious commitment. We feel very close to each other.
MUM. *(To Christina.)* I don't think you realise what you're letting yourself in for. We're a very tight-knit community, we might seem very normal at first glance, but actually we're very different. Having a relationship is hard enough, there are enough problems without putting these enormous difficulties in your way.
CHRISTINA. We know that.
MUM. And what about the children? Have you thought about them?
DANNY. It's early days yet...
MUM. You have to think about these things. Have you thought about what it might be like for them having a Jewish father and a Christian mother?

Christina and Danny come out of the scene and speak the following rhyme, as if to a child, with appropriate hand gestures.

CHRISTINA. There's the church...
DANNY. *(Slightly embarrassed.)*... Or synagogue...
CHRISTINA. There's the steeple...
DANNY. ...The sort of roof bit...
CHRISTINA/DANNY. ...Look inside, and there's the people...
DANNY. ...with the men on one side and the women on the other.
CHRISTINA. What?

Back to the main scene.

CHRISTINA. Any children we may have, Danny can raise them as Jews, it's not a problem.
MUM. I'm afraid it is a problem. According to our laws, if the mother isn't Jewish, then the children aren't Jewish.
DANNY. That's what the orthodox think...
MUM. That's the way it is.

CHRISTINA. I would be perfectly happy for them to be brought up as Jews, they can have a *barmitzvah*, they can go to... go to...sh..sh.. *(She prepares to make a big verbal leap. She is going to say 'shul' instead of 'synagogue'. She shares her mental preparation with the audience.)* I'm not going to say synagogue. I'm going to say *'Shul'. Shul*. I've said it to Danny. I can say it now. 'They can go to *shul'*. *(She turns back to Mum.)* ... they can go to...synagogue. *(To herself.)* Frig it!
MUM. What about circumcision? Would you let your son be circumcised?
CHRISTINA. Circumcision?

Danny addresses the audience in presenter mode.

DANNY. Is it (a) A holy covenant between God and his people; (b) A cultural rite of passage marking the child's entrance into the community; or (c) A barbaric and archaic act which has no relevance or meaning nowadays. Answers on a postcard please to Christina...

Back to the main scene.

CHRISTINA. The thing is, I personally have no religion. I won't be advancing any alternative.
MUM. You're Christian, aren't you?
CHRISTINA. No. I don't believe. I don't go to church.
MUM. But you were brought up as Christian?
CHRISTINA. We were all made very aware of what we were, but I wouldn't call bunking off Sunday school for five years being brought up Christian...
MUM. You celebrate Christmas?
CHRISTINA. I send a few cards...
MUM. You have a Christmas tree?
CHRISTINA. Yes, but...
MUM. There you are then.
CHRISTINA. It's only a Christmas tree. It's not even Christian, it's pagan. It doesn't mean anything.
MUM. Not to you, maybe. But to us. To us it means something.

The lighting switches to the area where the detective is monitoring developments. The main scene stays half-lit. Inspector enters. His ear is still bandaged, his cold is still there and he is also wearing a neck-brace.

INSPECTOR. How's it going?
DETECTIVE. Jesus, boss! What's happened to you?
INSPECTOR. Oh. I went to see my mum in the home. She managed a game of dominoes.
DETECTIVE. That's nice.
INSPECTOR. Not really. *(He indicated his neck-brace.)* She's a very poor loser. May I?

He takes the equipment off the detective. The headphones are obviously a problem, but he tries his best. We return to the main scene.

MUM. What about conversion? Have you thought about that?
CHRISTINA. Yes, but I'm not really interested.
MUM. I thought you weren't a Christian.
CHRISTINA. I'm not.
MUM. So what have you got to lose?
CHRISTINA. I don't want to belong to any religion. I just want to be kept out of it.
DANNY. Christina feels she would be doing it for the wrong reasons.
MUM. Then your children won't be Jewish.
DANNY. There are Liberal Synagogues...
MUM. If the mother's not Jewish, then the children aren't Jewish.
CHRISTINA. Shouldn't it be the type of Jewish upbringing which counts, the quality of the upbringing, not simply the number of Jewish parents...
MUM. Listen, darling. That just goes to show, you don't know. How could you? We carry with us thousands of years of persecution and pogroms. That's something you can't just wipe away, you can't just pretend it didn't happen...
CHRISTINA. Obviously, I don't know what it's like to experience...
MUM. Exactly, darling. You don't know. You can never know. Being Jewish is not something you can just pick up like that. It's something you're born into.
CHRISTINA. I come from Belfast. I've seen the pain which these divisions can cause. And I just think that sometimes it's better to put all those things behind us.
MUM. Put those things behind us! How can we? How can we put them behind us! That's what we are! We are different! We are all those things - the past, with all its suffering and pain and joy. We mustn't forget that.

Forget the past and you forget yourself.That's what you're doing, Daniel.
DANNY. No, I'm not.
MUM. You're cutting yourself off from us.
DANNY. I'm not cutting myself off from you. You're cutting yourselves off from me, telling me I cant be a Jew, I can't remain part of the community.
MUM. But you can't if you marry out.
DANNY. That's not true!
DAD. Daniel! Your mother's right.

His father has spoken. Daniel is stunned. The lights come up on the policemen, equally amazed.

INSPECTOR. We might have to make a move here, Dave.

The lights dim again on the policemen and we return to the family. However, from this point on the lights gradually fade back up on the policemen until they become part of the main scene.

MUM. I want you to understand one thing, Daniel. If you move in together, you can forget about seeing us again. Don't expect to have anything to do with us. There are millions of gentiles, but there are so few of us. Can't you see the problems she's causing?
CHRISTINA. The problems I'm causing! There wouldn't be any problems, if you people didn't behave like this.
MUM. 'You people'! What do you mean 'you people'? You mean the Jews? The dirty Jews, the Yids!...
CHRISTINA. ...I didn't mean that...
MUM. ...Well, why not just come out and say it?

The three of them talk at the same time.

CHRISTINA. That's not what I meant.
DANNY. She didn't mean it like that.
MUM. You hear that, Daniel? You hear what she's saying?...
CHRISTINA. ...For heaven's sake...
MUM. ...What did I tell you? Your girlfriend, she's all sweetness and light at the moment, but you wait, you wait till the first time you have an argument and you're shouting and screaming at each other, you listen whether she doesn't call you a 'dirty Jew'...

CHRISTINA. I didn't mean it like that.
MUM. ...Do you think I'm making this up? I've seen it happen.
DANNY. ...That's not how she meant it...
MUM. If ever they come for you, Daniel - and it might happen, remember that - if ever they come for you, do you think she'll get in the cattle-truck with you. Oh no! She'll just stand there, smiling, whilst they take you away...
CHRISTINA. ...How can you say that!...
MUM. ...I tell you I've seen it happen. Why should she be any different? Look at what they're doing to each other in Ireland...
CHRISTINA. ...How dare you!...
MUM. ...You can say you're not a Jew as much as you like, but you'll always be a Jew to them.
CHRISTINA. Now you listen to me! You think just because of what you've been through you have the right to say or do whatever you want. Well, you don't! Because nothing justifies racist behaviour, and that's what this is. Racism!
DANNY. ...Chrissie!...
CHRISTINA. All this chosen people stuff! It's just the same old sectarian shit under another name. She's a racist, that's all.
DANNY. Chrissie, please!...
MUM. See, Daniel. Scratch the surface and what do you get. They all hate us deep down.
CHRISTINA. No, you are a selfish bullying racist, trying to load your screwed-up shit onto another human being.
MUM. You hear how she speaks to me?
CHRISTINA. Come on, Danny, let's go. I feel a burst of really anti-Semitism coming on. Danny!

She leaves the room.

INSPECTOR. Dave!
DETECTIVE. Daniel Feinman, I'm arresting you in accordance with Deuteronomy chapter 7, verses 1-3, Numbers 25: 1-8, Exodus 34: 15 and numerous other counts. You have the right to remain silent but if you do the fact that you remain silent will be noted by a jury and might be used in evidence against you.
MUM. You happy now, Daniel? You see how she talked to me? Maybe I am selfish, a racist, all the things she called me. But it doesn't matter. I survived when so few others did. I know what I feel and I have to do what I think's right. I have to repay my debt. Yes, it's a debt. I have to

put back a Jewish life where so many were taken away. Now, I only have one child, but he can have children, and his children can have children, and so our numbers will return and we can laugh in Hitler's face. I have to do that. Otherwise, why was I spared?

CHRISTINA. *(From the hallway.)* Are you coming? Danny? Danny!
MUM. Daniel.

He gets up, walks to the door and opens it, but his exit is blocked by a wall of tupperware boxes. He closes the door again. From off-stage we hear Christina calling his name, as Mum and Dad leave the stage. The policemen set up the cell as at the start of the play, then leave Danny alone in the chair.

DANNY. *(Shouting off.)* I want to see a lawyer.
DETECTIVE. *(Off.)* No way!

The door opens and the inspector enters, still with neck-brace and bandaged ear, but without his cold. He begins preparing a line of coke.

DANNY. How long are you going to keep me here? *(The inspector is too busy preparing his coke.)* Excuse me? How long are you going to keep me here?
INSPECTOR. As long as it takes.

The inspector sniffs his line. The detective enters, carrying some tupperware and plastic bags. He has put on a bit of weight and is eating some shtrudel he has taken from one of the bags.

DETECTIVE. Alright, boss. *(He adds the new food parcels to one of the piles.)*
INSPECTOR. 10.21 D.C. Turner enters room.
DETECTIVE. Good stuff, this. Want some?
INSPECTOR. No thanks. I seem to have lost my appetite. This medicine you gave me is great. My cold's completely gone. What did you say it was called again?
DETECTIVE. Er...I've forgotten.
INSPECTOR. Oh. *(To Danny.)* Cigarette? (*Danny declines. He takes out a travel-pack of six tissues and offers one to Danny.)* Tissue? *(Danny*

declines. The inspector blows his nose momentously.) So. Daniel... *(He reads from a Bible.)* 'When the Lord your God brings you to the land that you are about to enter and possess, and he dislodges many nations before you - the Hittites, Girgashites, Amorites, Canaanites, Perizzites, Hivites and Jebusites, seven nations much larger than you, you shall not make marriages with them: do not give your daughters unto their sons or take their daughters for your sons.' You hear that, Daniel? 'You shall not make marriages with them.' Now, where's that from, Danny? Can you guess?

DANNY. The Bible.

INSPECTOR. The Bible. The Old Testament. The Torah. *'Lo tiskhateyn bom bit'kho* - you shall not make marriages with them'.

DETECTIVE. *(Aggressively.)* '*Lo takhsan imeyhem*'[11]! Get it?!

INSPECTOR. Dave, can you get us a drink of water?

DETECTIVE. I was just playing tough. It's my turn.

INSPECTOR. Dave.

He goes out.

INSPECTOR. 10.25 pm, D.C. Turner leaves the room.

DANNY. Who are you ?

INSPECTOR. Who are we? Jewish Affairs, Danny. That's who we are.

DANNY. Jewish Affairs.

INSPECTOR. That's right. As in 'Keep you affairs Jewish affairs'.

DANNY. What?

INSPECTOR. We make sure that Jews remain Jews, if you see what I mean.

DANNY. But you don't even look Jewish.

INSPECTOR. What do you expect? Black hats, beards, sidelocks? We're undercover, son. That's how we work.

DANNY. This is weird.

INSPECTOR. Kafkaesque, eh? You're in big trouble, Danny.

Detective pokes his head round the door. He is about to speak but the inspector holds up his hand to stop him.

INSPECTOR. 10.26, D.C. Turner re-enters the room.

DETECTIVE. Boss, that's Jean on the phone. She says your eldest's going ahead with the operation - she just feels she was born in the wrong body and she feels happier this way.

INSPECTOR. Tell her I'll ring her later. *(Detective goes out.)* The ten

comm... oh, 10.26, D.C. Turner leaves room... The ten commandments, Danny. They're divided into two sections. Did you know that? The first five are between Man and God and the second five are between Man and Man. Now the fifth commandment's very interesting because it seems like it's a commandment between Man and Man, but our Rabbis tell us that it's so important that it's included in the section between Man and God. And do you know which one that is, Danny? Well? Do you?
DANNY. 'Honour thy father and thy mother'.
INSPECTOR. That's right. 'Honour they father and thy mother'...

Detective returns with a glass of water.

DETECTIVE. 10.28, D.C. Turner re-enters the room.
INSPECTOR. Honour thy father and thy mother, Danny. Do you do that? Do you honour them? *(Danny shrugs.)* Is that why you're with Christina? Is that something that makes them pleased? Something that makes them proud? You know how your mother feels. Have you ever once thought about her, about what you're doing to her? Because one day, you'll be a dad, then you'll know. Oh, yes! You'll know the hurt you children can cause! The pain, the disappointment, the heartbreak. But do you ever think about us? About how we might feel, about what you might be doing to us? Oh, no! As long as you can do what you want, as long as you're OK, that's all that matters, isn't it...

He breaks down. The detective hands him a tissue.

DETECTIVE. It's alright, boss, it's alright. *(He helps the inspector to his feet and out the door, singing to calm him down. To Danny, once the inspector's left.)* Happy, now? That's how your mum must feel. But do you care? Like fuck you do. You know, your dad had made himself ill working to send you to good schools, your mum makes all that lovely food, most of which you don't even appreciate, and this is how you repay them. *(Menacingly.)* Well? Come on then? What have you got to say for yourself? Speak up! Hello!!
DANNY. Look, I'm not saying it's...

The inspector re-enters and goes over to a corner. Over the next exchange he prepares some more coke.

DETECTIVE. 10.30, D.I. Richardson re-enters - no, 10.31 almost.
DANNY. I'm not saying...

DETECTIVE. 10.31.
DANNY. I'm not saying it's their fault, but they sent me to public school, to university, they pushed me into the British system, and then they're surprised when I end up meeting a non-Jewish girl and marrying out.
DETECTIVE. So, we are going to marry out?
DANNY. Living together out then.
DETECTIVE. *(Pauses for a moment, then, suddenly, rising to a crescendo.)* 'An abomination is committed in Israel; for Judah hath profaned the holiness of the Lord and hath married the daughter of a strange god. And the Lord will cut off the man that doeth this, yea, cut him off from the tabernacle of Jacob and from all his people, and from the Lord himself.'

The detective is in religious ecstasy. The inspector takes a sniff.

INSPECTOR. Wow! Night Nurse eat your heart out! *(He pokes his head out the door.)* Marlene!...
DETECTIVE. *(Still in ecstasy.)*... 10.32, D.I. Richardson pokes his head out the door!...
INSPECTOR. Which cell should we put him in?
DETECTIVE. 10.32, D.I. Richardson puts his head back in the room and closes the door!
INSPECTOR. 10.33, D.I. Richardson sits back down.
DETECTIVE. So what's wrong with the Jewish girls, Danny? Too ugly? Too loud? Too much like your mum? Or don't they put out? Is that it?
INSPECTOR. ...D.C. Turner poised like a panther...
DETECTIVE. ...Won't let you near them until you're married, and then it's through a hole in the sheet? Eh? I bet Christina's not like that.
INSPECTOR. ...D.C. Turner floating like a butterfly, stinging like a bee...
DETECTIVE. She's fit looking. You've done well there, mate. I envy you. I bet she does all sorts of things the Jewish girls would never do...
INSPECTOR. ...behind suspect, leaning over dramatically...
DETECTIVE. I bet she loves your little circumcised putz, eh, Danny? Bet she'd bend over backwards for you? That's why you're with her, isn't it? Isn't it?

Silence.

INSPECTOR. ...Dramatic pause... Suspect on the ropes... I'll go and see about the cell.

He leaves.

DETECTIVE. 10.35, D.I. Richardson leaves the room.

The detective gets a chocolate bar out of his pocket. He brandishes it at Danny, takes a bite and leaves the room.

DANNY. *(Shouting off.)* I want to see a... 10.36, both policemen left the room... I want to see a lawyer!

We hear the detective, off stage, laughing at this ridiculous idea, then some ghostly music.

DANNY. What's going on? Who's there?

A ghostly apparition appears. A man in beggar's clothing.

MESSIAH. I am the Messiah, born on the day the Temple was destroyed to bring redemption to the world. But this I cannot do if you turn away from your people.

He vanishes. Another apparition appears. A traditional Hasidic Jew.

GREAT GRANDFATHER. I am your great-grandfather, the *Tsolniker Rebbe*[12]. Who will say *kaddish*[13] for me and my children if you turn away from your family? Do not condemn me to eternal wandering.

He vanishes. Another apparition appears, dressed in a Dickensian cloak.

GHOST. I am the ghost of Christmas past...and I think I'm in the wrong play.

He exits. We hear mum's voice.

MUM. *(Off.)* Daniel! Daniel! Sorry to disturb you. *(She enters.)* I've brought something for you.

She gestures off stage. Christina enters to 'Ride of the Walkyries', pushing a wheelbarrow full of food parcels. She is dressed in fantasy Nazi gear - leather boots, teddy, swastika armband, SS hat. She dumps the food and poses.

MUM. Well? What do you think, Daniel? She's a lovely girl.
DANNY. No! This is wrong!
MUM. I understand, Daniel. You've tried with Jewish girls, but you just don't fancy them. It's a chemical thing between you and Aryan women. So enjoy!
DANNY. No, this is not what I want. *(Mum exits. Danny looks at Christina.)* Oh, God! I wish they'd never invested Claudia Schiffer! Or Michele Pfeiffer. Or Anthea Turner. Or Virginia Bottomley...

The detective opens the door.

DETECTIVE. Feinman! Your lawyer's here! *(Danny is transfixed by Christina.)* Oy! Feinman! Your lawyer! *(Christina exits. Danny looks towards the door. Detective shouts off.)* In here! No! Here!

Moses enters, the detective closes and locks the door loudly behind him. Moses stands there shyly. He is reminiscent of an accountant or an academic - the very opposite of Charlton Heston - and speaks with a speech impediment.

MOSES. S..s..so sorry. All these cells look the same. H..How..How do you do, Mr Feinman. I'm Moses. I'll be representing you.
DANNY. Moses what?
MOSES. Just Moses. Moshe. It's from the Hebrew meaning 'to draw out' - '*Ki min-hamayim m'shishihu*'[14] - because they drew me out of the bulrushes.
DANNY. Wait a minute. Are you telling me you're the Moses? From the Bible?
MOSES. Well, I wouldn't like to say the Moses, but I'm certainly the one from the Bible. May I sit down? *(He sits down and opens his briefcase. He starts looking through papers for the relevant documents. In the process, he empties some of the contents of his case onto the table [packed lunch etc.] This is not a hot-shot lawyer.)* Right. Where are we now?... I'm sure it's in here somewhere... *(He brings out a couple of letters.)*... I must remember to post these...
DANNY. I'm very honoured you're representing me, but you're not

exactly how I imagined Moses.
MOSES. *(Still involved in his preparations.)* Really?
DANNY. Yes. I mean, Moses the lawgiver, the thunderer, the man who caused the Red Sea to part. Where's your beard, your manly chest, your big booming voice...?
MOSES. Bloody Charlton Heston. Everywhere I go, it's the same old story...
DANNY. Sorry, I didn't mean to upset you.
MOSES. It's alright. I understand. I was convinced God had got the wrong man myself. I told him so - Exodus 3, 11. I don't know if you've noticed, but I've got this stammer...
DANNY. Yes. That must be a problem in court.
MOSES. Well, I do tend to get a bit nervous in public. My brother Aaron used to do all the speaking for me. I just sort of did the tricks.
DANNY. So he'll be helping us in court?
MOSES. Oh, no! He doesn't approve of mixed marriages. Now where is that blooming folder, pardon my French...
DANNY. Tell me something, Moses. Why are you defending me?
MOSES. *(Still searching.)* Everyone has the right to a defence - even people who enter mixed-faith relationships.
DANNY. OK, but what happened to 'Thou shalt not marry out', 'thou shalt not give thy daughters to their sons', all that stuff? You wrote that, didn't you?
MOSES. It was dictated to me.
DANNY. Yes, but they're your laws, the laws of Moses, the five Books of Moses. You were getting people swallowed up by the earth for breaking them, stoning them and everything. So shouldn't you be prosecuting? Why are you defending me?
MOSES. Because I married out.
DANNY. Hello! You married out!
MOSES. Twice, as a matter of fact. Once in the desert before the Burning Bush, and once later on to an Ethiopian woman.
DANNY. You married out!
MOSES. Yes.
DANNY. Twice!
MOSES. Yes, alright!
DANNY. And you weren't punished?
MOSES. No. Aaron and Miriam, my sister, and quite a few others tried to kick up a stink the second time - said I wasn't worthy of leading the Children of Israel, that sort of thing, but God struck my sister down with leprosy and it sort of blew over after that.[15]

DANNY. Of course.
MOSES. A lot of us married out in those days. Joseph, several of his brothers, King Solomon - he had hundreds of wives, none of them Jewish. Even King David might not count as Jewish nowadays - his great-grandmother, Ruth, was a Moabite. See, we didn't have that matrilineage thing - the line going through the mother. Made things a lot easier.
DANNY. But if all these people married out, including you, the most righteous man who ever lived, the man who came closest to God...
MOSES. *(Blushing.)* Stop it!...
DANNY. ...If you all married out and we're still here today, then it can't be such a bad thing.
MOSES. Well, it's not quite that clear. There are certain apparent contradictions between the laws laid down in the Torah, the Five Books of Me, and some of the actions of its principal characters.
DANNY. I know, but...

Christina enters carrying a small table and some figures. Over the next few exchanges she sets up a crib in a corner of the stage. Danny watches her whilst Moses talks.

MOSES. The prohibitions are very explicit. And it's not just the Torah. It's the later writings as well - the Book of Ezra, the Talmud, the Gaonim.
DANNY. Yes.
MOSES. And then there's history. The prosecution will argue - and they've got a good case - that whenever Jews have started to marry out in large numbers, they have ended up disappearing. The only way to protect our tradition and our heritage is to protect our numbers. You can see their point. Right. Down to '*takhlis*'... to business. *(He has found what he is looking for - a folder.)* Now... Oh! *(He takes out a copy of 'Hello' magazine.)*... How did that get there?... somewhere I've got a list of our witnesses so far - ah, here we are: witnesses for the defence: your cousin Derek - the one who married the Filipino; the head of the Yehushua Second Coming Church of California, Rabbi Yamamoto, and Arthur Miller.

He hands Danny a tiny piece of paper. Danny is very disappointed.

MOSES. Not much, I'm afraid, but it's a start. I also have a list...

somewhere... *(More searching through files.)* of the opposition's witnesses. Ah, here we are. *(He pulls out a thick wad of papers.)* Rather a lot, I'm afraid. All the big names - prophets, Rabbis, martyrs. A bit like God's on 'This is Your Life'.

He thinks this is terribly funny and laughs uproariously. Danny is looking at Christina.

MOSES. What's the matter? You look like you've seen a burning bush.
DANNY. What if I've made a mistake?
MOSES. What do you mean?
DANNY. What if my mum's right? What if I am rushing into things? Maybe Christina can never understand what it's like to be Jewish.
MOSES. *(Starts packing up his things.)* I can't help you there, I'm afraid. I'll defend you, but you must make your own mind. Just be true to yourself. Remember what Hillel said: *'Im eyn ani li, mi li* - If I am not for myself, then who will be for me?'

Christina starts humming 'Away in a Manger'.

DANNY. *'U'kasher ani l'atzmi, ma ani* - And if I am only for myself, then what am I?' Don't I have to think about my parents, my community?
MOSES. And what about Christina? Don't you have to think about her?
DANNY. Yes.
MOSES. *'Im lo akshav, ey matay* - if not now, when?'

Moses leaves. Danny looks at the kneeling Christina. The scene changes into Danny's (and Christina's) flat. He walks towards her.

DANNY. Hi. *(She doesn't reply.)* I'm sorry.
CHRISTINA. You stayed. Why didn't you come with me when I left?
DANNY. I'm sorry. I... she said some terrible things. You mustn't let her get to you.
CHRISTINA. I won't.
DANNY. I should have known. She's been through this thing, she...
CHRISTINA. You know why I left Ulster. It's because I realised that I wasn't as liberal and right-on as I liked to think I was. My mother was at Enniskillen when the bomb went off. She wasn't injured, not physically, not directly. But she changed. She used to be so generous, welcoming.

She used to laugh all the time. All the time. And then she just became frightened. She never went out, she hardly ever said anything, she just sat at home and... and it was like she waited for the cancer to come and get her. And I hated them for what they did to her. I felt such rage, such anger. I was no different from my dad or my uncle or any of my country cousins marching in their orange lodges, shouting their 'fuck you's' at the 'Catholic bastards'. It had been there inside me all the time, just beneath the surface, ready to spew up at the first opportunity. And that frightened me. So I ran away. I just ran away. I didn't want to be like that, so I just changed my accent and got the fuck out of there as quickly as I could. I've been offered the Belfast job again.

DANNY. Why didn't you tell me.

CHRISTINA. I was going to say no.

DANNY. And now? *(She shrugs.)* If it's to do with what happened, I'm sorry, I didn't think that...

CHRISTINA. There you go again. It's always your fault, always about you. Well, this is about me for a change. You know when I left your parents' place part of me felt quite pleased. I thought: yes! At last! I'm the victim! I'm being discriminated against! It felt good. I could really get into that feeling, really get hooked on it. It's very tempting.

DANNY. I don't understand...

CHRISTINA. It's easy to feel proud of yourself when you're a victim, but real identity's a bit more complicated. And that's the challenge, isn't it? You've helped me a lot, Danny. You're so rooted in your background. It's a pain in the arse, but it's a good thing to be.

DANNY. You're going to take the job, aren't you?

CHRISTINA. You could always come with me. *(Danny is unable to say 'yes'.)* I thought so. Pity. We could have had such a good time. We could have had some lovely Jewish Orange children. Some lovely Jaffa Oranges. Pity.

They look at each other.

* * * * * * * * * * *

We hear some Klezmer music as the scene changes to Danny's parents' place. Plastic food bags fall down from the ceiling so that the stage becomes littered with them. The detective, now really quite obese, Danny's mum and dad are seated round the table, well into their meal. Danny leaves Christina and joins them. He is very quiet and sits in a similar position to his dad. Christina leaves the stage.

MUM. That's a terrible thing to happen.
DETECTIVE. Yes, it was a shame for him. I mean, the chances of it happening must have been millions to one. One minute he's walking along, minding his own business, the next a poodle falls out of a twelfth storey window, lands on his head and kills him stone dead.
MUM. Terrible.
DETECTIVE. Poodle got up and walked away. He was just in the wrong place at the wrong time, but somehow, it sort of feels right that he went like that.
MUM. When's the funeral?
DETECTIVE. Don't know. They lost the body. *(Mum looks surprised.)* It's a long story.
MUM. Poor man. Right! Who's for some seconds. Danny? *(Danny gives little of no response.)*
DETECTIVE. I'll have some, if I may.
MUM. *(Getting up.)* Bit of everything?
DETECTIVE. Don't worry. I'll get it.

She sits back down again. The detective goes off to the kitchen with his plate.

MUM. You know, Daniel used to write detective stories. Have you still got them? He should show them to you, Dave, you might enjoy them.
DETECTIVE. *(Returning with more food.)* That'd be nice.

Awkward pause. The only sound is the detective eating.

MUM. I saw Corinne yesterday in the supermarket. She sends her love. *(Pause.)* I've got her new number, do you want it?
DANNY. No.
MUM. I invited her round for *shabes* next week.
DANNY. What?
MUM. She's coming round next *shabes.*
DANNY. Why?
MUM. I thought you might like to see her.
DANNY. I'd like to see her on a one-way flight to a war zone.
MUM. I've invited her parents as well.
DANNY. What about the Rabbi? Is he coming? And the caterers? Have

you sorted them out?
MUM. Well, somebody has to. Look at you. It's been weeks now. I thought you'd put all this behind you. Such a face on you, my poor boy! Such a tragedy you've suffered. Please God you should be spared a real tragedy!
DANNY. Oh, here it comes. It's Holocaust time!
MUM. I beg your pardon?
DANNY. I was wondering what had happened to it. We've been here over an hour and there's been no mention of the Holocaust. You're slacking, you're losing your touch.
MUM. I will not be spoken to like that.
DANNY. You know what your problem is. You want to be the only one who's suffered, the only one who's ever known any pain. Well, I'm fed up with it! I'm fed up with feeling a failure because I haven't been through what you've been through, because I haven't suffered like you suffered.
MUM. What are you talking about?
DANNY. You know, ever since I was a boy I have had these daydreams about being in a car crash of getting some terrible disease or anything, anything that would make me feel that I'd suffered as well. I feel so bloody guilty all the time that I've had such an easy, unsuffering life. But this is my life. I'm sorry, there's nothing I can do about it, that's just the way it is.
MUM. Daniel, I never...
DANNY. ...And I can't make it better for you. I've tried, but it's just not possible. Not unless I put my head in a bloody oven, it's just not possible.
DETECTIVE. Oy! That's enough, son!
DANNY. *(To detective.)* Shut up! *(To mum.)* And you think this is something I want to pass on to my children? This morbid, fucked-up disease. I'd rather see the whole thing die out, really I would. If we can't pass on a positive, constructive form of Judaism, just your terrible, clinging, choking Holocaust obsession, then the whole fucking thing deserves to die out and good riddance to it.

He gets up and goes.

MUM. Daniel!...

DAD. *(Holding back Danny's mum.)* Leave the boy alone.

* * * * * * * * * * *

A brief burst of 'tradition' bridges into the next scene. The parental abode is replaced by a desk and chair, where the angel who approached Abraham earlier is seated. Abraham comes up to him. The music cuts.

ABRAHAM. I demand to see God.
ANGEL. Do you have an appointment?
ABRAHAM. I don't need one. I am Abraham, father of his chosen people.
ANGEL. *(Looking through an appointments book.)* It's just that he's quite busy at the moment preparing a spate of natural disasters... How about Tuesday next?
ABRAHAM. I want to see him now!
ANGEL. Well, what's it about!
ABRAHAM. My people.
ANGEL. What's wrong with them?
ABRAHAM. Have you any idea what's happened to them over the past few thousand years? Pogroms, persecutions, massacres. They have been treated like animals - worse than animals.
ANGEL. But they've survived.
ABRAHAM. Yes.
ANGEL. Thousands of years. An '*Or lagoyim* - a light unto the nations'. Apart from Robert Maxwell. So what's the problem?
ABRAHAM. Look at this. (*He gets out a thick booklet.)* It's the updated list of my descendants. That's me, Isaac, the twelve tribes *(he flicks through the book)* the Middle Ages, the Hasidim - then what? Look! Dov-Ber Halpern, Rachel Halpern - married Michael Feinman - their son Daniel Feinman and then it stops. It just stops.
ANGEL. Ah, yes...
ABRAHAM. And it's not just him. *(Turning over various pages.)* Look: here, and here, and here. Within a few generations that'll be it. I'll have no descendants left. What about my covenant?
ANGEL. Your covenant?
ABRAHAM. Yes. My agreement. With God.
ANGEL. Ah, that. Didn't you read the small print?

ABRAHAM. No.
ANGEL. Ah, well if you'd read it, you'd have seen that the number of your descendants can go down as well as up?
ABRAHAM. As countless as the sand in the desert, that's what I was told.
ANGEL. Look. I understand your concern but I'm afraid there's nothing we can do about it. It's the inevitable result of free will, the enlightenment and the great taste of crispy bacon.
ABRAHAM. But what about my people? What about the Children of Israel?
ANGEL. Who understands God's plans? Listen, your people are not the same as they were two, three thousand years ago. They're always changing, always redefining themselves. There have been crises like this before - worse. The destruction of the Temple, the exile from Spain, the false messiahs. And every time your people have emerged changed and renewed. Maybe that's what'll happen this time: maybe it's time for one of those changes, time to adapt to the modern world once more. Then again, maybe you shouldn't have agreed to the covenant in the first place. Maybe you should have just invested in the privatised utilities like everyone else.

The scene begins to change into Danny's flat.

ABRAHAM. Now he tells me!

* * * * * * * * * *

Danny's flat, though with everything packed up. Suitcases and boxes in the middle of the stage. Abraham and the angel leave. Danny is sweeping the food parcels and tupperware boxes off the stage. He exits with them, leaving the stage empty. The doorbell rings.

DANNY. *(Off.)* Can you get that?

Christina enters and opens the door It's Moses.

MOSES. Hello! Christina?
CHRISTINA. Moses. Hi! Come in. Danny won't be a sec.

MOSES. I've heard a lot about you.
CHRISTINA. Likewise. Read all your books. I'd offer you something to drink, but we're all packed.
MOSES. That's alright. *(A slightly awkward moment.)* I'm very pleased about you and Daniel. Getting back together again.
CHRISTINA. Against my better judgement.
MOSES. You don't mean that, do you?
CHRISTINA. No. He's begged and grovelled and I've nobly forgiven him. Actually we were over in Belfast last month, found a lovely flat and everything. And a *shul* - Liberal, of course. They seem very welcoming.
MOSES. To you as well?
CHRISTINA. Yes.
MOSES. That's good.

Danny enters.

DANNY. Moses! Hi! Glad you could make it. How are you?
MOSES. Fine!
DANNY. I've got something for you. *(He searches in one of the boxes and brings out the bag full of bottles.)* They're homeopathic remedies. They're for all sorts of things - stress, anxiety, assertiveness. You'll love them.
CHRISTINA. You giving them away?
DANNY. Yes.
CHRISTINA. It won't last!
DANNY. *(To Moses.)* Here, take them.
MOSES. Oh, no. I couldn't... well, maybe... no, I better not.
DANNY. *(Holding one of the bottles up.)* White chestnut - indecision. Just follow the instructions.
MOSES. Alright then. Thank you. *(He takes them.)* So, have you got a job to go to?
DANNY. I'm going to try writing for a bit, see how it goes. If not: desk near the door. I'm sure I'll find something. It's a new beginning. A *'shekheyonu'*. Would you say the blessing over us before we leave.
MOSES. Of course.
DANNY. *(To Christina.)* Do you mind?
CHRISTINA. No.
MOSES. *(Covers his head; Danny and Christina hold hands.)* '*Borukh ato adonoy eloheynu melekh ha'olam shekheyonu v'kimonu v'higionu lazman hazeh. Omeyn* - Blessed are you, Lord our God, King of the Universe who has protected us and kept us and brought us in health to

this season. Amen.'

Danny and Christina kiss.

MOSES. *(Taking a drop of homeopathic remedy.) L'khaim.*

Lights down.

THE END

Glossary

1 Literally: 'Air-person', a dreamer.

2 Lit: 'Keep well!'

3 Intelligence.

4 Reading from the Torah.

5 Madness.

6 May you have a longer life (a format response on talking about the dead).

7 Ceremony after a funeral.

8 May he rest in peace.

9 Lit: 'Taste of paradise'.

10 Literally: 'And they shall eat garlic' - the 'garlic' refers to 'oneh' (Talmud Baba Kama, 82A) - 'Oneh' are the commands referring to giving sexual pleasure.

11 Lit: 'You shall not marry them'.

12 Hasidic Rabbi.

13 Memorial prayer for the dead.

14 Literally: 'Because I drew him out of the waters' (Exodus 2:10)

15 Number 12.

THE PALESTINIAN GIRL

(SHOOTING MAGDA)

by

Joshua Sobol

Translated by Miriam Shlesinger

I wrote *The Palestinian Girl* to find a reason for making theatre in a complex and absurd context such as the Israeli-Palestinian entanglement, and to find an adequate form to deal with different levels of our contemporary reality.
The Palestinian Girl was first produced by the Haifa Municiple Theatre. It opened there on 10th October, 1985.

Director	Gedalia Besser
Set	Adrian Vaux
Costumes	Edna Sobol

CAST

DAHLIA/MAGDA	Leora Rivlin
SAMIRA	Salwa Nakam
BENESH/RODNEY	Roberto Plak
FAHED/ADNAN	Makram Khuri
DAVID /UDI	Yiftah Katsor
ADA/MIRYUM	Shosh Shlam
ITZAK/EFRAYIM	Yossef Bashi
HAVKIN/HERBERT	Kay Lautman
YONA/ AVI	Gideon Shirin
SINGER	Tami Alon
BURI	Erez Shafrir

CHARACTERS

BENESH, a director. His nickname, Benesh, is actually a corruption of his surname, Beinish. Together with Samira, Benesh wrote the filmscript of *Magda*., based on Samira's own story. Besides being director of the film, he also plays the role of Rodney, a British playwright, who was Samira's lover. Benesh is forty eight and married. For the past three years he has been having an affair with Dahlia.

DAHLIA, an actress, forty years old. Plays the role of Magda, the dramatic persona representing Samira. Magda is twenty three, the same age as Samira when the story takes place.

SAMIRA, a young Arab actress, twenty-five years old. The co-author, with Benesh, of the film-script Magda. In the film she is the one who reads the lead-in texts, in which she tells her story. These texts serve to introduce the scenes.

UDI, an actor, about thirty. He plays the role of David, who is twenty-five in the filmscript. David is a law student and a member of an ultra-rightwing organization. Udi himself holds radical leftwing ideas.

YITZHAK, a thirty-year old actor who plays Ephraim, a fifty-year old colonel (reserves) and David's father. Yitzhak is an expert at buffoonery, which is why he was chosen to play Ephraim, who appears in the film dressed as a clown, having just returned from a Purim masquerade party.

ADA, Udi's real-life mother, and David's mother in the film. Ada teaches creative drama classes, as does Miriam, David's mother in the film. She was cast as Miriam both because of the film's limited budget and because of her suitability for the part.

FAHED, an Arab actor, forty-two years old. He plays Adnan, Magda's boyfriend in the film, a twenty-five year old drama student.

YONAH, a thirty-five year old filmmaker. A good friend of Benesh's. In the film, he play Barry, a student, originally from the States, and a member of an ultra-rightwing group.

PAUL, the production's musician and pianist. He also plays the part of

Avi, member of the rightwing group and Barry's accomplice in his hooliganism.

HAVKIN, a onetime small-parts actor and a dancing teacher who barely makes ends meet by teaching dancing at acting schools. He is an old man, without family and utterly alone. In Vienna in the thirties, he was an Ausdruck-Tanz (Expression-Dance) dancer. In the film, he plays the part of Herbert, a former dancing teacher in whose studio Magda supposedly re-lives the story of the film.

A SINGER, she does vocalizations of the music played by the pianist.

SETTING

The plot is set in a television studio, where the television film, *Magda* is being shot. The plot of the film becomes a part of the play. The set is that of the television play, *Magda*, surrounded by the typical paraphernalia of a television production, such as video cameras and recording equipment.

The plot takes place over a single twenty-four hour period, during which the play is shot from start to finish on a shoestring budget.

The circumstances : time is short and the filming must be completed by the following morning, since the budget did not allow for more than one day of shooting, and the studio must be vacated within 24 hours.

ACT ONE

Scene 1

Outdoors. Night. On the lawn. Commotion. Yelling. Swearing in Hebrew and Arabic by everyone around the set. The participants are not yet visible. Just when the racket has reached its peak, a sheep is hurled onto the stage. This is Magda, covered from head to toe in a sheepskin. She falls on the lawn, screaming.

MAGDA. Adnan! Adnan! Help! Leave me alone! Help!

Enter three toughs: David, Barry, Avi. They are screaming.

DAVID. Traitor.
BARRY. Terrorist.
AVI. Stinking leftist.

David beats Magda, who is trying to get up off the floor. He is yelling. Kicks her. She screams.

MAGDA. Help! They're killing me! Help!
DAVID. *(Still kicking her.)* You Jewish traitor. Whoring with Arabs, you filthy bitch! I'll show you 'Nuernberg Corner of Auschwitz'!
MAGDA. *(Under the barrage of their attacks.)* I'm not an Arab! I'm a Jew. I'm a Jew!
BENESH. *(Shouting.)* Cut!

The action stops. They all step out of their parts. Work lights go on.

DAHLIA. *(Pushing her head out of the sheepskin. Turns to David.)* Can't you control yourself? Do you know you're really hurting me?
UDI. Complaints - to the director.
DAHLIA. *(To Benesh.)* I don't have to take any more of this. He's really killing me.
BENESH. And you're killing me. How many more times are we going to have to take this lousy scene until we're lucky enough to hear the text the way it should be?
DAHLIA. Wasn't I coming across?
BENESH. What were you saying? Do you know what you were saying?
DAHLIA. When?
BENESH. Before I said to cut. What was the last sentence you said?
DAHLIA. I'm not a Jew, I'm an Arab. I'm an Arab.
BENESH. You wish! You said the exact opposite.
DAHLIA. I did not.
BENESH. Samira, what did she say?
SAMIRA. *(To Dahlia)* You said: "I'm not an Arab, I'm a Jew. I'm a Jew.
DAHLIA. *(To Benesh)* Just a minute. Don't I know what I said?
BENESH. You know what you think you said.
ADA What's the point of bickering? Why don't we just listen to the recording.
BENESH. That's all we need now - to spend time on playbacks.

ADA. It'll take less time than this shouting match, believe me. (*To the recording technician:*) Let's hear the recording.
UDI. *(As the technician runs the tape back.)*. 'Mother, you don't have to be in the middle of everything.'
ADA. Udi, my love, I know what I'm doing.
BENESH. We're very short of time. We've got to finish shooting by tomorrow morning. We've been through every scene a thousand times. Every step. Now that we've reached the shooting stage, everyone keeps getting mixed up.
ADA. Benesh, you're working with people, not computers. And even computers make mistakes.
BENESH. What am I asking, for heaven's sakes? Just concentrate.
HAVKIN. It's getting late. So concentrate.
TECHNICIAN. Can I play you the recording?
ADA. Go ahead.
RECORDING. (*Magda screaming.)* I'm not an Arab! I'm a Jew! I'm a Jew! *(Benesh shouting.)* Cut! *(The technician stops the tape. Silence.)*
BENESH. All right. Back to your places. We're shooting the scene from the top.
DAHLIA. *(Stepping out of the sheepskin.)* I can't do it.
BENESH. Dahlia -
DAHLIA. I just can't go through that scene again. I can't.
ADA. Weren't you going to call a break?
BENESH. We'll run through the scene once more properly. Then we'll take a break.
DAHLIA. (*To herself.)* I can't stand it. I can't.
ADA. (*To Benesh.)* You've been working four hours straight. There's no point in putting the pressure on when people are exhausted. It'll just make things worse.
YONAH. (*To Benesh.)* Give us a break. Everyone's starving.
BENESH. (*Glancing at his watch.)* OK. Time out. But don't start preparing any gourmet dinners.
ADA. (*Announces.)* Listen, everybody: there are box lunches ready in the canteen. Sandwiches with Bulgarian cheese and vegetables. There's coffee in the black thermos, tea in the red one.
BENESH. You're all back here in fifteen minutes. We'll go straight into the Independence Day ball scene.

They all leave, except for Dahlia, and Ada who lingers behind.

DAHLIA. (*To Benesh.)* Can I talk to you for a minute?

BENESH. Let's go get some sandwiches. I'm famished too.
ADA. I'll have them bring you some sandwiches. (*Ada leaves. Dahlia and Benesh are left to themselves).*

Scene 2

Dahlia and Benesh on the set.

DAHLIA. Good thing we have a personal attendant. Otherwise I'd never get to talk to you.
BENESH. She's OK, that woman.
DAHLIA. Sure. Everyone's O.K except me.
BENESH. Poor Dahlia. Is that the game we're playing? Fine, I'm all yours.
DAHLIA. Thanks a lot. Go ahead and eat with whoever you feel like.
BENESH. Good timing is an important quality not only in acting; in life too. Good timing shows that you're with it, that you're tuned into people, not just busy with yourself.
DAHLIA. I know I'm complicated, and that I've got a sick personality.
BENESH. You simply refuse to accept responsibility.
DAHLIA. Responsibility, responsibility. You've got one answer to everything: responsibility. I can't accept responsibility when I've got that one sitting there, staring at me all the time.
BENESH. Who's 'that one'?
DAHLIA. You know perfectly well.
BENESH. She has a name, doesn't she?
DAHLIA. Samira, all right?
BENESH. No, it's not all right.
DAHLIA. So it's not all right.
BENESH. Why do you call her 'that one'?
DAHLIA. Are you picking a fight?
BENESH. First you say 'all right'. I say it's not all right. So, it's not all right. Just what's coming off with you?
DAHLIA. I've got a headache and I'm not up to explaining every word I say.
BENESH. First you want to talk to me. The next minute you tell me to go ahead and eat with whoever I feel like.
DAHLIA. You were getting on my nerves.
BENESH. Do you have a headache or was I getting on your nerves?

DAHLIA. What do you want?
BENESH. You're hiding.
DAHLIA. You're very open.
BENESH. I think I am.
DAHLIA. Really? Then, get rid of her.
BENESH. I beg your pardon.
DAHLIA. I can't do the part with her looking at me.
BENESH. Everyone's looking at you. Why is she the only one who bothers you.
DAHLIA. I'm not playing everyone. I'm playing her. When she looks at me, whatever I do dosen't feel right.
BENESH. That means you're not really concentrating on the job.
DAHLIA. I certainly am concentrating on the job'.
BENESH. What are you talking about?
DAHLIA. Benesh, do me a favor. Not a personal one. I'm asking you as an actor of yours. Keep her away from here, at least while we're shooting.
BENESH. I can't. It's her story. She wrote the script.
DAHLIA. She doesn't have to be here the whole time.
BENESH. I need her for the lead-ins.
DAHLIA. You can shoot those separately.
BENESH. It won't turn out the way I want. You've seen how she works. She reacts to the scenes, she adlibs the text. It comes out natural, spontaneous. If I record her part in isolation, it'll be dead. It's impossible.
DAHLIA. She makes me freeze. I keep feeling unnatural.

Samira appears in the distance, carrying a couple of box lunches and two bottles of beer. They don't notice her.

BENESH. Dahlia, between us, you're a creature of the stage. Why should she be giving us a hard time?
DAHLIA. Is it so hard for you to give her up for a while?
BENESH. Impossible. Besides, she'd be terribly hurt.
DAHLIA. If she were a Jew you wouldn't think twice.
BENESH. She isn't a Jew.
DAHLIA. *(From a distance.)* I've brought you something to eat.

The two of them fall silent. Samira hands Dahlia the box lunch and the beer.

DAHLIA. Thanks.

Takes the food and walks away, but stays within earshot.

SAMIRA. *(Handing the food and the beer to Benesh.)* I've got to take a few hours off.
BENESH. What happened?
SAMIRA. I've got a problem with my apartment. I'll be back this evening.

She walks over to her corner, packs her text and a few belongings in a knapsack. Meanwhile, Havkin appears and corners Benesh.

HAVKIN. Forgive me for butting in. I've still got a problem with the last scene. I don't understand...
BENESH. *(His mind is on Samira, who is busy gathering her things.)* What don't you understand? It's Christmas eve, you hear someone crying, you go in, you see a lonely girl, you invite her over to your place.
HAVKIN. But what do we actually do in the scene?
BENESH. You meet.
HAVKIN. But I don't understand. Don't I remember inviting her, or am I just pretending? It's only been one day - Am I senile? There's something unclear about the character.
BENESH. That's right. Something unclear about the character.
HAVKIN. Something confused...
BENESH. That's right. Confused.
HAVKIN. What should I do about it?
BENESH. Go along with it. *(Calls Samira, who is on her way out.)* Samira! Samira! *(Exits.)*

Scene 3

Havkin looks around him, at a loss, and notices Dahlia.

HAVKIN. I don't get it. Did I say anything to upset him? I don't get it.
DAHLIA. What don't you get? Samira has some problems with her apartment.
HAVKIN. That much I know. Her lover, that no-good English playwright stood her up on Christmas eve. She's sitting in her room,

crying and I go in there and invite her over to my studio.
DAHLIA. That's right.
HAVKIN. But the following morning, I come into the studio, I see you, and I don't even recognize you?
DAHLIA. Believe me, Havkin, I wish I had your part. Just let the text lead you along, and it'll be smooth sailing.
HAVKIN. The text is a problem in itself... I don't understand. Am I senile?

Paul enters, finishing a sandwich.

PAUL. Are we rehearsing the scene?
DAHLIA. Give us the accompaniment. We'll run though it.

Paul sits down at the piano and starts playing the waltz. Dahlia assumes the role of Magda. Havkin becomes Herbert. Magda starts dancing.

HERBERT. One-two-three, one-two-three.
HAVKIN. Help me with the text, if I forget.
HERBERT. One-two-and, one-two. Good...
HERBERT. In a big circle, nice and wide, use up the space, all of it. Free and easy. Throw your weight back. Leave it behind you. All of it. That's the way. Relaxed and easy.
HAVKIN. What comes next?
DAHLIA. *(Still dancing in the role of Magda.)* Life happens from one minute to the next!
HERBERT. Life happens from one minute to the next!
DAHLIA. And burns out from one minute to the next.
HAVKIN. I remember. That's line is certainly philosophical.
HERBERT. That's fine, that's fine.
HAVKIN. Life really does burn out from one minute to the next.
HERBERT. That's fine. Nice big circles, use up the space, that's right. One-two-three, one-two-three... A big circle, nice and big. Let yourself go. Majestic movements. You're a princess now. A queen. The world is yours. You cross over borders. You sweep over ice. Over water. Air. You're a solitary bird. All alone in the sky.
HAVKIN. That's rather poetic, actually.
HERBERT. Way, way up. The wind is with you. Take to the wind. Spread your wings. Wide. Nice and open. Glide. Float. Forward. Forward. You're creating space. Work your way into it.

HAVKIN. Real Ausdruck-Tanz...
HERBERT. Behind you there's a fire raging. A landslide. Destruction. Roads, buildings turning to dust. Forward, forward. Up and away.
HAVKIN. I can't help myself...

He joins in the dance, completely carried away.

HERBERT. Living is getting away. From one minute to the next. That's good. Excellent. Excellent!
HAVKIN. I remember the whole monologue.
DAHLIA. Go on with the text.
HERBERT. Where did you learn to dance like that?
MAGDA. From you.
HERBERT. You were a student of mine?
MAGDA. Yes.
HERBERT. Hello, Student.
MAGDA. Hello, Teacher.
HAVKIN. He's not senile.
DAHLIA. Of course not.
HAVKIN. He's just an old devil with a sense of humor.
DAHLIA. You said it!
HAVKIN. How does it go after that?
DAHLIA. Were you a student of mine in Vienna.
HAVKIN. What?... Ah!...
HERBERT. You were a student of mine in Vienna?
MAGDA. No, here. In London.
HERBERT. Just when did you study with me?
MAGDA. Yesterday.
HERBERT. What's your name?
MAGDA. Magda.
HERBERT. Hello, Magda.
MAGDA. Hello, Herbert.
HERBERT. Where do we know each other from?
MAGDA. From the staircase.
HERBERT. You're the girl on the staircase
MAGDA. I'm your neighbor on this floor. I live right across the hall from you.
HERBERT. Hi, Neighbor.
MAGDA. Hi, Neighbor.
HERBERT. Who told you my name?
MAGDA. You did.

HERBERT. When?
MAGDA. Last night.
HERBERT. Was I stoned?
MAGDA. It was Christmas Eve.
HERBERT. I was stoned.
MAGDA. And I was crying.
HERBERT. Why?
HAVKIN. What a naive question. Maybe he really is naïve?
DAHLIA. If it works for you, use it.
HAVKION. If it works for me... I'll be dead soon. It works for me.
DAHLIA. We'll all be dead soon.
HERBERT. Where were you fifty years ago?
MAGDA. I wasn't born yet.
HERBERT. Have you got a place to sleep?
MAGDA. At your place.
HERBERT. Since when?
MAGDA. Since last night.
HERBERT. Did you sleep well?
MAGDA. I hope I didn't yell in my sleep.
HERBERT. You're the girl who yelled last night.
MAGDA. I'm sorry.
HERBERT. I always forget the line after that.
DAHLIA. The fight you'll keep losing...
HERBERT. Yes!

Enter Samira. She returns to her usual place, puts down her bag and takes out the things she packed earlier. She is behaving as if she decided to come back. Dahlia notices her, but dosen't react directly.

HERBERT. The fight you'll keep losing is the one against yourself.
HAVKIN. *(Pondering that line.)* How does that tie in?
MAGDA. I'm not fighting against myself. I spend my whole life fighting against what they're trying to make of me.
DAHLIA. *(Addressing her remarks to Samira.)* Declarations, declarations. I can't believe the things that I'm saying.
HERBERT. That battle is doomed too. If you don't know what you want to be, you'll wind up having others call the tune.
MAGDA. I want to be Magda.
DAHLIA. That's another line I hate.

Samira lights up a cigarette and stares at Dahlia without saying a word.

HERBERT. What is Magda?
MAGDA. Magda is something that nothing sticks to. No label. Magda is the kind of stuff that can't be frozen in any form. Magda isn't the result. She isn't the continuation. Magda is what happens from one minute to the next. Magda is something that dosen't belong, something that'll never belong to anyone... *(She stops and goes back to being herself.)*
DAHLIA. I can't go on with that monologue. I can't say it. *(Turns to Samira.)* Is that really the way you feel about yourself?
SMAIRA. Look... *(Hesitant, then resolute.)* I wrote the script together with Benesh.
DAHLIA. But it's about you. It's your story.
SAMIRA. It's based on my story.
DAHLIA. That monologue is by Benesh.
SAMIRA. That's right.
DAHLIA. Naturally, as if I didn't recognize him? It's just what Benesh enjoys thinking about himself.
HAVKIN. Shouldn't we get on with the scene?
DAHLIA. I can't. I don't know how to go on at all.

Benesh enters holding a cup of coffee and a cigarette. He sees that they are immersed in their work, and sits down on the side. He listens. But does not interfere.

DAHLIA. You know, Havkin, I'm in a much lousier position that you are. The part of Magda is so contrived. It's such patchwork... *(She expects a reaction form Benesh, but he keeps silent.)*
If I acted on my instincts, I'd quit the production right now.
HAVKIN. What's the matter with you? What are you talking about? You'll do the part beautifully!
DAHLIA. How can I? The way the character is written is so shallow. Making declarations about herself. She doesn't develop at all. I don't understand her, and I told you: I don't believe a word she says.
HAVKIN. And what about you? Are you so understanding? Do you really believe every word you say? Take me. Here I am, a man of sixty-eight. Yes, that's right. And what do I know about myself? Very little. To be precise, only the biographical details and the few things I don't keep from myself. But what do I keep from myself?- Do I know? And I'm no slouch. I'm not coarse or thick-skulled either. I'm a gentle and sensitive person. I like to dance. I like music, art, books. I like to observe people.

This morning, for instance, I went outside and stood in the bus-stop. Two girls walked by, still fresh from a good night's sleep. One of them was sort of plump. Sensual. And they were singing some song. Suddenly this boy came towards them in the opposite direction. Not much of a man. Skinny, with glasses. But a male. And suddenly the girl was singing that song differently. Something inside her came alive, something got into her body. And it was perfectly timed. You know what I mean... And it wasn't that way with the other one. You could tell right away which of the females had caught the male. All because of that timing of hers. What do you call it - synchronization?

BENESH. 'Timing' will do.

HAVKIN. And you could see a human being in the mainstream of life. And what does she know? Instincts. It's all instincts. No really. I'm a man who's seen a thing or two in life. Married three times. Divorced once, widowed once, and now taking care of a wife who is sick... senile... Not to mention my share of affairs. And what do I know about myself as far as morality is concerned? Do I know how I'll behave if I fall in love again? Take me, for instance. I'm a shallow person too, making declarations about himself. And what do you mean about a character developing? Who develops anyhow? What I am today is what I was at twenty. Believe me. Nothing really changes. Except for the face, which keeps getting older. Character development is the concoction of theoreticians. Back then, I used to loose my head when I'd fall in love, and I could still do the same today. God have pity on anyone who develops out of that.

(To Benesh) I'm sorry to be using up production time.

BENESH. You're not using up time. It's part of the production.

DAHLIA. Why did you say earlier that you'll be dead soon?

HAVKIN. I haven't got anyone left to offer my love.

SAMIRA. Maybe you don't want to?

HAVKIN. Who wants what I have to offer?

PAUL. *(From his seat at the piano.)* Is that any reason to die?

HAVKIN. Do you know any better reason?

PAUL. I'm not on love with anyone and I'm not about to die on account of it.

HAVKIN. Oh, well, with you it's just temporary.

PAUL. No it isn't. I haven't been in love for years.

DAHLIA. Me either. I'm careful not to fall in love.

SAMIRA. How can you play Samira then?

DAHLIA. Do you think I don't do your part well too?

SAMIRA. Magda isn't exactly me.

DAHLIA. I don't introduce my personal life into my work either.
SAMIRA. That's not the problem.
DAHLIA. Then what is?
SAMIRA. Maybe I shouldn't tell you. I'm liable to spoil things.
DAHLIA. On the contrary. If you tell me, you might do me some good.
SAMIRA. You stay out of it. Nothing happens to you. Nothing hurts you.
DAHLIA. I really think the best thing for the production would be for me to call it quits. No harm would be done. On the contrary. You're here anyway. You're an actress. You know your text. I'm sure you understand it better than I do. Why don't you do the part yourself?
SAMIRA. I can't play myself. I won't believe my lines. And I want you to play me.
DAHLIA. Why? Why is it so important to you that I do the part?
SAMIRA. I want a Jew to play Magda, and if you think about it, you'll know why. I'm sure you can do a very good job too, especially after hearing you earlier.
DAHLIA. What did you hear?
SAMIRA. I think you've got a problem of truth and falsehood. I think you got to come to grips with some ethical questions and ask yourself if every word you utter is true, or if you're not just making all sorts of empty declarations about your feelings and your views while your behavior keeps exposing something entirely different.
DAHLIA. I know. I'm completely empty and I don't have anything to give people.
SAMIRA. That's an easy way of avoiding the truth. And it's another mask that you've got to tear off yourself if you really want to know who you are.
DAHLIA. Mind being more specific?
SAMIRA. When we met, you declared that you're against the occupation, against having one people rule over another and a whole list of lofty declarations.
DAHLIA. I stand behind everything I said.
SAMIRA. How do you intend to set things right and to free society of lies and depravity if you're just as depraved?
DAHLIA. I beg your pardon?
SAMIRA. I get in your way when you're playing me. You'd like me not to be here. Why don't you have the guts to tell me so straight to my face? Why do you try to work it out behind my back, with Benesh?
DAHLIA. You're right.
SAMIRA. I overheard you. Don't start explaining. If I were a Jew, it

would have been much easier for you. For me too. Sorry, I'm not a Jew. No, don't apologize. Words don't mean anything, only deeds. You're not a politician and I don't expect you to remake the world. But you're an actress and could do Magda the way she is. Warts and all. With whatever problems she has. Or you can cop out. But then at least you'll know what you're doing and who you are.

DAHLIA. I've got plenty to say to that, but we'll carry on with this argument some other time.

(To Benesh.) I'm ready. Go ahead and roll.

BENESH. To your places, everyone. *(As they all return to their positions, he turns to Samira.)* I'd like to include that conversation in your last scene with Rodney, before you and he say good-bye for good.

SAMIRA. It's more or less what I really told him.

BENESH. Why didn't you tell me about it when we were writing the script?

SAMIRA. I forgot.

BENESH. Sit down and write it.

SAMIRA. Now?

BENESH. Just a minute. *(To everyone.)* Listen, everybody - we're starting with Samira's story. We go straight into the scene with the dancer caller, and don't forget to make plenty of noise. *(To Yitzhak)* Haka'leh, you lead the scene through to 'Etz Ha-Rimon' and if all goes well we move right into my scene with Dahlia. Yonah... where's Yonah?

YONAH. Right here.

BENESH. When I come in as Rodney, you take over the set.

YONAH. Aye, aye, sir.

BENESH. Is Samira ready?

SAMIRA. I'm adlibbing.

BENESH. Tell the story in the simplest possible words. Just the way it happened. Sound rolling?

TECHNICIAN. Rolling. 10, 9, 8, 7, 6, 5, 4, 3, 2, 1. Go.

BENESH. Now get this - We don't stop until I say so. Let's go.

Scene 4

Samira is telling her story. A close-up of her face appears at the same time on a giant video screen.

SAMIRA. It was the eve of Independence Day. They were having a big party on campus. Adnan and I were preparing a small number.

Benesh signals to Yitzhak, who steps onto the set in the role of a dance caller, holding a microphone. A well-known folkdance tune ('Hey Harmonica') is blaring on the p.a. system. A singer enters. She's holding a wireless microphone and scatting to the music. Meanwhile, Samira walks over to her corner, to write out the dialogue between herself and Rodney.

DANCE CALLER. Where's your holiday spirit folks? Where's the good mood? Did you leave it back in the reserves? Back on the Beirut-Damascus road? I see a whole bunch of you just sitting there near the cafeteria. Are you from the chronic-care ward? Or the Society for the Handicapped? What is this folks? A nursing home or a university? Everyone, without exception, come join the dancing.

He gets off the stage and starts to sing Naomi Shemer's 'Shir Ha-Shuk' ('Song of the Marketplace'). The singer joins him and the two of them move off the set as though heading to liven up the celebration at some other end of the lawn. The actors keep passing back and forth in front of the camera, to create the effect of a large crowd of dancers. On the gigantic video screen, meanwhile, there appears a documentary sequence of large crowds of dancers. Now the dance caller returns and announces, on-camera.

DANCE CALLER. And now - the men all turn to the right, the girls to the left. Everybody takes a partner, and let's all form couples for 'Etz Ha-Rimon'.

The singer preforms the song 'Etz Ha-Rimon' with the dance caller humming along. The music and the singing fade out. Meanwhile, Benesh has changed clothes and gone over to Dahlia. The cameras follow them as they head for a different corner of the set, dancing. Benesh is playing Rodney and Dahlia is Magda. They go on dancing. Rodney leads Magda to the front of the stage.

Scene 5

Rodney and Magda are dancing. Far off, the melody of 'Etz Ha-Rimon' continues playing softly.

MAGDA. Where are you leading me?
RODNEY. To London.
MAGDA. Watch out, I might just take you seriously.
RODNEY. I've been following you all evening.
MAGDA. This party has much more interesting subjects than me, if you're from the Secret Service.
RODNEY. You don't know everything there is to know about yourself.
MAGDA. Go ahead and tell me something I don't know.
RODNEY. How long will you give me?
MAGDA. Thirty seconds.
RODNEY. You get exactly two questions.
MAGDA. Who are you anyway?
RODNEY. Rodney Lawson.
MAGDA. What are you doing here?
RODNEY. Looking for material for a BBC series I'm doing.
MAGDA. You a playwright?
RODNEY. We agreed on two questions. That's the third.
MAGDA. Never mind that. I'm an actress.
RODNEY. You don't say! Why do you think I've been watching you?
MAGDA. What, you knew?
RODNEY. I've got an eye for that sort of thing. I can smell an actress from miles off. *(Pulls out a flask.)* Do you drink?
MAGDA. Thanks, perfect timing. I'm on in a few minutes and I'm going to need all the courage I can get. *(Takes a sip, hands back the bottle. He takes a sip.)* Well, then. Are you here to find a theme for a play?
RODNEY. Yes. I've got the writer's blues, as they say. I sit down at the typewriter and I just can't get started. *(Smiles.)* I'm in trouble. I can't churn out any more of those idiotic dramas about marital woes and cheating spouses. It's all too close to my own life for me to be able to see the point. *(Takes another sip.)*
MAGDA. Why? Do you think your life is pointless?
RODNEY. I don't think so, I know so. You have no idea just how empty life can become. Here in Israel, you people live a life that's tense,

dangerous, full of contradictions. Almost everything you do has some meaning - political, moral, existential...
MAGDA. What do you want to write about?
RODNEY. A love story between a nationalist Arab girl and a nationalist Jewish boy.
MAGDA. Couldn't you find anything more complicated to write about? In any event, you're going to have to make it all up. In real life it could never happen.
RODNEY. Why not? Couldn't you see yourself falling in love with an Arab?
MAGDA. I'm not good for your story. I **am** in love with an Arab.
RODNEY. Is that so?... Would you be willing to tell me your story?
MAGDA. What made you choose this party at the university tonight?
RODNEY. A friend of mine. A British journalist who lives in Israel. He told me there's going to be a fight between Jews and Arabs here tonight.
MAGDA. What'll it be about?
RODNEY. The Arab students have prepared some number that's going to break up the party.
MAGDA. What?!
RODNEY. Would you mind introducing me to your boyfriend, the Arab?
MAGDA. There he is

Adnam appears, carrying some furs over his arm.

MAGDA. Adnan, there's a British playwright here who'd like to meet you.
RODNEY. *(Holds out his hand.)* Rodney Lawson.
ADNAN. Adnan.
RODNEY. Why don't we go sit down somewhere quiet.
ADNAN. I'm sorry, maybe later if that's OK with you. We're very busy right now. We've got a performance in a few minutes.
RODNEY. After the performance then, here?
ADNAN. Fine. See you later.

Rodney leaves. Benesh steps out of his role as Rodney and replaces Yonah as director. Fahed abandons the role of Adnan for a minute and turns to Benesh.

FAHED. Should we go ahead?
BENESH. As long as you've stopped, wait just a minute. Dahlia, wait a while before you put on the fur, to make it clar that you're scared.

DAHLIA. Did you notice the changes I made?
BENESH. Yes, yes. It was excellent. Keep on along the same lines. Can we go ahead?
TECHNICIAN. Sound rolling.
BENESH. Let's get going everyone. It's going fine. Don't stop until I say so. Roll 'em.

Benesh signals to Yitzhak, who steps onto the set in the role of a dance caller, holding a microphone. A well-known folkdance tune 'Hey Harmonica' is blaring on the p.a. system. A singer enters. She's holding a wireless microphone and scatting to the music. Meanwhile, Samira walks over to her corner, to write out the dialogue between herself and Rodney.

DANCE CALLER. Where's your holiday spirit folks? Where's the good mood? Did you leave it back in the reserves? Back on the Beirut-Damascus road? I see a whole bunch of you just sitting there near the cafeteria. Are you from the chronic-care ward? Or the Society for the Handicapped? What is this folks? A nursing home or a university? Everyone, without exception, come join the dancing.

He gets off the stage and starts to sing Naomi Shemer's Shir 'Ha-Shuk' (Song of the Marketplace). The singer joins him and the two of them move off the set as though heading to liven up the celebration at some other end of the lawn. The actors keep passing back and forth in front of the camera, to create the effect of a large crowd of dancers. On the gigantic video screen, meanwhile, there appears a documentary sequence of large crowds of dancers. Now the dance caller returns and announces, on-camera.

DANCE CALLER. And now - the men all turn to the right, the girls to the left. Everybody takes a partner, and let's all form couples for 'Etz Ha-Rimon'.

The singer preforms the song 'Etz Ha-Rimon' with the dance caller humming along. The music and the singing fade out. Meanwhile, Benesh has changed clothes and gone over to Dahlia. The cameras follow them as they head for a different corner of the set, dancing. Benesh is playing Rodney and Dahlia is Magda. The go on dancing. Rodney leads Magda to the front of the stage.

Scene 6

Adnan puts down the furs. They are in the shape of a sheepskin and a wolf's fur. Both are made as an all-in-one outfit, including the animal heads.

ADNAN. *(Inspecting the furs.)* I've been looking all over for you. I thought you'd run away. Then I find you here with that British guy.
MAGDA. Adnan, I'm scared.
ADNAN. You seem to be having a pretty good time acutally - dancing, laughing, drinking. From what I can see, you're really enjoying the whole business.
MAGDA. That Englishmen knows everything, do you know that?
ADNAN. Great. You should be ashamed of yourself.
MAGDA. You idiot. I wasn't the one who told him. He told me. He heard it from one of the journalists. If they know, then the fascists know too for sure...
ADNAN. *(Handing her the sheepskin and climbing into the wolf outfit.)* Take it easy. Our people invited the foreign press.
MAGDA. I thought you and I were the only ones who knew...
ADNAN. I'm not ashamed of our performance. Put on the fur.
MAGDA. Why didn't you tell me you were spreading the word?
ADNAN. I didn't tell them everything. Get into your costume.
MAGDA. Adnan, I don't like it when you do that sort of thing, without asking anyone, and hide it even from me...
ADNAN. I know what I'm doing. Hurry up and get dressed.
MAGDA. There's going to be bloodshed...
ADNAN. By the time they realize what's happening, the show will be over. They won't catch on until later. Don't worry.

Scene 7

The dance caller appears, holding a microphone. As he announces the next number, Adnan and Magda finish putting on the furs. They are now completely covered, as a sheep and wolf.

DANCE CALLER. Ladies and Gentlemen, students and hoi polloi. I'd now like to call upon the members of our Theater Group who have prepared a special performance for the Independence Day ball. Let's have a big round of applause, Ladies and Gentlemen!

He applauds. All of the others in the production also applaud and try to make as much noise as possible, for the effect of a large gathering.

DANCE CALLER. Actors, the stage is yours!

The applause continues. A sheep climbs onto the stage and dances a 'debka'_to the tune of 'La-Ma'ayan Bah Gedi Katan' ('A Small White Kid Approaches the Stream'). The sheep walks to the river bank and drinks. The wolf appears.

WOLF. Oh, it's so hot in this country. I'm so thirsty. Is there any water around here? Where is there some water? *(Spots the river.)* Oh, a river... *(The wolf walks down to the river. He is about to start drinking when he spots the sheep and stops.)* What are you doing here?
SHEEP. Drinking.
WOLF. Why here of all places?
SHEEP. This is the river that I've been drinking from since the day I was born. My father and his father and his father before him all drank from this river too.
WOLF. Why does it have to be upstream? You're deliberately contaminating the water that I use for drinking. You want me to eat you up?
SHEEP. God forbid, no... I'm sorry... I'll go drink downstream. *(The sheep passes the wolf and goes on to drink downstream.)*
WOLF. I told you you're contaminating my water and you still persist. I'll have no choice except to eat you up.
SHEEP. How can I contaminate the water you drink upstream when I only drink downstream? You have no reason to eat me up.
WOLF. You dare to argue with me. There's another reason for eating you up.
WOLF. I'm hungry - there's a second reason for eating you up. I'm strong - there's a third reason. And if that's not enough, we wolves get a craving for skewered mutton on our holidays. When I see a sheep like you... *(Starts singing to the tune 'Heigh-ho' .)*

Heigh-ho. Heigh-ho.
This lamb has got to go.
No matter why.

He'll leave or die.
Heigh-ho. Heigh-ho.

Everyone in the audience starts screaming 'Stop them! Get them off! Kill them!' All hell breaks loose. Catcalls and whistling. Samira faces the camera and tells her story. A close-up of her face appears on the giant screen.

SMAIRA. What went on after that was unbelievable. The lawn became a battlefield. Bottles and glasses went flying in all directions. I tried to run away but I tripped over my fur. I tried to get it off but the zipper was stuck. I didn't see anything after that. All I knew was that they were hitting me all over. *(David, Barry and Avi surround Magda and drag her to the front of the stage.)* I flelt myself being pushed and dragged. I called out to Adnan but he didn't answer.
MAGDA. Adnan! Adnan!
BARRY. *(Echoing her.)* Adnan! Adnan!
DAVID. You Arab-whoring slut!
MAGDA. Leave me alone. What do you want from me?
DAVID. Who was that Arab son-of-a-bitch?
MAGDA. If you know his mother...
DAVID. Every Arab is a stinking son-of-a-bitch.
MAGDA. They used to say that about the Jews once. You know who?
DAVID. Shut up, or we'll set you on fire right inside that fur!
AVI. Give us the name and address of that Arab motherfucker you've been shacking up with.
MAGDA. *(Still in the sheepskin.)* Nuernberg Avenue Corner of Auschwitz.
DAVID. What?!*(Kicks at the fur.)* I'll show you Nuernberg! You no-good Jewish traitor! Whoring with Arabs.You filthy bitch. *(Bashes the fur.)*
SAMIRA. *(In a flash on the screen.)* Suddenly I realized they were taking me for a Jew. I screamed as loud as I could:
MAGDA. *(From within the sheepskin.)* I'm not a Jew! I'm not a Jew! I'm an Arab! *(Sticking her hand out of the fur, holding up her ID card.* Here's my ID card!
BENESH. *(Meanwhile, Benesh - who has become Rodney again for his next scene - shouts in his capacity as director.)* Why don't you get out of that fur?
DAHLIA. I can't! It's tangled. I can't find the zipper. My head. I haven't got any air, damn it. What's wrong with it? What's going on?

She takes a step, collapses and lies motionless.

BENESH. Cut!
UDI. *(Forsaking the part of David.)* Someone get some water!
BENESH. Never mind the water. Get a knife. We've got to cut through the costume.
ADA. *(Running up to them.)* Here are the scissors.

Benesh takes the scissors, slits the fur legnthwise, helps Dahlia to sit up, shakes her and slaps her cheek. Dahlia comes to.

DAHLIA. Where am I! What happened!
BENESH. Are you all right?
DAHLIA. What...? *(Yonah rushes over to the cameraman.)*
YONAH. (Whispers an order to the cameraman.) Roll'em! Action! Keep rolling! *(Signalling to the sound technician.)* Sound! Roll it!
TECHNICIAN. It's rolling!
ADA. Udi, stop dreaming. Hurry up and get an ambulance!
DAHLIA. No, no... Not an ambulance...
YONAH. *(From a distance, ordering.)* Move back, move back. Give her some air! *(They obey without realizing that he's filming. They move back. Only Benesh, dressed as Rodney, and Dahlia dressed as Magda, remain in the focus.)*
BENESH. *(Busy tending to Dahlia, rubbing her temples, opening her blouse.)* Let me do it. Don't get in the way?
DAHLIA. What are you stripping me for?
BENESH. To give you some air.
DAHLIA. My head is spinning.
BENESH. Should I get a doctor?
DAHLIA. No. I'll be all right in a minute. I'm OK.
BENESH. Sure you're OK... You fainted!
DAHLIA. I'm sorry... How did it come out?
BENESH. Great. You were terrific.
DAHLIA. I'm glad...Water... My mouth is dry...
YONAH. Samira! *(Signals her to introduce a piece of narrative.)*
SAMIRA. *(Blending in. The camera angles in on her. She recounts).* Rodney took me home in a cab, to my apartment. He helped me up the stairs. He was very gentle. He helped me undress and put me into bed. He brought me some water. *(Ada brings Benesh a glass of water, which he brings to Dahlia.)* He made me some coffee, lit me a cigarette...

(Benesh gradually enters the role of Rodney. He lights up a cirarette for Dahlia.)
SAMIRA. *(Continues.)* He asked me what else he could do for me. I told him: 'Get me citizenship papers and a British passport.' 'Sorry,' he said. He didn't understand. I told him, 'I'm a Palestinian' 'You're not Jewish?'. 'No, I'm really sorry. I'm a Palestinian Arab.' Then he said; 'Why that's wonderful!' 'What is!'. 'That you're a Palestinian. I'm really glad.'
YONAH. *(Waving his hands to Dahlia and Benesh and whispering.)* Go on! Go on!

Dahlia grasps the situation. She realizes that Yonah is seizing on the opportunity to film a scene of 'cinema verite'. She busts out laughing and is too weak to control herself. Samira stops talking. Yonah, exasperated, waves his hands at Benesh and prods him from a distance.

YONAH. Keep going! Keep going! *(Benesh has made the complete transition to Rodney and Dahlia has become Magda.)*
RODNEY. Why are you laughing?
MAGDA. *(An improvization of Dahlia's.)* I can't help laughing... I can't help laughing at how happy it makes you... *(She notices how happy Yonah is and laughs even harder.)*
RODNEY. *(An improvization of Benesh's.)* What's so funny about my being happy?
Magda. Because I'm not exactly thrilled to be a Palestinian...
RODNEY. I want you to know how I feel about your problem... I'm convinced the Israelis are making a terrible mistake.
MAGDA. Sure, a terrible mistake. They beat me up as a Jew.
RODNEY. They're behaving towards you the way the anti-Semites behaved towards the Jews.
MAGDA. Is that so? Are you an anti-Semite?
RODNEY. God forbid. I'm a socialist. Of course, I'm an anti-Zionist, and a stauch supporter of the Palestinian cause.
MAGDA. Really? Then will you marry me?
RODNEY. What!? We hardly know each other...
MAGDA. We don't actually have to live together. All I want is a passport and citizenship. People get married for a lot less, don't they? You'll be able to divorce me as soon as you want. I promise.
RODENY. *(Whom Benesh is using to get his own ideas across.)* Are you sure you're all right?

MAGDA. You're a regular escape artist. I see... I've never been more clear-headed than right now. You're really prepared to do anything for me.

RODNEY. *(Here Benesh is conducting a direct dialogue with Dahlia.)* Look... I'm in the process of separating right now...

MAGDA. *(Also conducting a direct dialogue with Benesh.* 'Process of separating...' Don't bother with that line. I'm not going to sit around and wait. Me you can tell the truth to.

RODNEY. I love you.

MAGDA. Liar.

RODNEY. As an actress. Finish studying, come to London and I'll take care of you.

MAGDA. *(This time she really is Dahlia speaking directly to Benesh.)* I love you to, as a director.

RODNEY. *(Reminding her)* A playwright...

MAGDA. Sure, sure. You're one of those people who only love themselves. Just my luck, I always wind up with that kind of men... the kind that can twist my feelings just like that...

BENESH. *(Forsaking the character of Rodney completely, and stopping the scene.)* OK Dahlia, let's hold it righ there...

YONAH. Cut! *(To Benesh.)* You've got a piece of cinema verite. I should be so lucky in my film!

BENESH. *(Hugging Dahlia. There's warmth between them.)* Now you really can take some time off. You've earned it.

DAHLIA. Why? I could have gone, you kow, but you had to cop out, as usual...

BENESH. All right, lay off...

ADA. Come on, Dahlia, let's get you something hot to drink. *(As she walks out, Dahlia passes Samira.)*

SAMIRA. *(To Dahlia.)* The two of you got a pretty good improvization going there.

DAHLIA. You did something to me. Touched some spot in me...

HAVKIN. There's supposed to be a dance at this point. *(Cornering Benesh.)* No really, I mean it. If I'd known this is all I'd have, I wouldn't have taken the part. *(Makes them all his audience and talks about Benesh for all to hear.)* The whole play, he tells me, is set in your dance studio in London. So I sign on! I take the text, I go home, I sit down to read it... *(Starts laughing a strange kind of laughter, mingled with near-crying.)* From one page to the next, I kept getting more and more upset. Once dance at the beginning, one dance at the end, and that's my whole part.

UDI. You've got that scene in the middle too.
HAVKIN. With no dancing.
UDI. A dramatic scene.
HAVKIN. With no dancing.
YITZAK. Where do you want to fit in more dancing. This isn't a musical.
HAVKIN. What do you mean where? If you ask me, I'd finish the fight scene with a dance.
YITZAK. This time you're really going too far.
HAVKIN. Now you listen here.
YITZAK. How can a fight scene end with a dance? Just who's going to do the dancing?
HAVKIN. The three thugs, that's who! Do you know what Ausdruck-Tanz is all about? Expression-Dance! Couldn't you find the music for that? You took this Viennese dance instructor, this Herbert, from the twenties... I'm sure he must have been an Ausdruck-Tanz dancer. You take those three thugs, give them the right kind of music, and you bring out the whole character! *(To Paul.)* Couldn't you find the music for that?
PAUL. Why not? Here it goes.

He sits down at the piano and starts playing a wild, violent rendition of 'Joshua Fit the Battle of Jericho'. The singer scats along. Havkin starts swaying to the beat of the music. Udi joins in. The two of them drag Yonah into the dance. The others form a kind of improvized band, banging on whatever they happen to find. Someone takes over the lighting and creates a nightmare effect. Havkin becomes Herbert and calls out the steps, as he continues to dance and lead the others.

HERBERT. Sharp movements - *eins Zwei drei!*
Head high - *eins zwei drei!*
Back straight - *eins und zwei!*
Stomach in- *eins und zwei!*
Eyes ahead - *eins zwei drei*!

The dance develops into a real Ausdruck-Tanz number in which the three dancers externalize a character and psyche which draw upon the feelings of weakness, fears, self-hatred, the availability of a vulnerable victim (at his point, Dahlia may join in the dance, personifying the weak victim), brutality against one's victim, a feeling of strength that fills the attackers, the togetherness of a gang united behind its leader. The dance now engulfs the others, who join in, one by one, as the group grows into a drove-on-the-rampage, tightly packed, unvarying, steeped in repressed violence.

ACT TWO

Scene 1

The scene opens with the sound of knocking on the door. The set is dark. The light is on Samira who is facing the camera.

SAMIRA. The following morning I woke up and my whole body ached. Someone was knocking on the door. I got out of bed and put on a robe. Then I realized that I could hardly stand up. I felt a strong pain in my back, on the lower righthand side. I dragged myself to the door.

The light on the set goes on. Magda walks to the door. Knocking again.

MAGDA. Who is it? Rodney? I'm coming.
VOICE. *(A sheep bleating.)* Baaah...

Magda opens the door. Enter a sheep - i.e. somone wearing the sheep costume that Magda wore the night before. The sheep launches into a ridiculous dance and sings in an oriental accent.

The song is a well-known oriental style ditty about a little white kid.

SHEEP. 'El ha-ma'ayan / Ba gedi katan / ba gadi lavan...'
MAGDA. Adnan? You sure know how to make a quick getaway! Where's the foreign press? We'll give them a show that really breaks up the party... What's this I see? Heïgh-ho, heigh-ho...
(Stepping out of the sheepskin is David. He is laughing.)
MAGDA. *(Recoiling.)* What are you doing here?
DAVID. Appearing. *(Holds out his hand.)* I'm David.
MAGDA. I don't want to know you.
DAVID. Why not? Know thine enemy.
MAGDA. Get out.

DAVID. Is that your oriental hospitality? Not very impressive.
MAGDA. Very funny.
DAVID. With the law to defend us
No barb will offend us.
MAGDA. I don't find your barbs very amusing.
DAVID. You're pretty when you're mad.
MAGDA. You're not.
DAVID. Sorry. What can I do? A guy can't be held responsible for his face.
MAGDA. That's where you're wrong. A person **is** responsible for his face.
DAVID. Maybe. Let's not get into any philosophical arguments.
MAGDA. Why not? Aren't you responsible for the words you use either?
DAVID. What's the matter with you? Don't you have any sense of humor?
MAGDA. I have enough sense to know that you're not even responsible for your own arms and legs, or your head either for that matter.
DAVID. Listen, today is Independence Day. I'm in no mood to fight. All I came for was to apologize for the mistake we made when we beat you up, and to give you back this fur and your ID card. *(He pulls her ID card out of his pocket and gives it to her.)*
MAGDA. You could have mailed it back, or just thrown it away. An Arab's ID card dosen't mean a thing to you anyway, right?
DAVID. Wrong. I'm treating you with respect. I only beat you up because I thought you were a Jew. One of those bleeding-heart leftists from the Theater Department. Remember - as soon as I found out you were an Arab I stopped. Didn't I? Listen, an Arab with sound nationalist views I can definitely understand and appreciate. If I were an Arab, I'd behave the same as you. I think there's a good reason for mutual respect between us - the kind you find between two honorable enemies.
MAGDA. You're wrong.
DAVID. Why? We're enemies on the political plane, but personally I've got nothing against Arabs. Especially not against nationalist Arabs.
MAGDA. I'm not a nationalist.
DAVID. What do you mean? Then why did you put on that show last night?
MAGDA. Because it was a parable that gave a true picture of the situation.
DAVID. Oh, cone on! There's truth and there's truth.
MAGDA. That may be your way of seeing your own life. There can only

be one truth.
DAVID. Sorry, what you call your truth is no more than the outward expression of your own nation feelings.
MAGDA. I don't know what you're talking about.
DAVID. What do you mean? Don't you have any nationalist feelings?
MAGDA. Do you?
DAVID. Of course I do. What do you mean...
MAGDA. I feel sorry for you.
DAVID. Why's that?
MAGDA. Apparently, you don't even know what feeling means.
DAVID. Just a minute. I want to get this straight. Don't you love your own people?
MAGDA. Do you love yours?
DAVID. Of course I do!
MAGDA. Then I guess you don't even know what love is.
DAVID. Is that so?
MAGDA. If you love three million people and you've got three million loves then you don't really have a single love. I can't love more than one person, and when I do, I don't have any love left over.
DAVID. With me it's just the other way around. I love wine, I love women, I love chickens, I love fish on the grill...
MAGDA. You love to babble away without thinking. You're a naive kid.
DAVID. Lady, I'm not a kid, and I'm not naive. I'm twenty-five already.
MAGDA. And you don't know who you are.
DAVID. I know exactly...
MAGDA. If you knew you you were, you wouldn't let people with the conscience of a pimp use you for unethical purposes and turn you into human trash.
DAVID. How's that again?
MAGDA. You can hit me, if you want, and finish the job.
DAVID. I didn't come here to hit you. I'm rather enjoying our conversation actually.
MAGDA. Well I'm not. I don't have the patience for your kind of humour. My whole body aches and I don't have anything more to say to you.
DAVID. I told you I was sorry about the beating. I really am. I didn't sleep all night.
MAGDA. My heart bleeds. You want me to feel sorry for you. Do me a favor and go.
DAVID. Do you think it was easy for me to come here?
MAGDA. I'm not interested.

DAVID. Doesn't my coming here prove anything?
MAGDA. I find it suspicious.
DAVID. Somehow or other, I feel guilty towards you.
MAGDA. So go and nurse your guilt feelings somewhere else.
DAVID. Listen, I'm talking to you like one human being to another. Why do you answer me like that?
MAGDA. You're sitting across from me now, with your face all soft and gentle. But how can I forget the other face that you had. The meaness and the evil. And the beating you gave me. I don't like people who have a double standard. First they hit you, then they feel guilty and start whimpering.
DAVID. I really do feel guilty.
MAGDA. Your feelings are your own problem. Besides, you needn't **feel** guilty. You really **are** guilty.
DAVID. I know.
MAGDA. No, you don't. I'm not just speaking in general terms. I'm referring to something very specific that you have no way of knowing about.
DAVID. What exactly?
MAGDA. None of your business.
DAVID. Tell me please. I'm asking you. I'd like to know.
MAGDA. Why not actually? You should know. I have a kidney problem. My left kidney doesn't work properly. And now, thanks to your kicking, I've got strong pains in my right kidney.
DAVID. Are you sure it's the kidney.
MAGDA. I know my body well enough. I'm scared you might have wrecked it.
DAVID. I don't know what to say.
MAGDA. Then just shut up. *(She gets up.)* Now you really can go, and celebrate with your friends.
DAVID. *(Gets up too. Paces the room.)* What do you mean I can go... What do you mean I can go... I'm not about to go now... I couldn't... What do you... What am I... I'm not human trash yet... I'm... I did something to you, now I've got to take the consequences... Listen, you're getting dressed and coming with me right now.
MAGDA. Where to? Where to?
DAVID. What do you mean where to? To the hospital, that's where to...
MAGDA. I don't have health insurance. I haven't paid for six months.
DAVID. What?... I'll pay what ever it costs.
MAGDA. Leave me alone. You can keep your money.
DAVID. What do you mean 'leave me alone'. Forget it. Just stop telling

me to leave you alone and to keep my money and to go celebrate with my friends. What am I - a piece of shit? What am I - some kind of rat? You can't throw me out now. I'm not moving, got that? I'm not moving until you get dressed and come with me straight to the hospital. Oh, God, what did I do? Oh God. Hurry up and get dressed. What are you waiting for? Come on! Get dressed already! God... What are you looking at me for? Do you know you've got no sense of responsibility? You know what it means to get kicked in the kidneys?

Dahlia walks off the set. Ada and Udi rush over to her, take off her robe and quickly help her dress for the next scene. Meanwhile Samira is talking to the camera and Fahed is pacing in the wings preparing for his scene with Magda.

SAMIRA. *(To the camera.)* David was on the verge of hysteria. He was pacing the room like a wild animal. I'd never seen anyone in such a state. I have to admit I was pretty scared. David's concern was contagious. He almost forced me into getting dressed. We took his car, an old Renault 4 that he sold to pay my hospital bills. I spent a week in the hospital. David didn't budge from my bedside the whole time. He brought me a transistor radio. He bought me a Walkman and cassettes. He bought me a chess set and taught me how to play. I must admit the time really went by quickly. When it turned out my kidney wasn't damaged, he was happy as a child. He kept buying me present. A few days after I left the hospital, I met Adnan.
BENESH. Is Dahlia ready?
DAHLIA. Ready.
BENESH. Roll it. Move straight into the next scene. *(To Yonah)* Smooth as can be. At this rate, we'll be through on time.
YONAH. Knock on wood.

Scene 2

BENESH. Roll VTR. Yonah. VTR rolling. 4, 3, 2, 1, 0
DAHLIA. It's so empty here without you. I woke up last night and looked for you everywhere. Even in the bathroom. Then I suddenly remembered that you're in Lebanon. How are you? Hello... Hello... Damn it, the line's gone dead. *(Enter Fahed as Adnan. He meets Magda.)* Adnan?! Look who's come back from the cold...

ADNAN. You were in the hospital, I hear.
MAGDA. It's you they were after, but you disappeared. Someone had to take their beating.
ADNAN. Who beat you?
MAGDA. Someone who was in love with his people, like you.
ADNAN. Could you identify him?
MAGDA. What for? You want to get beat up too?
ADNAN. Tell us who it is. We'll finish him off.
MAGDA. Haven't enough people been hurt already? Do you have to drag even more victims into it?
ADNAN. I can't just ignore the fact that a Jew beat you up.
MAGDA. Pretend it was an Arab. Where we come from, men do still raise a hand on women sometimes.
ADNAN. He hit you as an Arab.
MAGDA. You're wrong. He hit me precisely because he took me for a Jew. When he found out that I was an Arab, he actually stopped.
ADNAN. Why are you trying to cover for him?
MAGDA. What's eating you? Your'e sense of honor?
ADNAN. You don't know what that means, do you?
MAGDA. Of course not. After all, I'm a woman... (*Fahed stops acting, abandons the characterization of Adnan.*)
BENESH. Cut! What's the matter, Fahed? I thought we'd overcome the problems with the text already.
FAHED. It isn't the text. There's something about the character that doesn't seem right to me.
BENESH. Now you tell me?
FAHED. One actor quit the production already because of that character. Now you're blaming me for agreeing to pinch-hit at the last moment?
BENESH. Rassan didn't leave because of the character.
FAHED. I've spoken to him.
BENESH. I don't know what he told you.
FAHED. Let's not talk about Rassan now. I don't want to get into politics. (*To Samira.*) Was Adnan your boyfriend?
SAMIRA. He was in love with me. But we were no more than friends.
FAHED. He heard you were in the hospital and he didn't go to see you?
SAMIRA. He was hiding. He was afraid the police were after him.
FAHED. Why doesn't he say so?
SAMIRA. He didn't say so because he was embrassed. By the time I met him, he already knew the police hadn't been looking for him at all. I found out about it but it wasn't until much later that I understood.
FAHED. Couldn't you find some way of working that into the scene?

BENESH. I don't want to show him as a coward.
FAHED. A coward? Do you know how the police behave towards Arabs they pick up?
DAHLIA. She told you the police weren't looking for him.
FAHED. How was he supposed to know they weren't?
DAHLIS. How was he supposed to know they were?
UDI. Have you ever lived as a second-class citizen? Have you ever lived like a minority that's regarded as a fifth column and an enemy of society?
ADA. Have you?
UDI. Oh, Mother, I can imagine what it's like.
ADA. Imagine, can you?
FAHED. He's right. That's just the way it is. You live in a constant feeling of insecurity. As soon as you see a police roadblock you get that empty feeling in the pit of your stomach. Anyone who's been involved in something like that Independence Day party prank has good reason to stay out of sight. *(To Benesh)* I don't understand why you didn't include it in the scene. Why doesn't he bring it up? To begin with, it's the truth and you get to show what the political situation does to people. Besides, it would make him stronger.
YONAH. On the contrary. The fact that he manages to hide both his fear and his shame makes him much stronger. From the dramatic standpoint, he has negative feelings about himself. They block his relationship with Magda and make him almost violent towards her.
FAHED. How will the audience know all of these lovely things. Are you going to just tell them?
YONAH. Act it out.
FAHED. '**You** act it out.' No, buster. That message is too complex and intricate to act out. The audience will see that Adnan is angry, that he's got a problem. That much I can work in, but how are people going to know the guy is angry with himself because he's been hiding, because he was afraid of the police and that he's ashamed to admit it because he discovered that it was unfounded fear stemming from his predicament as an Arab? How do you want all that information to get through simply by acting it out?
BENESH. It's not the information that counts here.
FAHED. And how the information counts! Forgive me, Benesh, when you decide to prsent an Arab, you've got a problem. You don't treat him as an equal.
BENESH. I don't treat the Arab as an equal.
FAHED. I'm not talking about your views. I know you're anti-racist.

But precisely because of your views, you fall into the trap. You don't want to present an Arab who behaves dishonorably.
BENESH. I'll grant you that much. The way things are now, with the anti-Arab racist attitudes, I'm about to present an Arab whose behavior is liable to make people feel contempt or scorn.
FAHED. I categorically disagree with you, even though I am an Arab. Maybe that's what we should be showing - that the dishonorable situation that people are forced into makes them behave dishonorably? *(Addressing everyone.)* As Jews, don't you understand that? *(To Benesh again.)* Why do you want to make this film about Samira anyway? Just because you happened to meet Samira on a flight from London to Israel and she told you her story? Why not make a film about yourself and you own situation?
BENESH. This is a film about me and my situation.
FHAED. I don't get it.
BENESH. Samira had the guts to fight for the freedom she didn't posess, the freedom everyone was trying to deprive her of. I don't have the guts to follow through on the freedom I do posess.
FAHED. What do you mean by the guts to follow through on your freedom?
BENESH. It's the guts to give freedom to those who depend on you.
UDI. Are you talking personally or in the political sense?
FAHED. Hold it. Let's leave politics out of this. Look at us. I'm an actor, you're a director. I depend on you. Have you got the guts to give me my freedom?
BENESH. Just what do you mean by that?
FAHED. Let me release Adnan from your concept of him.
YONAH. And enslave him to yours?
FAHED. Stop philosophizing. *(To Benesh.)* I'm Adnan. Give me the freedom to be the way I feel. Let me do an improvization on the scene.
BENESH. *(To Dahlia.)* Are you game?
DAHLIA. What the hell... let's try it... what could happen?
BENESH. Go ahead. Let me know when you're ready. *(Fahed walks off the set. Dahlia is about to leave too.)* Where to, Dahlia?
DAHLIA. To the john. Call me when you're ready. *(Exits.)*
HAVKIN. Just a minute.. Just a minute. Are we adlibbing?
ADA. As part of the scene, Havkin. As part of the scene.
HAVKIN. What's part of the scene... Who's part of the scene... If it's freedom we're after, then let's have freedom all the way. There's no half-freedom, just like there's no half-love.
BENESH. Havkin, we're trying something out.

HAVKIN. Trying something out? Of course we're trying something out. You think I'm in the theater since yesterday? You think I'd force my way in just to steal a scene. I'm just asking if I can join in when I feel the time is right - or should I go on sleeping?
YONAH. How can you join in when the scene is taking place in Jerusalem, and you're in London?
HAVKIN. Who's in London?
YONAH. Herbert!
HAVKIN. What does my being in London have to do with it? *(To Benesh.)* Didn't you explain to me that all of the scenes take palce in my London studio?
BENESH. Yes, but in Magda's memory.
HAVKIN. Yes, in Magda's memory...
BENESH. And this scene took place in Jerusalem.
HAVKIN. So...
YONAH. You know what, Havkin, just go on sleeping.
HAVKIN. You go on sleeping! I don't understand...
BENESH. Sh...Sh... Enough! We're starting.
HAVKIN. *(As he steps aside and Fahed enters as Adnan.)* I don't understand... There's something here I don't understand...

Scene 3

Fahed enters dressed as a Hasid from Me'ah She'arim, an ultra-religious neighborhood in Jerusalem. This includes a black robe, a fur hat, a beard and sidelocks. He is holding a prayer book and is absorbed in his prayers, swaying like a branch in the wind.

BENESH. *(To the cameraman.)* Roll VTR!
YONAH. VTR rolling.

The cameraman dollies in towards Fahed who is swaying to and fro in fervent prayer. Dahlia returns from the bathroom. She enters unwittingly, humming a song from the European hit parade, not realizing that they've started shooting. Suddenly, she sees the Hasid praying and bursts out spontaneously.

ADNAN. Shabess! Shabess!
DAHLIA. What's this?
ADNAN. Shush, you heathen.

DAHLIA. *(To everybody.)* Who is he? David? *(Suddenly she realizes that the camera is rolling and she cries out in dismay.)* Oh, no... You're shooting!

SAMIRA. Improvizing.

ADNAN. *(Whispering to her.)* Magda... Magda... *(She gives the others a perplexed look. Benesh nods to her and signals her to continue. She assumes the role of Magda and starts improvising.)*

MAGDA. Adnan?

ADNAN. Magda...

MAGDA. Adnan, I'm coming. What's this? Have you converted?

ADNAN. I heard you were in the hospital. I went to visit you but they told me you'd been discharged already.

MAGDA. What's this get-up?

ADNAN. I'm appearing in a film.

MAGDA. What film?

ADNAN. A piece of nonsense. The Jews are doing another production about the Arabs to calm their crummy conscience.

MAGDA. Any money in it at least?

ADNAN. Money, my foot! A bunch of down-and-outs making a two-bit video film.

MAGDA. Where've you been all this time?

ADNAN. Anyone ask about me?

MAGDA. Who should have asked?

ADNAN. The police.

MAGDA. The police? What're you talking about?

ADNAN. Didn't they question you?

MAGDA. About what?

ADNAN. About our Independence Day performance.

MAGDA. Of course not. What's got into you? They've forgotten all about it.

ADNAN. Damn that Fahed! If I catch him, I'll break every bone in his body. Boy, did he put one over on me, the bastard. 'Watch out, Adnan, don't show your face. The whole security service, the whole police force is after you...' *(Yonah and Paul enter the improvization as Barry and Avi. They walk onto the set, smoking cigarettes.)*

BARRY. *(To Avi.)* Look at her. Don't we know her from somewhere?

AVI. Isn't she from the university?

BARRY. Say, where do I know you from?

ADNAN. *(Bursts in as a Hasid:)* Shabbess! Shabbess!

AVI. What do you want?

ADNAN. Cigarettes on the Sabbath in our Holy City? Heretics!

BARRY. What's gotten into you man?

ADNAN. *(Begins ranting and raving.)* 'And if ye will not for all this hearken unto Me, but walk contrary unto Me, then I will walk contrary to you also in fury. And I, even I, will chastise you seven times for your sins. And ye shall eat the flesh of your sons, and the flesh of your daughters shall ye eat...and cast your carcasses upon the carcasses of your idols...'

AVI. Lunatic!

BARRY. Leave him alone. Come on.

ADNAN. 'Tfu! And I will scatter you among the heathen... and your lands shall be desolate and your cities waste, and ye be in your enemies' land and ye shall perish among the heathens and the land of your enemies shall eat you up, and they that are left of you shall pine away in their iniquity in your enemies' lands. Tfu!'

Avi. Lunatic!

BARRY. Leave him be. Let's go... *(They leave and Adnan shouts after them.)*

ADNAN. 'I will even appoint over you terror, consuption and the burning ague and cause sorrow of heart. And ye shall be slain before your enemies. And I will bring a sword of vengeance upon you and I will send the pestilence among you and ye shall de delivered into the hand of the enemy. Paskudnakes.'

MAGDA. Stop it, enough, they're gone. Calm down. ' I will even bring a sword of vengeance upon you and I will send the pestilence among you and ye shall be delivered into the hand of the enemy... '

ADNAN. What?

MAGDA. You're not the only one they forced to study Bible. I went through that too.

ADNAN. Are they the ones that hit you?

MAGDA. No, someone else.

ADNAN. Who?

MAGDA. What's it to you?

ADNAN. Am I your boyfriend or not? Tell me who beat you up and we'll finish him.

MAGDA. Haven't enough people been hurt? Do we have to have more?

ADNAN. A Jewish fascist beat you up and you want me to take it easy?

MAGDA. What's hurting you, your sense of honor?

ADNAN. You don't know what that means, do you?

MAGDA. All I know is this: when they were beating me up, you ran.

ADNAN. The only language they understand is the language of force. Tell me who it was and I'll finish him off.

MAGDA. I don't want to finish him off.
ADNAN. Why are you covering for him? I'll find him myself.
MAGDA. God help you if you lay a hand on him. You know me and you know what I can do.
ADNAN. What's this all about? You haven't fallen in love with him by any chance, have you?
MAGDA. It so happens I have.
ADNAN. With a Jew? The one who beat you up?
MAGDA. He didn't know what he was doing. When we're together, I'm not an Arab, and he's not a Jew. We're two people who've discovered one another.
ADNAN. You're the sharpest woman I know, but you don't have the slightest bit of poltical awareness. Politically you're no more than an infant.
MAGDA. And you. You're so smart but sometimes you're such a fool. Still, I'm not mad at you. You're jealous. That's human and natural. Politically or otherwise, the man in you is what's been hurt. I understand you.
ADNAN. I understand you too, woman. Power, that's what attracts you in a man. And as soon as you smell weakness, you spit and scratch and lick. In that area, when you match me up against your new man, I'm bound to lose. How attractive can the vicitm be, compared to the sex appeal of the hangman? He can walk around with a gun, in uniform, standing tall, head up high. And me, I've got to castrate myself, to lower myself, to bow my head and to keep out of sight so that he might condescend to give me a fraction of the right to exist. He's the master of the land, the king. And what am I? A servent, a beaten dog. Look at me: a lousy joke of a human being. I can understand your choice. *(Havkin jumps up and joins the scene.)*
HAVKIN. That's not true. What utter nonsense! First you be a victim for two thousand years, then you'll understand how much sex appeal there is in weakness.
ADNAN What are you doing here?
HAVKIN. *(Embarrassed.)* What? *(Realizing he has entered a scene where he doesn't belong, Havkin becomes Herbert and introduces some anger into the character.)*
HERBERT. What are **you** doing here? You're in my studio.
Adnan. We're in Jerusalem, sir.
HERBERT. *(Pointing at Magda.)* In her memory you're in Jerusalem. You only can exist in her imagination. But she's in my studio in London.
ADNAN. *(Actually Fahed, who dosen't know how to continue the*

improvisation, indicates this directly.) Sorry, I don't know you and I have no interest in knowing you.

HERBERT. So fuck off! *(To Magda.)* You've got company. I've got to tell you he's an intruder in my house and he's got the gall to tell me he doesn't know me!

FAHED. A victim for 2,000 years. They've slashed off three zeroes, in case you don't remember.

MAGDA. I though you were asleep...

HERBERT. How can anyone sleep with him standing there carrying on at the top of his lungs?

(He's stuck, trying to figure out a way to end his part of the scene. He then finds a solution.)

Incidentally, I think someone is looking for you.

MAGDA. For me? Now?

HERBERT. Yes. Someone came, knocked on the door. I open up and ask 'What do you want?' 'To see her.' 'Who?' 'The girl who's living with you.' What should I tell him?

MAGDA. Tell whom?

HERBERT. The guy who's looking for you.

MAGDA. Nobody is looking for me at three am on Christmas Eve in London. Herbert. Come, let me walk you to your bed. *(Dahlia wants to get out of the scene too and to end the improvization, but now Benesh enters in the role of Rodney, surprising them both.)*

RODNEY. Magda?

MAGDA. Rodney!

RODNEY. I've been looking for you everywhere. I knocked on this door out of sheer desperation.

HERBERT. Oh, there he is. *(To Rodney.)* She didn't want to believe me.

MAGDA. Why are you chasing me?

HERBERT. He wants you. That's obvious.

MAGDA. *(To Rodney.)* I told you it was all over between us.

HERBERT. I guess you didn't sound very convincing.

MAGDA. So what brings you here at such an hour? Your wife fall asleep again?

RODNEY. I'm in the middle of filming a new television play.

HERBERT. Are you married?

RODNEY. Would you mind excusing us?

HERBERT. Sir, I don't know you. If anyone has any excusing to do, surely it's your wife. Want to call her and apologize?

RODNEY. *(To Magda.)* Can we go somewheres private?

HERBERT. Don't worry. I don't see very well.

RODNEY. Sorry, sir. We have something private to discuss. Would you mind leaving us alone.
HERBERT. By all means. *(Turns to go.)*
MAGDA. No, Father, you stay here.
RODNEY. 'Father'?
MAGDA. I'd like to introduce you. My spiritual father, Herbert. My ex-lover, Rodney.
HERBERT. Hello, ex-lover.
RODNEY. Hello, spiritual father.
HERBERT. You, I haven't adopted yet.
RODNEY. What's this supposed to be.
MAGDA. Recreation. Like your love.
HERBERT. If you're not in a hurry to get home to your wife, you're invited.
MAGDA. He's never in a hurry to get home to his wife before he sleeps with me. Only after.
HERBERT. The old story.
MAGDA. The old story.
RODNEY. Ha ha. I love jokes, you know.
MAGDA. Sure, I know. Wasn't I your last joke.
RODNEY. That's not true. You weren't my last joke.
MAGDA. Wasn't I? Is there a new one? What's her name?
RODNEY. I knew you wouldn't go back to Israel. I'm awfully glad you've stayed.
MAGDA. I know you're glad. You think everything will go back to being just the way it was. You'll come over, spend an hour with me, then you'll begin stealing looks at your watch.
RODNEY. No, that's over.
MAGDA. That's right. As far as I'm concerned, that miserable chapter is over.
HERBERT. *(Taking over the role from Rodney.)* We'll open up a new leaf.
MAGDA. How well I know these conversations.
HERBERT. Let's draw a line over everything that's happened.
MAGDA. Let's forget the past.
HERBERT. Fine. I've forgotten already. Don't you believe me?
MAGDA. I believe you. I believe every word you say.
HERBERT. The past is dead.
MAGDA. Dead and buried.
HERBERT. I'm going to cut off all my other ties. It'll take a week, two weeks... then I'll be all yours. We'll go out togther, we'll have a good

time, we'll live together. *(To Rodney.)* Forgive me for stealing your text.
RODENY. Steal away if it makes you happy.
HERBERT. It isn't only yours, and stealing from a thief doesn't count. *(To Magda.)* Want to dance?
MAGDA. By all means!

Herbert motions with his hand. Paul sits down at the piano and starts playing Edith Piaf's 'Rien de Rien'. The singer joins in. Herbert and Magda dance. Rodney leans against the door, watching them.

RODNEY. Bravo, bravo! Like a couple of lovebirds. Let's go out Magda. Let's go get something Chinese in the Soho.
MAGDA. Maybe something Middle Eastern?
RODNEY. Fine, just say where.
Magda. In one of the restaurants of the Old City or in Eastern Jerusalem?
RODNEY. What are you talking about. What's the matter with you?
MAGDA. In Jerusalem, in my own apartment.
RODNEY. And I'm at the North Pole.
MAGDA. I can feel the cold all the way to here.
RODNEY. What's happening to you? *(Samira gets up. Walks over to face the camera and talks.)*
SAMIRA. I'm in my room, in Jerusalem. I'm having a conversation with my boyfriend Adnan. David is on reserve duty in Lebanon. I went down to the pay-phone because I'd set a time with David. That's when I met Adnan and took him to my room. Do you remember him? You met him a year and a half ago, at the Independence Day party at the university. He's in jail now. Got ten years as an accomplice to a murder. They killed the Jewish thug who kicked me in the stomach and killed my baby. Mine and David's. David was a total wreck. He's in some *yeshiva* in the ultra-religious neighborhood. A born-again Jew. I saw him right after I got out of the hospital. I was in for a long time. He wanted me to convert and then we'd get married. He loves me. Adnan's willing to forgive me too. Everyone's willing to forgive me. One says to convert, the other says to come back to Islam, the third one coaxes me to London, to be European. All I needed was to fall in love with someone from India. I'm much in demand, what can I do? I was a wreck when I got out of the hospital. I headed for London. You remember how you invited me when we met at the university. That's when I came to you, Rodney. You said you were a confirmed believer in the Palestinean cause. You promised to help me find a job. I was a real mess when I first arrived. I

tired to pull myself together, but you got me this room in Covent Garden and made me your mistress. Except that now we're in Jerusalem with Adnan.

MAGDA. *(Actually Dahlia to Benesh, directly.)* Between you and me, it's the same story with us, give or take a few minor details.

RODNEY. *(Actually Benesh, who is trying to stop the improvization now that the earth is beginning to burn under his feet.)* That'll do. Why don't we stop there?

DAHLIA. No. This time I'm going to tell you everything.

BENESH. Wouldn't you rather save it for some other time, in private?

DAHLIA. You're not going to get another chance. I can see exactly how things are between us. Right now! I'm going to tell you everything right now!

BENESH. You can't do this...

DAHLIA. Can't I? Why not? Because that's the way the master wants it? I certainly can and I will! Just what do you think I am, another character in one of your dramas?

BENESH. No. I don't have any characters that are vulgar in my dramas.

DAHLIA. So this time you will, and I'll show you just what vulgarity really is. I'll pick up the phone to your wife.

BENESH. You'll do no such thing.

DAHLIA. Just you try me.

BENESH. That'll be the end. I mean it. You know I'm capable of throwing you out, just like that. Which would be a pity. You know that no man ever loved you like I did and no man ever will.

DAHLIA. You've done a good job. 'Be sociable. Have a Pepsi.' And go.

HERBERT. Do you know the way out, or do I have to show you?

BENESH. *(Briefly resuming the role of Rodney.)* Thanks. I'll find my way out.

He steps off the set, then takes a cigarette. His hands are shaking with excitement as he lights up. Dahlia is crying, her face buried in her hands. Herbert hurries over to her side, takes a long elegant coat off a hanger in his apartment and wraps it around Magda. Meanwhile, Yonah is preparing to hand the director's baton back to Benesh

YONAH. Benesh...

BENESH. Keep going, keep going... I need a cigarette...

Yonah continues to serve as director, pointing the cameramen in the right direction from behind. Meanwhile, the scene between Herbert and Magda continues.

HERBERT. *(Trying to comfort Dahlia; i.e., Magda.)* There, there. Take it easy. *(He wraps the coat around her, takes a period hat from the thirties and puts in on her head. She continues crying.)* There, there... Come on...

He leads her to the mirror, facing her reflection. Dahlia is surprised to see herself dressed up as an elegant Viennese lady from the thirties. She starts laughing through her tears. Herbert is encouraged by her laughter. He hands her a pair of long gloves. She puts them on. He wraps a beautiful old cape around his shoulders, a white shawl around his neck, a top-hat on his head. He stands at her side and the two of them look like a glamorous Viennese couple from the thirties. Paul draws inspiration from the picture and begins picking a tune on the piano - a nostalgic Viennese waltz. The singer scats to the music. The dance starts out softly but gradually grows into a shattering, buring waltz.

HERBERT. Viens, mon amour! *(He leads Dahlia into a dance to the beat of the waltz. As they dance, Havkin forgets about Herbert, and what we see are Dahlia and Havkin laying their souls bare.)*
DAHLIA. Why are you dressing me?
HAVKIN. Isn't it pretty?
DAHLIA. Who are you, really?
HAVKIN. I'd like to be the story of your life. No man has ever loved you the way I did, and no man ever will.
DAHLIA. What would I do without you at such a terrible time in this stange place?
HAVKIN. We were bound to meet. It was the inevitability of chance.
DAHLIA. I don't understand you.
HAVKIN. Every meeting takes place by chance, but when you meet the right person, the inevitable happens.
DAHLIA. *(Suddenly stops dancing.)* I'm all alone. You have no idea how lonely I am. I haven't a soul in the world.
HAVKIN. That's not true. *(Havkin embraces her. He kisses her on the lips passionately, like an ardent young lover.)*
DAHLIA. What's come over you?
HAVKIN. You've done a good job. 'Be sociable. Have a Pepsi!'
DAHLIA. I'm sorry... *(Reaches out to stroke his face, but he pulls back.)*

HAVKIN. *(One by one he removes the items of Viennese clothing. He bends over.)* I'm an old man. I know that. I'm not asking what I would have asked thirty or forty years ago. Now let me crawl quietly back into my corner. By myself. I haven't a soul in this world. Good night... *(Herbert wlks away from the set.)*
YONAH. Cut!

All those present burst into spontaneous applause, gather around Havkin and lavish their praise on him. He is very excited.

BENESH. Let's take a break, everybody!

They all amble out. Remaining on the set, in separate corners are Udi and Samira. Also on the set are Dahlia and Benesh.

Scene 4

BENESH. *(Walks over to Dahlia.)* Dahlia...
DAHLIA. Leave me alone. *(Turns to leave.)*
BENESH. Wait a minute, Dahlia...
DAHLIA. Don't worry. I won't tell your wife. I'm not that vulgar. *(She leaves. Benesh follows her.)*
BENESH. Dahlia, I'll wait for you in the cafeteria. *(Exits.)*

Udi, holding a cigarette, walks over to Samira.

UDI. Got a light? *(She lights his cigarette, and one for herself.)* Thanks. What's with your apartment?
SAMIRA. What do you mean?
UDI. I heard you were having some problem.
SAMIRA. No, that was a white lie. I was looking for on excuse to get away from here for a while.
UDI. Why?
SAMIRA. Because of Dahlia. She thinks I have something going with Benesh.
DAHLIA. Well, don't you?
UDI. Everyone thinks you do.
SAMIRA. After that business with Howard, I keep away from married men.

DAHLIA. Who's Howard?
SMAIRA. That's Rodney, in the script.
DAHLIA. Did it happen just that way?
SMAIRA. Not exactly. But pretty much. Benesh apparently put a lot of himself into the part of Rodney.
DAHLIA. What's it like seeing your own story being filmed?
SAMIRA. It isn't exctly my story. Dahlia puts a lot of herself into Magda too.
DAHLIA. So what's it like to see others hitching a ride on your story?
SAMIRA. Interesting. Suddenly you realize that we're not so different from one another.
UDI. And me? Do I remind you of David or isn't it the same story at all?
SAMIRA. You'd be surprised. You're very much like him. You even look like him. Sometimes when I look at you, I see him.
DAHLIA. Are you still in love with him?
SAMIRA. No. I feel sorry for him.
UDI. Why?
SAMIRA. David is a man who'll never know who he is.
UDI. Is there such a thing?
SAMIRA. Sure there is. A person who never comes to terms with moral questions. A person who only acts on his emotions.
UDI. That's someone spontaneous, isn't it?
SAMIRA. Are you developing the character or are you talking with me?
UDI. Both...
SAMIRA. He's a person who's torn between confilicting desires.
DAHLIA. You talk a lot about morals... That subject's on your mind a lot..
SAMIRA. If you were the target of repression and exploitation, you'd be sensitive to people's moral or immoral behavior too and it would be on your mind a lot.
DAHLIA. It's damned hard getting near you...
UDI. Yes, it really is.
SAMIRA. Are you sure you want to?
UDI. In order to know that, I have to try, don't I?
SAMIRA. Go ahead and try.
UDI. Would you be willing to help me?
SAMIRA. How can I help you?
UDI. Let's begin with that scene of the phone-call from Lebanon.
SAMIRA. How can I help you?
UDI. I'll do my text and you throw in Magda's.
SMAIRA. No problem. *(She takes the text, opens on the relevant page.)*

Go ahead. *(Udi recites David's text. Samira* recites *Magda's.)*
DAVID. Hello. Hello. Magda?
SAMIRA. *(Reading from the script.)* David? Where are you calling from?
DAVID. *(Half acting.)* From the outpost. We've got a phone connection for half an hour. Lucky I caught you. How are you doing?
SAMIRA. I miss you.
DAVID. I miss you too. Terribily.
SAMIRA. What? I can't hear you .
DAVID. I miss you too. Terribly. How's our apartment doing?
SAMIRA. It's empty. It's awfully empty without you. Last night I woke up and looked for you in bed, everwhere, even in the bathroom. Then I suddenly remembered you're in Lebanon. What are you doing?
DAVID. Dying.
SAMIRA. What?
DAVID. Dying to see you.
SAMIRA. I want you here next to me. Can you hear me? Now!
DAVID. I keep picturing you. It takes so much out of me emotionally.
SAMIRA. What? I can't hear you. What did you say?
DAVID. I said it uses up such a lot of energy to create a picture of you in my mind.
SAMIRA. Yes, it's crazy.
DAVID. What a tremendous waste of energy. I know just when my energy is going to run out. If I don't get to see you by then, I'll start to die. You hear me?
SAMIRA. I hear your voice, but I can't see you. I miss you so much. I can't touch you. You took everything I love with you. But I can still feel you.
DAVID. Go on. I hear you.
SAMIRA. Everything in the apartment reminds me of you. It's so hard being without you, and I want you back right now. I want to feel you. How are you?
DAVID. A soldier in my platoon ws killed two days ago.
SAMIRA. You've got to come back to me, you hear me? I want you back safe and sound, beside me.
UDI. *(Abandoning his impersonation of David.)* Lebanon was an eye-opener for me too.
SAMIRA. Did you take part in the war?
UDI. No. I was in an entertainment troupe with two other actors from the theater. We had nothing to give. None of us was an entertainer. So we put on segments from Kafka's_*The Trial.* One day they sent us to some

God-forsaken spot. When we got there, it turned out to be a makeshift POW camp. A kind of small, improvized barbed-wire pen. We appeared on a small platform, concocted out of some ammunition crates. The audience consisted of a dozen oddballs whose job was to interrogate the prisoners. They sat there in front of the fence. Behind it, on the ground were the prisoners. A few dozen men - filthy, unshaven, their hands tied and their eyes covered. I can picture it all as if it were happening right now. There I am on the platform, recounting the story of the gates and the guards while those investigators sit there across from me, staring, their eyes red from sleepness nights. Behind them was the fence, and behind it, the prisoners, with strips of rags on their eyes. And there I stood, spitting out those words by Kafka...

SAMIRA. And what did you do?

UDI. Nothing. What did I do? I finished and got off the stage. What could I do?

SAMIRA. You could have said what you thought.

UDI. I wish I knew what I thought. We live in a fog. Nothing's clear-cut.

SAMIRA. And that suits you fine.

UDI. No. Why do you think that suits me?

SAMIRA. Why are you taking part in this film?

UDI. It's an important film...It's important for the public to know the truth.

SAMIRA. Are you discovering any truth in this file that you didn't already know?

UDI. Look...the very fact that we're dealing with this subject... Jews, Arabs... It's a subject that our whole future depends on.

SAMIRA. Why don't you think things through?

UDI. Wait a minute. In your story do you discover any truth that you didn't know before?

SAMIRA. No. I'm afraid I've failed. I admit it. When I was immersed in my work, I didn't notice. Now that I'm sitting on the sidelines watching the results, I can see the whole story's there but the truth doesn't come through.

UDI. If I were you...

SAMIRA. What would you do?

ADA. *(Peeping out behind the set.)* Udi? Is that where you are? They're looking for you. Come and get dressed.

UDI. In a second.

ADA. With you, a second is half an hour.

UDI. Lay off, Mother. Just a second. I'll be right there. *(To Samara.)* My mother was all I needed here. What did I bring her into the production for, anyway?

SAMIRA. I don't know. I didn't bring my parents in. (*Fahed appears, holding the script. He is memorizing the text.)*

FAHED. Sorry. Am I interrupting anything?

SAMIRA. No, we were working on the text.

ADA. (*Off-stage.)* Udi!

UDI. I'm coming! (*Exits.)*

FAHED. Am I interrupting anything? Would you work with me too? *(Fahed is eating nut chocolate throughout ther scene.)*

SAMIRA. *(Taking the text.)* Where from?

FAHED. *(Pointing to the line in the text.)* Where he stopped.

SAMIRA. *(Reading from the text.)* What's up? Am I being blackballed?

FAHED. Hold it. Just where is this happening?

SAMIRA. In the street. He's been avoiding me. I run into him in the street. He's just walking by, reading a book.

FAHED. In the street?

SAMIRA. Yes. He'd always walk with a book in his hand, immersed in it, paying no attention to what was going on around him, living in a dream world. It was Da'ud.

FAHED. Da'ud?

SAMIRA. Yes. Adnan in the script.

FAHED. I see...well, let's begin (*He takes the text and walks as he reads.)*

SAMIRA. What's up? Am I being blackballed?

ADNAN. (*(Lifting his head from the text.)* Oh it's you? When are you converting?

SAMIRA. I'm not converting.

ADNAN. Is the fascist planning to become a Moslem?

SAMIRA. There's no need. There are enough Moslem fascists without him.

ADNAN. So how will you work it out? Are you going to have a progressive Jewish lawyer draw up a contract allowing you to live together?

SAMIR. We don't need a contract. We'll go on the way we've done until now.

ADNAN. And when there is a baby, are you going to raise him as a Jew? As an Arab?

SAMIRA. When these's a baby, we'll try and raise him as a human being.

ADNAN. That fascist has turned you into a cosmopolitan. You're half-

Jewish already.
SAMIRA. That fascist is no fascist and I'm not half-Jewish.
ADNAN. You're naïve. You don't know what you're doing. Politically, what you do is meaningless.
SAMIRA. Why bring politics into this?
ADNAN. I don't know. I'm talking nonsense. You're getting me mad and you're making me talk nonsense, which on;y gets me madder...
SAMIRA. Why don't you come and visit us, Adnan.
ADNAN. No way! Absolutely not...
SAMIRA. Do we have the plague?
ADNAN. Listen... Maybe I'm not so free-thinking, so liberal... *(In an outburst.)*
ADNAN. I'm sick and tired of following the cultivated rules of western civilization.
SAMIRA. Why 'western civilization' all of a sudden?
ADNAN. I don't know. I don't want to see you with him. I'm jealous, OK?
SAMIRA. That's a shame. I happen to be very fond of you, as a human being.
ADNAN. 'As a human being'. Boy, you sure know how to turn the knife...
SAMIRA. Adnan...
ADNAN. Forget it. Go to him. He'll make you feel better.
SAMIRA. He's in Lebanon.
ADNAN. Here's hoping he never comes back.
SAMIRA. Adnan!
ADNAN. What's got into me!
SAMIRA. What do you think of the script?
FAHED. One hell of a script. *(Gathering up the chocolate crumbs from the aluminum wrapper and licking his fingertips.)*
SAMIRA. I'm asking seriously.
FAHED. Seriously, I can't tell you.
SAMIRA. Why not? Afraid of hurting my feelings?
FAHED. Don't be silly. I simply haven't read it.
SAMIRA. You haven't read the script?
FAHED. No. Why are you staring at me like that. Don't take it to heart. I never read scripts. I just read my own part.
SAMIRA. Terrific. And even that, only at the last minute, I see.
FAHED. If I have no choice.
SAMIRA. You probably even makes an ideology out of it - arriving nice and fresh for the actual shooting...

FAHED. Who's fresh? Can't you see how tired I am?
SAMIRA. And you think you're going to change things that way?
FAHED. Who has any intention of changing things? Lady, things have changed me. I used to be all gung-ho once, like you, but now... for years, I've been too tired. Boy, am I tired. *(Laughs.)* But don't worry. Your script isn't the only thing I haven't read. You're in good company. I haven't read Shakespeare in years either. Or Ibsen. Or Chekhov. Actually, since I graduated from university I haven't read a single play, except the ones I took part in. I'm in the actors' guild at the theater. What do you think we talk about at meetings? Work-hours, premiums, promotions... Who has the time to read anything... At our last meeting, someone suggested that the actors should have a say in deciding on repertoire. Why shouldn't they put on a play by Wedekind. Everyone was in favor. Me too, even though I'd never read a single work of his and I got the impression the others hadn't either. Still, the name has a nice ring to it. Wedekind. That's a playwright's name for you. When did he live?

Enter Benesh and Yonah followed by the entire cast, just back from their break. Yonah is in the middle of a sentence.

YONAH. You can take it from me, I tell you. If you go on at this pace, we'll be through shooting by 5 a.m. and by 8 o'clock, you'll be able to give them back the studio the way we said we would.
BENESH. Take the cast and set them up for the scene. *(As Yonah goes about organizing the next shots,Benesh turns to Samira.)* Samira, get ready with the lead-in for scene twelve.
SAMIRA. Aren't you doing a re-take of the phone-call from Lebanon and the meeting with Adnan?
BENESH. No. We saw yesterday's rushes and decided to do without it.
SAMIRA. There were quite a few inaccuracies in the text...
BENESH. Never mind, it comes across clearly.
SAMIRA. I was sure we'd re-do those shots. You said...
BENESH. We'll see. We'll see... If we have any time left over, then maybe... How's it going, Yonah?
YONAH. All ready? Let's begin.
BENESH. *(To Samira.)* Do you need to go over the text?
SAMIRA. No, no. I remember it. *(She walks over to the camera and begins talking.)*

Scene 5

Samira is talking to the camera.

BENESH. Roll VTR.
YONAH. VTR rolling.
SAMIRA. David got back from the army on the night of Purim. He had a beard. He was in a strange mood. 'Do you mind my uniform?' he asked. ' I don't care what you've got on.' He suggested trhat we go out right away to 'meet the two criminals who are to blame for my existence.' He was referring to his parents. He always called them by all sorts of strange names instead of simply referring to them as 'my parents'. I asked him if he'd told them yet that I was an Arab. 'No,' he said. 'They'll find out the hard way.' I said I didn't want to go to see them because I didn't want any part in his games with his parents. To which he replied that they would be a part of our game. He insisted that we dress up as a couple of born-again religious Jews. I told them, 'David, hold it'. We got to David's parents' house very late at night.

Magda and David go in. Magda is dressed in the modest garb of a very religious girl, with a kerchief on her head. David is in uniform. He has a beard and is wearing a skullcap. Samira continues with her story.

SAMIRA. The apartment was very dark. David rang but there was no reply. He used his own key to unlock the door, and we went in. We waited over an hour for them to arrive. They'd been to a Purim masquerade party put on by the drama club where David's mother served as an instructor.
MIRIAM. David? Dudale.
DAVID. Hi Mom. Hi Dad.
EPHRAIM. Hi son.
DAVID. Let me introdue you. Magda -
MIRIAM. Delighted. Miriam.
EPHRAIM. I'm Ephraim. Nice to meet you. You're still in the reserves?
DAVID. I'm though.
EPHRAIM. Welcome.
MIRIAM. Duvidel. You've lost weight.
DAVID. No I haven't.

MIRIAM. Hasn't he?
EPHRAIM. No. Yes. Maybe a little.
MIRIAM. Have you eaten anything?
DAVID. I'm not hungry.
EPHRAIM. He's not hungry.
MIRIAM. There's fish in the fridge.
DAVID. I told you Mother. I'm not hungry.
EPHRAIM. Sit down. Why are you standing?
DAVID. How's business Dad?
EPHRAIM. Pretty good. Can't complain. How's school?
DAVID. OK.
MIRIAM. You met at the university?
DAVID. That's right.
MIRIAM. Good. Then I'll get the fish.
EPHRAIM. Yes, yes, get the fish. Are you staying over?
DAVID. We'll see.
EPHRAIM. Don't go back to Jerusalem tonight. Stay here.
DAVID. We'll see.
MAGDA. We'll see.
MIRIAM. You prefer *gefilte*?
MAGDA. I prefer fish.
MIRIAM. *Gefilte* **is** fish, stuffed fish.
MAGDA. I see.
MIRIAM. The non-*gefilte* kinds has lots of little bones in it.
MAGDA. I'll have *gefilte*.
MIRIAM. Ephraim prefers the non-*gefilte* kind. But he's an expert. You should see him clean a head. David, I'll give you some...
DAVID. *Gefilte, gefilte*. Magda and I have known each other for almost a year.
EPHRAIM. Is that so? Is it serious between you two?
DAVID. You might say so.
EPHRAIM. Good, good. Well, go ahead and eat.
DAVID. We met at the Independence Day ball at the university.
EPHRAIM. That's a nice occasion for meeting people.
DAVID. Remember the fight at the ball that night?
EPHRAIM. The fight? No... What about?
DAVID. Arabs students started a provocation.
EPHRAIM. Oh... well, no wonder there was a fight.
MIRIAM. Your name is Magda, right?
MAGDA. Yes, Magda.
MIRIAM. So how do you like the fish, Magda?

MAGDA. A bit... sweet.
MIRIAM. Not sweet enough?
MAGDA. No, no! It is sweet enough.
MIRIAM. That's the way my mother used to make it.
MAGDA. Really? It's very... special...
EPHRAIM. Magda...
MAGDA. Yes?
EPHRAIM. I knew a girl called Magda once.
DAVID. Really? You never told me.
EPHRAIM. Her real name was Magida. She was the great-great-granddaughter of the renowned rabbi, the Magid of Mezerich, so they named her after him. Magida, Magda.
DAVID. Magda is not related to the Maggid of Mezerich.
EPHRAIM. She isn't?
DAVID. No she's not a member of the Maggid's family.
EPHRAIM. I'm no great admirer of the Maggid.
MIRIAM. What are you studying?
MAGDA. Acting.
MIRIAM. Oh, that's nice. I teach creative drama.
MAGDA. Do you like your work?
MIRIAM. Yes, very much.
DAVID. We're thinking of getting married.
EPHRAIM. When?
DAVID. We haven't set a date yet.
MIRIAM As far as we're concerned, you can live together without getting married.
EPHRAIM. Sure, we're free-thinking people.
MIRIAM. If I were your age, I wouldn't dream of getting married. I'd go for free love, living with whoever I love. Marriage? That institution hasn't a foot to stand on.
EPHRAIM. It hasn't any feet at all.
MIRIAM. I'm surprised at you two.
DAVID. But we want to get married.
MIRIAM. If it's what you want, go ahead.
EPHRAIM. Sure. Go ahead if you want to.
DAVID. Do you want to meet Magda's parents?
EPHRAIM. No.
DAVID. No?
EPHRAIM. No, on the contrary, why shouldn't we.
MIRIAM. I suppose we'll have to eventually, if you decide to get married.

EPHRAIM. Sure we will. Sooner or later.
MAGDA. Isn't it funny how a fight can lead to a wedding.
EPHRAIM. Well, life is full of surprises.
DAVID. We were in a fight together.
EPHRAIM. Well, you know what they say - the first step is always the hardest.
MIRIAM. I'd be happier if you stayed away from that sort of thing.
DAVID. Why's that? You think we should just let the Arabs make a mockery of the holiday?
MIRIAM. Dudaleh, you're a student now. You should concentrate on your studies. If there's any unrest, there are people in charge of keeping the peace.
DAVID. What do you think, Dad?
EPHRAIM. Just a minute. Got a bone here. What did you want to know?
DAVID. If you think we should let the Arabs make a mockery of the holiday.
EPHRAIM. Listen, I don't spend all day thinking about it. There's law, there's law enforcement, there's the security forces.
DAVID. My parents are very moderate people. They belong to what's called the Silent Majority.
EPHRAIM. That's how it is.
MAGDA. I don't get it. *(Everyone freezes, looking at her.)* I don't get it.
MIRIAM. What don't you get?
MAGDA. He calls you 'the two criminals'... *(Laughs.)* The two criminals who are to blame he's alive...
EPHRAIM. *(Laughs.)* We like using nicknames in our family - Miruskah, Dudaleh, Froilech
DAVID. Hold it Dad. I want to get this straight. A bunch of Arab students use the Independence Day celebration to make fun of the holiday...
MAGDA. What do you want him to do?
EPHRAIM. No, really, what do you want me to do? Did I send them?
DAVID. Are you phased out? Are you on drugs, Dad?
EPHRAIM. On drugs? What do you think I'm taking?
DAVID. Do I know? Hash? Marijuana?
EPHRAIM. We're on fish.
DAVID. You're behaving as though you're on a trip.
EPHRAIM. *(Still containing himself, but only barely.)* Trip, shmip...
MIRIAM. Ephraim, you're eating the fish with the bones.
EPHRAIM. The hell with the fish. The hell with the bones.

MIRIAM. Ephraim, the boy's home on a visit.
EPHRAIM. Home? Does he have any idea what a home is?
MIRIAM. Ephraim, we decided something.
EPHRAIM. You decided!
DAVID. What did you decide? What about?
MIRIAM. Dudaleh!
DAVID. Don't you call me Dudaleh any more. Got that? Don't you dare call me Dudaleh. David! David!
EPHRAIM. You decided! Freedom! Now look what your freedom's got you! A guy tries to hold on to his sanity, and they tell him he's on hash! A trip! He just dosen't know where to stop. That's the result of your freedom. A house that's free is no place to be!
DAVID. Wait a minute. What did you decide?
MIRIAM. Nothing.
EPHRAIM. The boy's home on a visit... Don't I know this character. You got yourself out on a limb. Now don't expect me to pull you down. Got that?
DAVID. What are you talking about?
EPHRAIM. I'll tell you just what I'm talking about. Light and darkness can't live together. And if you think you're so smart, it's because nobody ever told you 'no' on account of that genius who brought you up by the book instead of giving you a few sound spankings when it might still have done some good, damn it!
MIRIAM. Ephraim, have you gone mad?
EPHRAIM. You've gone mad yourself. Go find your Dr. Spock now!
DAVID. I want to know just what you decided!
MIRIAM. He's stoned out of his mind. He dosen't know what he's saying. Wasn't it bad enough the way you embarrassed us before the entire faculty and student body?
EPHRAIM. You wanted a clown? Fine! She forced me into this get-up.
MIRIAM. He gets right up there on the stage and starts singing the funeral hymn... Unbelievable.
EPHRAIM. She thinks she can just get the whole world to do what she wants! Why blame me when it's your dumb students that insisted on wearing pajamas? Death makes me laugh, it's not my fault.
MAGDA. Not me. Death doesn't make me laugh.
DAVID. Just wait a minute. Who went out on a limb?
EPHRAIM. You did!
DAVID. I went out on a limb?
EPHRAIM. Who else?
MIRIAM. Ephrarim...

EPHRAIM. Always smoothing things over. You think you can smooth everything over. You've stuffed the fish, now eat them yourself.
DAVID. I stuffed the fish?
EPHRAIM. And how you did! Nobody's going to eat them for you. Running from one extreme to another. First a pacifist...
DAVID. He's digging up archaeological finds.
EPHRAIM. And how a pacifist. A conscientious objector, no less. A draft dodger.
MIRIAM. He was rebelling against his father. Ephraim was a company commander in the Armoured Corps then.
EPHRAIM. With him everything is a rebellion. He's so busy rebelling that he'll marry the daughter of the Rabbi of Lubavitch.
DAVID. Me marry the daughter of the Rabbi of Lubavitch?
EPHRAIM. Yes, you marry the daughter of the Rabbi of Lubavitch .
DAVID. Me?
EPHRAIM. You'd marry the Rabbi of Lubavitch himself. You haven't by any chance joined some Indian sect or become a vegetarian, have you?
DAVID. No, but I'll tell you what I **have** done.
EPHRAIM. What?
DAVID. I've come to the conclusion that Arabs and Jews can live together in this country.
EPHRAIM. You don't say? What ever made you think that? The Lebanese experience?
DAVID. That too.
EPHRAIM. And what else?
DAVID. Magda. She's opened my head.
EPHRAIM. Is that so? Is that what you think too?
MAGDA. Yes, me too.
EPHRAIM. Fascinating. And just what opened your head? The beating he gave you on Independence Day?
MAGDA. What? What did you do?
EPHRAIM. I've always said the only thing the Arabs understand is force.
MAGDA. Leave them alone, David. Let's get out of here.
DAVID. I didn't tell them.
EPHRAIM. What did you think kid? That you could keep us from finding out that you're shacking up with an Arab. Your friends told us everything.
DAVID. You knew. You've known the whole time... And still you've been acting it out, with your hypocrisy...
EPHRAIM. What did you think kid? That we still get all shook by your

nonsense? What did you think, that you can still impress anyone with those whims of yours?
DAVID. *(To Miriam.)* That's your doing. 'It's just a stage.' I can just hear you: 'It'll pass...'
EPHRAIM. Yes, that's right. Just like all the other whims passed eventually. You'll live with an Arab, you?
MIRIAM. Ephraim, don't answer him!
EPHRAIM. *(Mimicking her.)* 'Don't answer him. Don't answer him.'
EPHRAIM. Don't I know you by now? You got scared by your own nerve! Just look at the hero who's going to go living with an Arab. I could see straight through you from the very beginning. Coming home when it got to be too much: Mommy, Daddy, help!
DAVID. Ha! Ha! So you've finally come out of your holes.
EPHRAIM. A big mouth, that's all you've got.
DAVID. It stinks, eh? It stinks! At long last. So you're opening your filthy trap for once! Go ahead! Have a field day while you're at it! A free house! A tolerant house! Say it! An Arab! Scared you, didn't it? Of course it did. Bringing a monster into your cozy little nest? Shitting into your homemade soup. That's the truth, isn't it? A filthy Arab! Go ahead and say it! *Gefilte! Gefilte!* Are you going to ostracize me or what? Going to go into mourning over me? Disinherit me? I don't give a shit about your money! Wouldn't take a penny from you anyhow! You can stuff it with your stinking money! Get your Dr. Spock to have me committed! Scum, that's what you are! You rotten old pair of no good... *(Pulls back, grabbing his gun.)* You'll pay for this... You'll pay for this! *(Runs off.)*
SAMIRA. There's no truth in this film any more.
HAVKIN. Is your whole life nothing but truth?
BENESH. Havkin...
HAVKIN. No, I want to understand. *(To Samira.)* Is there really that much truth in your life? Or maybe your life, like all our lives, is an ocean of trivial moments with you jabbering on about this and that and doing thousands of meaningless things. That's what I'd like to know.
SAMIRA. If you really want to know, the part of Herbert wansn't even supposed to be in the story.
BENESH. Lay off of that now!
SAMIRA. Why? 'Cause it makes you ucomfortable?
HAVKIN. Wait a minute. What's the problem with Herbert?
SAMIRA. There never was such a person.
HAVKIN. What do you mean there never was?
SAMIRA. Herbert is a brainstrom of Benesh's.

DAHLIA. But look how much colour he adds...

ADA. And meaning...

SAMIRA. That wasn't why Benesh put him in.

HAVKIN. What was the reason then?

SAMIRA. Ask him.

BENESH. What difference does it make now?

SAMIRA. You're not prepared to back up the things you said.

BENESH. I'll back them up, I'll front them up, I'll side them up...

SAMIRA. Great. Go ahead and kid about it.

BENESH. I wanted your story to have one character with a bit of human warmth to it.

SAMIRA. That's a lie.

HAVKIN. And what's the truth?

SAMIRA. He wanted to find you something to do.

HAVKIN. What? What did you say? What did he want?

SAMIRA. He said you -

BENESH. Why don't you shut your ass!

Havkin. Hold it! Watch how you talk to her.

BENESH. You can shut up too.

HAVKIN. I don't get it. What did he tell you?

SAMIRA. He said he knows a desperate old actor.

BENISH. You stupid fool. You and your truth.

SAMIRA. Isn't that the truth?

HAVKIN It's the truth... I don't see why you have to argue about it. It's the exact truth. To hell with it 'An actor'... What's an actor anyhow? You think I'm an actor - that I can play all sorts of roles?... I can't even figure out the text... And I, for one, **did** read it. I read it!... But I don't understand it. I don't remember a thing... For heaven's sakes... The scene I just did... I don't know... Twenty-five or thirty years ago I could... Now, I just don't get it... Maybe I'm not a real person any more... Maybe I just thnk I am actually walking and eating and sleeping... The devil only knows... It's all so pointless... And I've got a wife at home... If I just had a bottle here, I'd get drunk. -

DAHLIA. That's enough, Havkin, take it easy.

HAVKIN Maybe none of us really exists. Maybe we just think we do...

DAHLIA. Take it easy, Havkin.

HAVKIN. It isn't me. I don't really exist after all. It's Doctor Chebutikin. I never did understand that monologue and now all of a sudden I do. There's a true giant, Chekhov... *(Turns to Samira.)* In order to create truth, you have to destroy a truth. *(Silence falls. They all stand around, their arms limp. Samira turns to leave.)*

UDI. Hey, Samira, where to?
SAMIRA. I'm a fool, haven't you heard?
UDI. Just a minute, Samira.
SAMIRA. You can stay here and finish up your part. It's an interesting one, isn't it, and that's what counts as far as you're concerned.
UDI. I'm going with you.
SAMIRA. You promised to back me up and you didn't say a word. You don't have an ounce of character.
UDI. I'm going with you, Samira. *(Yonah dashes out in front of them, blocking their way.)*
YONAH. Just a minute! Nobody's going anywhere.
SAMIRA. Get out of the way.
YONAH. *(Pushing her to the center of the set.)* Get back in position facing the camera, you hear me?
UDI. How dare you raise a hand to her?!
YONAH. Shove off, before I smash your face in!
UDI. What?!
YONAH. You get back to the camera on the double! If there's any place in this world that I hold to be sacred, this is it. You're going back there. What did you have in mind - that you can just go ahead and spit on people? Truth, untruth... If it's truth you're looking for, suck it out of your ass. You got more truth there than you have in your heads. People put everything they've got into this story of yours. This guy is my friend and he has to face all of you naked and at the end of his tether. And you have the gall to complain. He pulled Rodney in his direction? Rodney who, Rodney what? I don't give a shit about Rodney. You don't know who Yonah is yet. I'll break the bones of anyone who hurts him now. 'The truth!' You're afraid of how your story is going to wind up. You get up there in front of the camera right this minute, you hear me? *(Shoves Samira. Shoves off Udi who tries to interfere.)* You too! Protecting her honor... Do you have any idea what you're working on here?... I've read your text... *(To Udi.)* You think you're on some kind of pleasure trip, trampling on the pus and the guts of a disintegrating soul like David and keeping the precious integrity of your own sweet personality intact? Protecting her honor, no less... That man's life has been wrecked in this work. Where do you come off treating that part like it was some kind of windfall? What do you think? - That a person can dig out all of the wickedness and rot buried deep inside him without being torn to bits and coming within a hair's breath of being put away? How dare you come to this job like you were in a pharmacy? How can you possibly expect to play your last scene in the kind of amiable mood you arrived in from that

nature trip you took with her? Just what did you have in mind? Have you given any thought to the God-awful things you're going to have to bring to life in a few minutes, or are you completely immersed in thoughts of how to escape the confusion and madness within you? Idiot! If that's what you want, then go ahead and hold hands with her , and make out and have a good time! Protecting her honor... You should both be ashamed of yourselves, you stinking couple of bourgeoisie... Tfu! You make me sick! Go ahead! Go back on the set! And if anyone so much as utters the word 'truth' here, I'll break his bones! *(To the camera.)* Action! Go!

Scene 6

Udi stands stunned. Dahlia enters as Magda. She is aware of Udi's condition. Ignoring the text, she walks over to him, touches him, hugs him, shows him her affection.

MAGDA. It's good to have you back. I've missed you. Don't talk. You don't have to say anything.
DAVID. I'm such a good-for-nothing.
MAGDA. Stop it.
DAVID. Laughable and good for nothing.
MAGDA. We're together. That's what count. Let me help you.
DAVID. *(Still Udi speaking about his own situation in the scene.)* I can't... Help me get out of sight...
MAGDA. I won't let you go away again.
DAVID. You're afraid I'll do something to myself...
MAGDA. You want a spanking? You love me. You've got me. You've got a baby in my belly. You've got enemies who want to hurt you. You've got things worth protecting. Why get out of sight?
DAVID. What did you think I was doing all this time?
MAGDA. Trying to get your head straightened out. Thinking about yourself.
DAVID. How? How does a person think about himself. How do you do it? You tell me.
MAGDA. Simple. You try to open your eyes to what's happening to you.
DAVID. Yeah, sure.
MAGDA. You ask yourself what you really want.
DAVID. What I really want. What I really want.
MAGDA. You try to find out what other people want from you. Who is trying to use you and how... You focus on yourself - you're the object of

your own life... You -

DAVID. I can't think about myself. Ever. I try, but my thoughts run away with me. I tell myself: now you're going to think about yourself, only about yourself - nothing else. A minute later, I find myself thinking about all sorts of other things. Everything except myself. I try to take myself in hand. To re-focus my thoughts on myself. I force myself to concentrate on it. I call out my own name... and I find myself looking out at the sea, the hills, the sky... feeling so empty... scared.

MAGDA. For years, you had all those different heads inside your own. Getting rid of them can't be easy.

DAVID. How did **you** manage? How? How?

MAGDA. Me... I told myself at a very early stage... I remember... It was at night... My mother was crying... softly...crying... Then she fell asleep... She kepr sighing in her sleep... I couldn't fall asleep... I lay there in the dark on my back, staring into the darkness... Suddenly it was all clear to me... my whole existence... Magda, I told myself... Magda, you've been brought into a world where you will be exploited... you won't be free... you'll be forced to stoop down... to serve the will of others all through your life...until you die... and that's the only life you'll ever have... never in all eternity will you have another... And it should mean everything to you, this life of yours... it should be more precious than anything else in the world... and nobody should use your life for his own ulterior motives... Don't let anyone lie to you, you hear? Don't let anyone conceal his real intentions from you... *(Suddenly she turns sharply towards David.)* What do you mean you can't think about yourself.

DAVID. I'm trying to tell you the truth.

MAGDA. I believe you.

DAVID. You know why I didn't come straight to you? I was ashamed. I was ashamed of running away. I was ashamed of exposing myself to you that way. - Of all the stupidity! Like a spoiled child. Then, when I realized what I'd done, I was ashamed to come back to you. I said to myself: how are you going to be able to look her in the eye? I went into hiding. A whole week I stayed out of sight. You know where? If I tell you, you won't believe me.

MAGDA. Forget it. You don't have to tell me.

DAVID. Yes, I do. I felt so wretched.

MAGDA. Let's drop it. I don't want you to expose yourself on such a humiliating way.

DAVID. I have the humiliation coming.

MAGDA. Don't start feeling sorry for yourself and don't try to drag me

into feeling sorry for you, because I won't.
DAVID. You despise me, I know.
MAGDA. Don't tell me what I feel towards you.
DAVID. My running away was unforgiveable. I should have been with you and I wasn't.
MAGDA. You should have been wherever you wanted to be.
DAVID. It's unforgivable.
MAGDA. Who has to forgive you except me, in order you you to forgive yourself?
DAVID. Now you're treating me like a psychologist.
MAGDA. Go to hell, will you?
DAHLIA. A human reaction at last.
MAGDA. You're sneaky - You know that? I have to watch out with you.
DAVID. Nobody takes me seriously. I run away with a gun and you're not even scared 'cause you know just what I'm worth. *(Talks out into space, as if addressing evceryone who has affected his life.)* It won't do you any good. Some things just have to be punished.
MAGDA. And you're dying for me to punish you?
DAVID. Not you... It'll come, don't worry.
MAGDA. The black writing on the door?
DAVID. I don't give a damn about that. I know my old friends - Psychopaths, morbid cowards who aren't satisfied unless they manage to scare others too. Their heroism is the heroism of miserable sadists whi keep looking for a helpless victim to pounce on so they can feel a little more powerful.
MAGDA. I'm scared.
DAVID. The black writing on the door? Don't be. I might not know how to think about myself yet, but I do know how to fight. Let them just dare come. God., they sure won't get out of here in one piece.
MAGDA. *(Gasping and putting her hand on her stomach.)* Ah!
DAVID. What happened?
MAGDA. It kicked me.
DAVID. *(Patting her stomach.)* Are you kicking? So tiny, and already kicking? You little rascal. I'll never do to you what my father did to me.
MAGDA. Couldn't we go to sleep somehere else?
DAVID. No. This is our home. We don't have another. And this is the first time in my liife that I know exactly what I'm going to be fighting for.

As Samira goes on with her story, Yonah, Paul and Ada climb onto the set and tie up Udi and Dahlia. Dahlia lies down on the mattress. Udi sits on the floor. Yonah and Paul are kneeling next to him.

Scene 7

SAMIRA. They took us by surprise while we were sleeping. They got in through an open window, sneaked up to our mattress and started beating us in our sleep... *(She stops talking, then turns to Benesh.)* I can't continue.

BENESH. Go on.

SAMIRA. You cut whatever you want out of the story. You'll cut it all out.

DAHLIA. She's right.

BENESH. Wait a minute. What are you missing? Which scene are you missing now?

SAMIRA. I'm not missing anything.

DAHLIA. Why don't you say anything. The scene where Magda and Rodney split up.

BENESH. Oh, is that the scene you miss?

DAHLIA. No, execpt that without it the whole character of Magda is meaningless.

BENESH. Is that scene the one with all the meaning?

DAHLIA. Yes.

BENESH. And I'm telling you that scene is totally unnecessary.

DAHLIA. Why? Because it talks about you?

BENESH. Yonah, do we have enough footage?

YONAH. Footage, yes.

BENESH. All right. We'll rake that scene.

DAHLIA. I don't need that scene...

BENESH. *(Resolute.)* We're taking the scene.

YONAH. We have to put the London apartment set back up...

BENESH. Never mind the set. Do it in close-up, faces filling the screen, no background. *(To Dahlia.)* Let's go. Let's hear the lines without which the character has no meaning.

YONAH. Sound running! Shoot! *(Dahlia enters the part of Magda.)*

MAGDA. You know, Rodney. I don't understand the point of this life I'm living in London. If you love me the way you say you do, why do I keep coming up against a wall of *double entendres*. Do you love me, or don't you? Be indifferent. Say your feelings are dead, that what we had between us can't be revived.

RODNEY. I do love you.
MAGDA. Why does your behaviour prove the opposite? No feeling, no hope...
RODNEY. Don't we have it good when we're together?
MAGDA. Our bodies touch one another and tingle but I don't even know if that's truth or untruth any more... How do you feel about me? *(Shifts to Dahlia.)* The woman you got pregnant... The woman who miscarried...
BENESH. That's not your text.
DAHLIA. Those are the facts.
MAGDA. Rodney.
DAHLIA. Even if you'd rather avoid that memory -
MAGDA. Rodney.
DAHLIA. Those are the facts, and you were away from me just at the time when I was the most upset, the most vulnerable, the most frightened.
MAGDA. Rodney.
DAHLIA. And you can just carry on as though nothing has happened to you? Or to me? What a progressive person you are. A scathing critic of social injustice. A revolutionary. A Trotskyist. What not... What do you feel about all the months we've put into one another and into our relationship? I came from Palestine for you... 'Come, just come, and I'll help you.' What am I to you? - Some creature you can use when it suits you? You - a man who has everything. And give him more, just give him more - he takes, never asking who did the giving. Don't you think I'm a whole human being? Don't I deserve whatever a person in love can give someone he loves? Or is there something wrong with me? Why? -Is it because I'm a woman? Or because I'm not English? Not European? Different? Or maybe you simply aren't really in love? Maybe you're just lying? Not only to me; to yourself too. But if you're lying to me, tell me. Don't try to put one over on me and don't make me play the fool for the rest of my life.
BENESH. Have you had your say? Are you satisfied now? Can we move to the next scene?
DAHLIA. Why don't you answer me? Are you that much of a coward?
RODNEY. *(Alias Benesh who has made up his mind to hide completely behind the text Samira has written for Rodney.)* Listen, I'm a playwright. I write television plays and it's a shitty job. It's something that takes everything out of me. Sometimes, I catch myself red-handed, behaving abominably, and I say to myself: follow through on that, take it as far as it will go. But remember the details for the upcoming scene in your play.

If I botch up a personal relationship, I splatter the dregs over my next play. When I find myself being inhuman, I tell myself: raw material for a scene. I can't help it. All I can do is work a new scene around the defective stuff I'm made of. I create, and my life melts away. I destroy and wreck everything around me, and I turn the story of that destruction into an episode of Hearthrug Theatre. I'm not trying to make excuses. Of course you're right in everything you've said. When I'm dying, there's one thing I'll regret - that I won't be able to use such an interesting setting in any scene of any play. I guess I'm the kind of person who has no real substance. I guess my life itself is just an illusion. *(Suddenly he becomes genuinely enraged, no longer in the role of Rodney, and makes his exit in an improvization of Benesh.)*

BENESH. It's all a fake. All false. What are you asking me to do anyway? You want me to give you all the time I've got left to live? You want all of me to yourself? What right do you have? Who's a Trotskyist? Who's progressive? You're fighting me! You want to take me over. To tame me. To turn me into your plaything. You want me to give in. Can't two people find some other way of sharing their lives? Does one always have to be the master and the other the slave? And if the ultimate enslavement is death, can there be any life together without actually looking forward to the other one's death? Like that old couple playing the comedy of love, with all the niceties. Playing worn-out pranks on one another. Rehashing a textual cliché. - So hackneyed. - With each of the two clowns displaying flickers of independence for their awestruck friends in the audience. Each of them caught up in the same web that has entangled them together. That's what the play is - those two old rakes pretending to give each other what a person in love is capeable of giving the one he loves - whatever time he has left to live. And at the very same time they keep stealing a glance at one another out of the corner of an icy eye, laying low and waiting anxiously and egarly for the moment when the other one's eyes will look up to freeze all at once, in sudden death, and the comedy will be over. *(Turns to Dahlia through Magda.)* What it means, you ask?... What it means?...After everything we've been through, we still work together... You're hurt. - So am I. We may not be destroyed, but we're badly hurt. And just look what we're doing with our wounds - working together. And you still ask what it means? *(Samira steps into position and speaks to the camera.)*

SAMIRA. They broke in while we were asleep and started hitting us. When I came to, my head was roaring like an ocean. I could hear voices through the racket. I recogmized David's. He was talking with two strange men. He was saying some terrible thngs. I thought it was a nightmare. I tried to move my arm and realized I was tied up. I opened my eyes. David was tied up beside me. He was talking with two thugs. I couldn't delieve my ears. I wanted to scream at first, but I guess I was too stunned to make a sound. I kept still. I pretended I was still unconscious.

Scene 8

The apartment in Jerusalem. A mattress on the floor. David and Magda are tied up. Magda is pretending to be unconscious. David is talking in a whisper with the two thugs, Avi and Barry.

AVI. I don't believe you. I don't believe you.
DAVID. You really blew it, I'm telling you. What idiots! Do you know how long it took me to win this Arab chick over? And her friends too? Do you have any idea how touchy and complicated it's been? I'm just beginning to see some results and there you go, with your thick-headedness, throwing months of hard work down the drain!
AVI. If it's true, what you're saying, why haven't you said a word?
DAVID. Who to, you idiot, who to?
AVI. Don't you call me an idiot!
DAVID. Idiot! Who to?
BARRY. To one of our members
DAVID. You're a real asshole, you know that? If I'd said a word to anybody, it would have leaked for sure and the whole thing would go to waste. That kind of work can only be done solo, see what I mean?
AVI. But you were seen kissing in the street.
DAVID. You moron! I'm telling you I've been putting on an act.
BARRY. But the guys don't understand!
DAVID. What's more important? For the guys to understand or for us to get a hold on the traitors who collaborate with them? 'The guys' don't understand. Are we an underground or a youth movement?
AVI. But -
DAVID. Our members had better get used to the idea of not understanding all sorts of things. Carrying out orders, not asking questions.
AVI. I don't know whether or not to believe you.
DAVID. Go ahead. - Carry out your orders. - .Suits me fine. *(Silence.)* Why didn't I rub out the writing on the front door? Figure it out for yourself. Couldn't I have just taken some paint and gone over it? Why

didn't I? I was thrilled to bits when I saw that message. I told myself: they're finally helping me out.

AVI. What do you want me to tell the guys?

DAVID. Nothing! Got that? Not a word should leave this room.

BARRY. But she'll talk.

DAVID. Untie me and go. I'll untie her, I'll bring her to and I'll tell her I had it out with you.

BARRY. *(To Avi.)* What do you say?

AVI. I don't know...

DAVID. Beat it quickly before she wakes up. Go and tell the guys that you really let us have it and that you were interrupted in the middle. Sell them some bill of goods, what's the difference? When the time comes, when I have the whole list, we'll gather all the guys and I'll tell them about the whole operation myself.

BARRY. What about her pregnancy?

AVI. That could be a problem.

DAVID. Don't worry about it! Are you her father? We'll take care of the pregnancy and everything else when the time comes. Just cool it. There's not going to be any baby - if that's what you're worried about.

BARRY. Did you enjoy it at least?

DAVID. Want the details?

BARRY. You're a bastard, David. A real bastard!

DAVID. What did you think. With the kinds of methods our 'leader' was using, you suppose we would have gotten anywhere?

BARRY. He's really turned soft.

DAVID. Holding demonstrations, making headlines. What we have here calls for completely different methods. You just wait and see. When the time is ripe, we'll throw the old fogy out and take things into our own hands. If anyone opens his trap then, we'lll slash his face.

AVI. Listen... so help me... I don't know if I should believe you or not.

DAVID. Believe your ass, OK?

AVI. You're not human. You're a monster, you know that?

DAVID. Or maybe you think the Arabs are going to get on those trucks just because you ask them to. When the moment comes, we're going to have to be monsters.

AVI. I could never act like you. Not even to that Arab chick. She's human too, after all, isn't she?

DAVID. What do you think… that it's easy for me? Sure it's cruel, but we don't have a choice. If we want this country to be totally free of Arabs, we're going to have to learn to be cold as a stone.

BARRY. *(Enthusiastic.)* Sure! Cold as ice!

AVI. 'Eiskalt.'
BARRY. 'Eiskalt'. That's a terrific slogan.
DAVID. Scary, eh? If you'd seen the list of names I've got already and if you knew how many planted agents have been working from within our own ranks and who some of your so-called friends are, them you'd know what scary means.
BARRY. Who? Who's planted?
DAVID. You want to see the list?
BARRY. Of course I do?
DAVID. Then untie me and I'll show you something.
BARRY. Let him go.
AVI. You sure?
BARRY. Let him go.'Eiskalt.' *(Avi cuts through the ropes. Barry and Avi disappear.)*
DAVID. Magda, are you alright?
MAGDA. Keep away from me.
DAVID. Let me set you free.
MAGDA. Don't touch me, you monster.
DAVID. What's with you?
MAGDA. I saw you.
DAVID. You don't understand.
MAGDA. I heard you.
DAVID. Listen a minute.
MAGDA. I understand perfectly.
DAVID. Let me explain.
MAGDA. I can't stand hearing your voice.
DAVID. You think I meant what I told them?
MAGDA. Get away from me.
DAVID. I was pretending.
MAGDA. I don't believe a word you say anymore.
DAVID. What did you want me to do, you moron.
MAGDA. You're sick. That's what you are.
DAVID. God. How can I convince you? I was just pretending. Don't you understand what pretending means?
MAGDA. You were not! I could see you and hear you. It was you you... More **you** than I've ever seen you.
DAVID. You don't understand a thing. You're a real idiot. You're all screwed up.
MAGDA. A screwed up Arab. Say it.
DAVID. You're nuts. Let me untie you.
MAGDA. Get away from me.

MAGDA. Get away from me.
DAVID. Stop it. You're mad.
MAGDA. Mad. Sure I am. You drove me mad. I could die.
DAVID. Come on, stop it.
MAGDA. Kill me. Why don't you just kill me and finish off where your friends left off.
DAVID. Why do I deserve this? God, I deserve this. I did everything to save you. God, you've got to believe me. *(Avi and Barry reappear.)*
AVI. Traitor. You thought you'd fool us.
BARRY. Traitor. We'll finish you off.
DAVID. Psychopaths. Come on, psychopaths.
MAGDA. David... behind you. *(David swerves towards Barry and hits him. Barry falls on the ground. Just then, Avi hits David over the head from behind. David falls over. Avi kicks him in the stomach, then in the head. Barry gets up. His face is smeared with blood. He jumps on Magda.)*
BARRY. You filthy whore, I'll show you! *(He kicks Magda in the stomach. She gasps and lifts her still-tied hands to her stomach, then keels over.)*

Scene 9

As soon as Magda falls as a result of Barry's kick, Samira gets up and takes two or three steps towards the camers of give her lead-in. She mumbles something unclear. Her knees buckle and she turns full-circle, unsteadily, as though drunk. The lighting flickers to the rhythm of Samira's movements, alternately blinding and fading. Samira moves towards the cornerof the stage. Everyone rushes to her. She falls to the ground. Blackout.
A different light goes on. The light of a nightmare. The people in the nightmare are moving to the rhythm of a double-speed film. Their voices are high-pitched and screechy. Their speech sounds like a tape being played at twice the normal speed. The whole scene gives the feeling of a film being screened at double-speed. If this effect cannot be achieved with live actors on stage, the scene can be shot for video and screened on the large video screen at double speed.

RODNEY. Hello where are you calling from oh Heathrow it's wondeful to have you here got a pen and paper take down the address then I've rented a flat for you no I'm not living there myself yet that'll take another few weeks I'll explain when I see you this afternoon or tomorrow at the latest It'll be super believe me...

PSYCHOLOGIST. *(Ada in a white gown and nurse's cap.)* Good morning Samira did you have a good night you're looking wonderful here take these pills at the rate you're going you'll be better and out of here in just two or three weeks meanwhile there's someone here who's very eager to see you you may come in sir she's still in a very weak condition her defenses aren't too strong be gentle when you talk to her...

RODNEY. *(Shows up in underwear and dresses at breakneck speed.)* That was fabulous wasn't it where did I put my watch oh no it's six already with you time goes by so quickly sweetheart gotta run bye till next time darling...

ADNAN. *(Appearing in the garb of an ultra-religious Moslem. He is holding a strand of prayer-beads and shuffling the beads at a mad pace. As he talks he also keeps falling to his knees and stand back up again, in a frenzied re-entry into the Moslem praying position.)* Hello Samira don't you recognize me it's me Adnan what no I'm not hospitalized here I'm in jail we bashed in the head of the thug who killed your baby why are you laughing this is no get-up it's our national apparel.

ADA. *(In a flash-appearance of the psychologist.)* You've got to return to your national identity as a psychologist and a Jew I can tell you that assimilation isn't the solution... *(Vanishes.)*

ADNAN. I'm willing to forgive you all of it despite everything you did and despite the loose lifestyle I love you and I would marry you too of course you'd have to change the way you live and say goodbye to your European habits...

RODNEY. *(In an affectedly casual style of dress.)* I'm off to the film studio darling haven't managed to get you a job yet but be patient... *(He disappears.)*

ADNAN. Cut out smoking completely wine is out of the question of course not to mention those old clothes of yours... burn them all and start wearing our traditional outfits... living like a decent Moslem woman observing the religious laws and of course learning everything you need to now about religion and about the obligations of a Moslem wife... *(Leaps up in an odd movement.)* Why are you spitting you lunatic? *(He jumps back and forth as if to avoid Samira's spitting.)* You're crazy stop it you're crazy... *(Vanishes.)*

RODNEY. *(Dressed to the teeth.)* My wife's very vulnerable right now emotionally I can't just leave her she's human too you know but it shouldn't take more than another two or three weeks a month at the part in a television film this autumn... *(David is dressed as an ultra-orthodox yeshiva student. He is poring over a page of Talmud, jumping up to pray, laying phylacteries and removing them; in short, going through all the riual motions preformed by an observant Jew in the course of a single day. Meanwhile, Miriam and Ephraim, in clown's outfits, have undergone a Jewish metamorphosis of sorts and have become Jewish-theater clowns. They are carrying armfuls of dishes with various foods on them. Ephraim is juggling three bananas while Miriam is pulling bowls out of a basket and palcing them before David who is preforming the rituals.)*

MIRIAM. David darling David dear have some broiled chicken and here are some meatballs and meatloaf with lots of onion and garlic the way you like it and here's some *gefilte* fish for the Sabbath meal

DAVID. *(Preforming the rituals at breakneck speed.)* Take away your sacrilege

MIRIAM. David you've got to eat

EPHRAIM. *(Still juggling the bananas.)* How does that line of yours go without flour there is no *Torah*...

MIRIAM. I'm leaving you some apples and bananas too...

DAVID. I told you to take away your heathen abomination

MIRIAM. It's all *kosher* all *kosher* we *koshered* our kitchen at home ask Daddy

EPHRAIM. *Kosher* as can be and we put up mezuzahs on every doorpost including the bathroom you needn't be afraid to come home

DAVID. *(Hurling the dishes at his parents. They stagger and convulse in odd fits and jumps to avoid being hit. Rodney suddenly finds himself in the middle of the scene.)* You can take your meatballs take your meatloaf take your fish...

EPHRAIM. Honor your father and thy mother

DAVID. She is not my mother and you are not my father

RODNEY. *(Ducking the flying meatballs.)* In late July my wife will be getting a job in Portugal and then I'll move in with you at Covent Garden sweetheart see you next time

MIRIAM. You've been through a difficult time we understand

DAVID. Go away and don't let your feet profane this palce

RODNEY. *(Appearing with an extravagant sweater tied around his neck, waving in the air behind him.)* Yes darling autumn here is very long but you've got to admit it's the loveliest season of the year and that the afternoon hours are the most appropriate for lovemaking *l'amour l'apres-midi*

MIRIAM. *(To Samira who is out of sight.)* Go to him I beg of you

Samira you he'll listen to you're the only one who can get this obsession out of him and give us back our son Samira go to him

RODNEY. Why do you say concubine stop using such vulgar language the characters in my plays don't use such vulgar language are you short of money come on darling let's stop fighting I swear to you this Christmas we'll celebrate together in our apartment and by then I promise you'll have a passport and a job

DAVID. *(All the while swaying back and forth in frenzied orgastic movements of a person praying.)* Why did you come here Samira why I'm trying to get you out of my system and I can't sit here memorising verses and I keep thinking of you Hear Oh Israel I say at night and think of you I love you go away from here go I told you there's no escaping retribution and now I know there's a connection between all the events and the coincidences and that there's a supreme pretext now I know don't go to London convert we'll call you Ruth after Ruth the Moabite may she rest in peace and we'll be married in a proper Jewish wedding Samira..

RODNEY. *(Appearing in festive winter clothing, dancing and siging as he waves a small gift-wrapped box.)*

> Merry Christmas to you, Merry Christmas to you
> Merry Christmas dear sweetheart, Merry Christmas
> to you...

MIRIAM. Go to him. Go Samira you're the only one who can bring our son back to us

ADNAN. Get rid of cigarettes, the wine, learn the basic precepts of our religion

DAVID. You'll become a proper Jew and we'll get married

RODNEY. I can't stay now but I'll be back tonight she gets drunk easily and then she passes out for twelve hours I'll come and we'll have a wondeful time

HERBERT. *(Enters with a small Christmas tree.)* I'm a Jew in the Nazi sense not the Jewish one

RODNEY Merry Christmas

DAVID. Simply convert

ADNAN. And learn the duties of a Moslem wife

RODNEY. She gets drunk easily

ADA. *(As the psychologist.)* Identity Samira identity assimilation isn't the answer you've got to find your identity again because without an identity you understand identity is...

SAMIRA. *(Yelling as she comes to; as she yells, the light loses its nightmarish effect.)* Go away! Go away! All of you! Go away! Leave me alone all of you! Go away! Go away! Go away, you and your filth! Go! Go! Go... *(She wakes up and sees the others all standing over her.)* Magda is something that nothing sticks to. No label. Magda is the kind of stuff that can't be frozen in any form. Magda is just the opposite. Magda isn't the result. She isn't the continuation. Magda is what happens from one minute to the next and burns out from one minute to the next... Magda is something that dosen't belong, something that'll never belong to anyone. What's going on?

ADA. You fainted.

UDI. How are you feeling?

SAMIRA. All right. Strange. Like after a good sleep. Was I out for long?

YONAH. Seconds. Maybe half a minute. Can you stand up?

SAMIRA. I'm OK. As far as I'm concerned, we can carry on.

BENESH. What do you mean 'carry on'? We've finished the story.

SAMIRA. Finished?... Aren't you shooting the nightmare?

BENESH. Yesterday's rushes came out great. No need to do a retake.

SAMIRA. Then we're through.

BENESH. Yeah. That's it. We can start taking the set apart.

YONAH. Wait a minute. Who's taking thngs apart already? A job well done calls for a drink first! *(Pulls the cork on a bottle of champagne and hands the bottle to Benesh.)* Take a sip, wet your whistle and say a few words man!

BENESH. *(Passing the bottle on.)* What can I say... I don't know what to say...

HAVKIN. Stop that nonsense. Don't listen to him. Nothng to say, my eye!

YONAH. Havkin!

HAVKIN. Ladies and gentlemen, don't take youselves too seriously. We haven't exactly turned the world upside down. All we've done is tell a story and here's hoping we did a good job. Now we're excited and that's natural, but we'll be splitting up soon, each one of us returning to his own life. And we'll discover that we haven't moved any mountains. On the other hand, we'll discover that no abyss has opened up either. We're not about to change the world, for better or for worse. So let's forget about words. Have you forgotten where you are - the studio of Herbert! Someone who never even existed! And in Herbert's studio, when you run out of words, you dance! Isn't that right, Benesh?

BENESH. Ausdruck-Tanz.

HAVKIN. Exactly. Ausdruck-Tanz. Paul - music!

Paul sits down at the piano and begins to play Ravel's 'La Valse', The singer scats along and everyone joins in the Ausdruck-Tanz. Their manner of dancing gives each actor the chance to express his own particular character. Havkin directs the dancing, brings the characters together and uses the dance to convey the essence of the play.

THE END

Biographies

Derek Barnes was born in London and studied at the Royal Academy of Music and the London Opera Centre. He pursues an international career as a conductor of opera and music theatre, and as a composer and arranger. His most recent music for the stage was for the world premiere of Arnold Wesker's *Blood Libel.*

Carole Braverman was born in New York City. She has been Playwright in Residence at The American Conservatory Theatre in San Francisco and the Berkeley Repertory Theatre in Berkeley, California. Her early plays include *The Girl With a Sense of Fair Play, The Margaret Ghost* and *In Tiber Melting. The Yiddish Trojan Women* was produced in New York, London and Los Angeles. In London, it won the London Weekend Television's 'Plays on Stage' Award', and the Jewish Chronicle's 'Best Jewish Play Award'. She has recently completed a new play, *Vigils Under Threat* of *Death*. She lives in Andover, MA where she teaches English and Theatre at Phillips Academy.

Marion Baraitser's latest play, the adaptation of Olive Schreiner's *The Story of an African Farm* was developed at the National Theatre Studio and broadcast on BBC Radio 4. Short-listed for the Verity Bargate award early in her career, she has received Arts Council awards for her plays *Winnie, Mr Bennett and Miss Smith, Elephant in a Rhubarb Tree* and *LOUIS/lui.* She has edited *Plays by Mediterranean Women,* and *Contemporary Puppet Plays* (Harwood Academic Press). She has an MA in English Literature and taught the Diploma in Literature for London University's Extra Mural Department, and Creative Writing for Morley College. Her short stories have been published in *Metropolitan* and she has written for several journals and newspapers. She lives in London with her husband and four children.

Tony Hammond (MA Cantab) is Director of Education at the Spiro Institute. A lecturer in modern Jewish literature and history, he previously taught literature in universities and schools in France and the UK. He has done research in French Renaissance literature and is currently doing research on Midrash. He has been involved in a number of theatre projects, and is the author of *The Best of All Possible Worlds*, a verse drama based on *Candide*. He is married with three children and lives in London.

Sonja Linden's first play *Present Continuous* won a Fringe First Award at the Edinburgh Festival and was broadcast on BBC radio. Other plays include the youth eco-opera *Are You Sleeping in a Safe Place, Call Me Judas, The Jewish Daughter*, a sequel to Brecht's *The Jewish Wife* and most recently *Gradiva or The Love-Cure*, an erotic comedy about the relationship between Freud and Jung and their women, selected for the 1997 Writers' Guild Showcase. She co-edited *The Dybbuk of Delight*, the first British anthology of Jewish Women's poetry (Five Leaves Press, 1995), and *The Slow Mirror: New Fiction by Jewish Writers* (Five Leaves Press, 1996). Sonja Linden is currently Writer in Residence at the Medical Foundation for the Care of Victims of Torture.

David Schneider was born in 1963 and was brought up in North London. After taking a B.A. in Modern Languages at Exeter College, Oxford, David, the grandson of Yiddish playwright Abisz Meisels, stayed on to research a Ph.D. in Yiddish drama. He left Oxford in 1987 to become an actor and made his professional debut in Joshua Sobol's *Ghetto* at the National Theatre. Since then he has appeared in numerous stage and television productions, most notably *Friday Night Armistice, The Day Today*, and *Knowing Me, Knowing You* for the BBC. *The Eleventh Commandment* is his first stage-play

Joshua Sobol was born in Israel in 1939. He studied philosophy at the Sorbonne. He has written thirty-five plays so far, which have been translated into some twenty-five languages and produced all over the world. *The Palestinian Girl* has been produced in more than twenty theatres in Israel, Germany, Austria, Sweden, USA and Switzerland.

FORTHCOMING TITLES BY LOKI BOOKS:

- **NEW PLAYS FROM SOUTH AFRICA**

The best new plays, experimental and political from The Battersea Arts Centre's South African season including. the adaptation of Olive Schreiner's 'The Story of an African Farm' and 'beds on bricks' by Iindiza Theatre Company. (Autumn, 1998).

AVAILABLE FROM LOKI BOOKS

- **'DOLLY CITY'** by Orly Castel-Bloom. **ISBN:LOKI: 0 9529426 0 7: £7.99**

An irreverent and witty satire, an original and timely tour de force about the Yiddishe -mamma complex, and Israel today, by a triple prize-winning new young voice.
'A novel of Joycean insolence - A beautiful book whose non-conformism is a delight.' (*La Marsellaise*) 'Castel-Bloom writes with such freshness, such dash and panache that I was willing to follow her anywhere.' (Eva Figes)

APPLES FROM THE DESERT: SELECTED STORIES: SAVYON LIEBRECHT: ISBN: LOKI: 09529426 1 5:
Classic bittersweet tales of fury, passion and disenchantment by a popular second-generation Holocaust writer; 'A signpost of modern Hebrew prose' (Ha'aretz)

MEDITERRANEAN WRITERS TALK PEACE:
A collection of the finest work from top novelists, poets, journalists, playwrights, screen writers from Morocco to Israel.

All books available from good book shops, or from Loki
Books: 38 Chalcot Crescent, London NW1 8YD.
tel/fax: +44(0)171 722 6718
e-mail: all@lokibooks.u-net.com
web site: http://www.lokibooks.u-net.com
Trade: Central Books 99 Wallis Rd, London E9 5LN
tel/fax +44 (0)181 533 5821